Ingredients

CREATED BY PETER MIRAMS

ORIGINAL TEXT BY LOUKIE WERLE

TEXT REVISED AND EXTENDED

FOR THE UK BY JILL COX

KÖNEMANN

Concept: Peter Mirams

Editor: Judy Sarris

Art Director: David Leigh

Text: Loukie Werle, Jill Cox

Copy Editors: Peter Wilton, Lynda Wilton, Jane Rich

Ingredients sourced and styled for photography: Judy Sarris, David Leigh, Stella Murphy

Marketing Director: Stephen Balme

Production Director: Anna Maguire

Traffic Manager: Meredith Johnston

Published by JB Fairfax Press Pty limited, 80 McLachlan Avenue, Rushcutters Bay, NSW 2011, Australia. A.C.N. 003 738 430

ISBN of the German edition: 3-8331-1296-4

© 2005 Tandem Verlag GmbH

KÖNEMANN is a trademark and an imprint of Tandem Verlag GmbH

Printed in Germany

ISBN 3-8331-1456-8

10 9 8 7 6 5 4 3 2 1

X IX VIII VII VI V IV III II I

Introduction

When we were given the opportunity to create *Ingredients*, our editorial team's initial excitement gradually became tempered by the realization of what an awesome task it would be. How many ingredients were there? How did you define an ingredient? Which names, of the many in use in the world at large, should we choose to describe the same thing? We just had to take the plunge and begin a fascinating journey.

Our writer, Jill Cox — in conjunction with Loukie Werle, who had already supplied the information for our first book, *Australasian Ingredients* — began to research and write about the various food groups. Even she, with her very considerable experience in cooking and producing cookery books, was amazed by the huge volume of products available. The overwhelming range of varieties of some categories, such as cheese and fish, made it essential occasionally to condense them into useful and digestible (if you'll excuse the pun) selections.

With labelling and identification, our copy editors went to extraordinary lengths to distinguish between ingredients which are often confused, even by some food writers: cumin and nigella; spring onion and shallot; lobster and crayfish are examples.

While Jill and Loukie produced the words, art director David Leigh and I became intrepid shoppers, seeking out often-elusive ingredients for photography. We scoured local Asian markets for some of the more unusual spices, seaweeds, noodles and dried fish. We cajoled growers into planting and nurturing fresh herbs, which would normally have been out of season during our production schedule. We punished the budget to fly rarer species, such as witchetty grubs, by express to our photographic studio, and even, we humbly confess, had to scale a fence to 'borrow' a couple of berries from a bush bearing early fruit. Perhaps our punishment was the humiliation of being only too aware of the surprised whispers of bemused fellow shoppers in supermarkets, who clearly thought we had 'lost the plot' as we filled trolley after trolley with one of every ingredient on the shelves.

As you will see in the following pages, we have made a point of showing fresh foods as you would expect to buy them. I'm sure you will agree that photographer Paul Gosney has taken a wonderful series of shots, after overcoming all sorts of problems, such as fresh herbs instantly wilting under studio lights, odoriferous cheeses running amok in the heat, and fresh fish dripping infuriatingly over pristine, white backgrounds.

The resulting photographs, together with Jill and Loukie's commentary, provide an easily used, but comprehensive reference book for everyone interested in food and the incredibly wide range of wonderful ingredients available today. I hope it will be as fascinating for you as it has been for us.

JUDY SARRIS

Contents

Herbs, spices & seeds

Not so long ago, the most exotic flavourings to be found in an average pantry were salt, pepper and possibly garlic. Fresh herbs were a rare sight, except for perhaps a patch of mint or parsley growing outside the back door.

How times have changed! Thanks to the migration of different ethnic groups and the movement of people around the world in general, our culinary spectrum has grown enormously. We are now familiar with a wealth of flavours and aromas, and often cook with the herbs, spices and seeds associated with Italian, Greek, Moroccan, Spanish, Lebanese, Thai, Indian, West Indian, Chinese and Japanese cuisines, to name but a few.

There is nothing to match the flavour and fragrance of fresh herbs, which are easily available from any supermarket either in bunches or pots. Better still, they can be grown in the garden or a window box for snip-and-come-again freshness. Dried herbs are also a good option. However, they tend to be stronger and more pungent than the fresh variety, and so should be measured accordingly to maintain balance when cooking.

Balance and harmony is also especially important when it comes to spicing food. In countries where spices are integral to cooking, the art is learnt at mother's knee. Strong spices are hardly ever used on their own. When using cumin, for example, you'll often find a little coriander balances the flavour; Indian cumin beef curry being an exception.

To get the most out of your spices, before adding to a dish, dry-roast them by placing in a small frying pan over a moderate heat, shaking the pan frequently until the typical aroma is released and small wisps of smoke start to escape. Remove from the heat immediately, as burning turns them bitter. Grind in a pestle and mortar or in a spice blender. Include ground spices in the early stages of a recipe to bring out the full flavour.

BAY LEAF
Laurus nobilis
There is hardly a savoury dish which does not benefit from the addition of one or two bay leaves. An important part of bouquet garni, the leaves can be used fresh, straight from the tree or dried. A few bay leaves placed in a storage jar with rice will delicately flavour the rice and ward off weevils.

CORIANDER
Coriandrum sativum
Sometimes called **Chinese parsley** or **cilantro**, the leaf has a distinctive aroma. Used extensively in Mediterranean, Latin American and Asian cooking. People either love or hate this herb with a fierce passion. The roots and leaves are a 'must' in Thai green curry.

SORREL
Rumex scutatus
Mainly used in soups, omelettes, sauces served with cold fish and poultry, and sprinkled on boiled potatoes. The young leaves are a good addition to a mixed green salad.

FENNEL
Foeniculum vulgare
Use the chopped, feathery leaves in salads, particularly potato salad, with fish, in pasta sauces and rice dishes. A whole fish can be baked on a bed of fennel branches.

LEMON GRASS
Cymbopogon citratus
Popular in Asian dishes, this herb is slowly becoming mainstream. Use the bottom 10cm (4in) of the stalks only. Remove tough outer layers and bruise the tender inside with the blunt side of a chef's knife, before chopping or slicing finely. Use the leaves to infuse the water in which fish or chicken is poached or steamed, in syrup for fruit compotes, or in custards when making *crème brûlée* or crème caramel.

YARROW
Achillea millefolium
Used in mixed green salads.

TARRAGON
Artemisia dracunculus
Always look for French tarragon, which has a much more pronounced flavour than Russian tarragon. If Russian is all you can obtain, use more. Used in *fines herbes* blend, in béarnaise sauce, with fish, poultry, offal and egg dishes, and to infuse white wine vinegar.

ANGELICA
Angelica archangelica
Leaf, stem and flower all have a sweet flavour. Use chopped leaves in salads and stewed fruits. The stem is candied and used in desserts and for decorating cakes. Seeds, stems and roots are used to flavour liqueurs, such as chartreuse, Bénédictine and vermouth.

MARJORAM
Origanum majorana
Use with meat, poultry, vegetable and egg dishes, in soups and sauces, pasta and rice dishes.

LAVENDER
Lavandula angustifolia
Use the fragrant flowers sparingly in cakes, biscuits, jellies and ice cream. Vinegar may be infused with the stalks and flower heads.

9

CURRY PLANT
Helichrysum angustifolium
Its leaves release a typical 'curry' fragrance when lightly touched, making it an aromatic addition to the garden. Use when cooking rice, soups, stews and veal, and in stuffing for game. Note that the curry plant is not an ingredient in curry powder.

HORSERADISH
Cochlearia armoracia
Freshly grated horseradish is used to give piquant flavour to spreads and sauces that accompany roast or boiled beef, fish and chicken.

SWEET BASIL
Ocimum basilicum
Large, fleshy leaves, particularly popular in Italian dishes, such as pesto. Sweet basil combines well with tomatoes. To preserve the purple or bright green colour of the leaves, do not chop with a knife, but tear by hand. Use leaves only.

SALAD BURNET
Sanguisorba minor
Sprigs give a refreshing cucumber flavour to drinks, while leaves are used in salads and sandwiches.

BOUQUET GARNI

A flavouring for soups and stews made from a bay leaf and sprigs of parsley, thyme and marjoram, tied with a long piece of string for easy retrieval from the pot before serving. The Italian version of bouquet garni consists of bay leaf, parsley, oregano and garlic.

FINES HERBES

A blend of finely chopped parsley, chervil, chives and tarragon, used to flavour delicate dishes, such as omelette or a green salad. Mixed into a little melted butter and lemon juice, *fines herbes* is frequently used on grilled fish or steak and in emulsified, butter-based sauces, such as béarnaise and hollandaise.

MINT

Mentha

Use sprigs in drinks, and chopped leaves with lamb, vegetables, especially new potatoes and peas, and in fruit salads or to make mint sauce. VARIETIES: spearmint, applemint and peppermint.

GARLIC

Allium sativum

Garlic is used with almost anything, except maybe dessert. Its flavour depends on how it is prepared — cooked garlic being much milder than raw, chopped garlic. It can be used raw or fried, poached, roasted or sautéed, and can be cooked peeled or unpeeled. Choose a firm, hard head of garlic with no soft or discoloured patches. Do not refrigerate but store in a cool, dry place.

THYME

Thymus vulgaris

A versatile herb, it has strong, aromatic leaves that are used in soups, stews, bean dishes, or with meat of any kind, including terrines and pâtés. Also good with vegetables, particularly with roast potatoes.

11

ROSEMARY
Rosmarinus officinalis
Used with most meat, especially veal and lamb, poultry and game dishes, but the flavour is too strong for most fish. Use sparingly on pizza, focaccia, in pasta and risotto.

CHERVIL
Anthriscus cerefolium
Used in soups, sauces, egg dishes, salads, sandwiches, chicken and fish dishes. One of the ingredients in *fines herbes*.

PARSLEY
Petroselinum crispum
Most familiar variety of this important culinary herb. It has bright green, tightly curled leaves, and is hardy and highly nutritious. Finely chopped parsley leaves are among the mix in *fines herbes* and the stalks are used in bouquet garni.

MARIGOLD
Calendula officinalis
During the days of the Roman Empire it was known as **poor man's saffron** and was used to add colour and flavour to rice and fish dishes, cakes and puddings. Flower heads can be used fresh in salads or dried in soups and stews.

CONTINENTAL PARSLEY
Petroselinum hortense filicinum
The French use both leaves and stems of this flat-leafed variety in cooking. Italian cuisine uses only leaves; the stems are reserved for making stock. The French have their famous *persillade*, a finely chopped mixture of parsley and garlic, which is sprinkled on to all manner of dishes, such as meat or fried potatoes, just before serving. Then there is *gremolata* (without which osso bucco would not be complete), a finely chopped mixture of parsley, garlic and lemon zest, sprinkled on a dish before serving.

DILL
Anethum graveolens
Light green, feathery leaves and tiny green-yellow flowers. Used with fish and egg dishes or finely chopped in salads, especially good with cucumber or cottage cheese.

BORAGE
Borago officinalis
The finely chopped leaves, when young, taste good in salads and sandwiches. Use older leaves in soups. Whole leaves or sprigs are used in drinks or may be dipped in batter and deep-fried. The blue flowers may be used in salads.

SAGE
Salvia officinalis
Its powerful flavour tends to dominate. Used when cooking dried beans and fatty meats such as pork — goose, duck and oily fish, and with dishes of calf's liver or pasta.

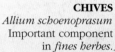

CHIVES
Allium schoenoprasum
Important component in *fines herbes*. Used to give a mild onion flavour, especially with eggs and salads. Use the pale purple or pink flowers in salads.

LEMON BALM
Melissa officinalis
Lemon-scented, tooth-edged leaves add a minty lemon flavour to meat, poultry and fish dishes, to fruit and vegetable salads, and to soups and puddings. Infusion of leaves makes a soothing tea.

RUE
Ruta graveolens
In Italy, where people are appreciative of bitter flavours, rue is often added to a mixed green salad.

OREGANO
Origanum vulgare
Used with meat, poultry, vegetable and egg dishes, in pastas, soups, sauces and rice dishes.

HYSSOP
Hyssopus officinalis
Use finely chopped leaves in pork, goose or duck stuffing,
and in gravy or soups. Use the flowers in salads.

SAVORY
Satureia spp
Use finely chopped leaves to
give a peppery bite; good with
dried beans and lentils, fresh
beans, and in crumb mixtures
for coating fish and meat.

LEMON VERBENA
Aloysia triphylla
To impart a lemony aroma,
place a few leaves in the
bottom of a cake tin or use to
flavour rice pudding or sweet
custards, such as *crème brûlée*
or crème caramel.

BERGAMOT
Monarda didyma
Used in summer drinks, tea,
salads, desserts and with meat
dishes. The flowers may be
used in a salad. Add a few
leaves to China or Indian tea
for the flavour of Earl Grey.

CARAWAY
Carum carvi
The young
leaves are used in
soups and salads,
and to sprinkle
over vegetables.

14

LOVAGE
Levisticum officinale
The finely chopped leaves
give a peppery celery
flavour to salads, soups
and meat dishes.

Add soft, leafy
herbs late in the
cooking process,
about 5–10 minutes
before the dish is
cooked. Woody
varieties, such as
rosemary or thyme,
can stand longer
cooking times.
Most of the herbs
in this section are
available dried, but
use fresh whenever
possible. Herbs are
easy to grow in a
small garden bed,
in pots, or even
in a sunny
window box.
If you have to use
the dried variety,
keep in mind that
the flavour is much
stronger. You will
need to reduce the
quantity by a third
or a quarter so, if a
recipe calls for 1
tablespoon of
chopped rosemary
leaves, use only
1–1½ teaspoons of
the dried variety.
Dried herbs lose
their potency after
a while, so check
the best-before date
regularly. If past it,
throw the herbs out
and buy a new
supply or, better
still, try using fresh.

ELDER
Sambucus nigra
Use the fresh flowers to
make wine or batter,
deep-fried for a dessert,
or to add flavour to fruit
jellies. The berries may
be used in tarts and
sweet sauces, for jams,
jellies and chutneys, and
also to make wine.

CHAMOMILE
Chamaemelum nobile
Use the small, yellow and white, daisy-
like flowers in salads. The dried flowers
of English chamomile are used to make a
soothing, herbal tea.

AMCHOOR
Mangifera indica
Mostly used in Indian cuisine; a lemon-flavoured seasoning ground from dried, unripe mango. If unavailable, substitute freshly squeezed lemon juice.

ASAFOETIDA
Ferula asafoetida
A sticky substance or powder made from the resin of giant fennel, which is no relative of the fennel we know. This foul-smelling spice is used in Indian dishes, often with beans, as an anti-flatulent, and by Brahmans, whose religion forbids them to use onions and garlic, as these are believed to inflame sexual passion. Only the smallest amount is necessary and, rather than adding it to the food itself, the resin is often shaped into a little ball and stuck to the lid of the cooking pot. The powder is added straight to the food. When cooking, this spice smells very pleasant, rather like onion and mild garlic.

BOUQUET GARNI, dried
Mostly used in stocks, casseroles and soups, dried bouquet garni consists of parsley, bay leaves and thyme wrapped in a square of cheesecloth and tied with string for easy retrieval from the cooking pot before serving.

ALLSPICE or **PIMENTO**
Pimenta dioica
This spice with clove, pepper and cinnamon overtones is used in marinades for meat and game. Lightly crush the whole berries to release the aroma. The ground spice is used in soups and sauces, rice dishes, pâtés and sausages.

CAPER
Capparis spinosa
The unopened, green flowerbuds of a shrub, native to the Mediterranean. Sold pickled, the smaller the caper the better. Capers are indispensable in steak tartare, tartare sauce and puttanesca pasta sauce.

ANISE
Pimpinella anisum
A small, hard seed with a spicy, sweet taste. Used in baking, especially biscuits and cakes, in preserving, such as plums and gherkins, in anise-flavoured liqueurs and drinks, and to mask the strong flavour of some cough medicines.

BLACK CUMIN
Cuminum cyminum
Also known as **royal cumin**. Nigella, a small, triangular, jet black seed, is often wrongly called black cumin. Real black cumin is used less frequently than white cumin because it has a strong flavour.

CARAWAY
Carum carvi
These brown, oblong seeds are crucial ingredients in seed cakes and sauerkraut, and are commonly used on breads, in spreads, such as Liptauer cheese, with potatoes, goose, duck and pork. Widely used in making liqueurs.

16

CARDAMOM
Elettaria cardamomum
Sold as seeds or in pods. Colours vary from black to green to white. Remove seeds from the pods before using. Most common in Indian and Sri Lankan curries. Good with vegetables, fruit pies and meat dishes.

CELERY SEED
Apium graveolens
The celery plant is a native of Italy. Its rather bitter seeds are dried and mostly used in casseroles and soups. Also used to make celery salt, which may include some of the leaves and roots of celery.

CLOVE
Eugenia aromatica
A clove loses its potency after prolonged storage. Test in water: if fresh, it will sink or float upright; stale ones lie on the surface. Use whole or ground in meat and marinated fish dishes, pastries and mulled wine.

CAROM
Carum ajowan
This celery-seed look-alike is closely related to cumin; the seeds, with their thyme-like flavour, are mostly used in Indian cuisine to flavour curries, chutneys and pappadams.

CHILLI PEPPER
Capsicum annuum, var. *frutescens*
Chilli or cayenne pepper is the dried, ground fruit of the various capsicum plants. Buy dried chillies whole, in flakes or as a powder. Use in curry pastes, Thai soups and South American dishes, such as chilli con carne, as a fiery flavouring.

CORIANDER
Coriandrum sativum
Always grind coriander yourself after briefly dry-roasting; the store-bought, ground product loses its vibrancy quickly. Widely used in curries, Middle Eastern spice mixes and pickling mixtures.

CASSIA
Cinnamomum cassia
Also known as **cassia bark** or **bastard cinnamon**, the flavour is much the same as cinnamon. Use whole in meat dishes, curries and coffee, and the ground cassia in cakes and pastries or to enhance the flavour of chocolate and fruit dishes.

CINNAMON
Cinnamomum zelanicum
The dried bark of the cinnamon tree is curled into quills and cut to equal lengths. Use broken into smaller pieces in curries and compotes, together with lemon zest and cloves in mulled wine, and ground into a powder in puddings and cakes.

CUMIN
Cuminum cyminum
Without it, Middle Eastern and Latin American food would be dull. It is a popular flavouring in Indonesian cuisine and is nearly always in curry powder. The whole seeds are present in Dutch Leyden cheese. Roasted cumin is a great addition when sprinkled over fresh fruit.

CURRY LEAF
Chalcas koenigii
Related to the lemon tree, the fresh or dried leaves of the curry plant are added to curries. Curry powders and pastes may contain an amount of ground curry leaves.

DUKKAH
A Middle Eastern spice mix, usually consisting of coriander, cumin, sesame seeds and hazelnuts. These are all roasted before being coarsely ground and seasoned with salt. Use as a dip for fresh bread with olive oil, and sprinkle on *fattoush* — the Lebanese bread — cucumber and tomato salad.

FIVE SPICE POWDER
Used in Chinese cuisine, especially with meat, poultry or fish dishes, this is a mixture of Sichuan pepper, star anise, fennel, cloves and cinnamon.

CURRY POWDER
Curry powder may contain any of the following: ground turmeric, cumin, coriander, cardamom, chilli, fennel seeds, cloves, fenugreek, tamarind, poppy seeds, saffron, pepper, nutmeg, mace, curry leaves, garlic and ginger.

FENNEL SEED
Foeniculum vulgare
Used in pickling, in Indian cookery, as a flavouring for bread, and in the pharmaceutical industry for gargles. The seeds, which have a slight aniseed flavour, are also used in certain liqueurs.

GALANGAL
Languas galanga
A member of the ginger family, but differing in flavour when dried, the powdered form of this root is also sold in local Asian markets as *laos*. Use in Indonesian hot and spicy dishes and Malaysian fish and seafood dishes.

DILL SEED
Anethum graveolens
Used in soups and stews, for pickling, and, particularly in Scandinavia, in the preparation of salmon and crayfish. Said to have a generally soothing effect, dill is an important ingredient in infants' gripe water given to relieve colic.

FENUGREEK
Trigonella foenum-graceum
The seeds have a sweet, curry-like aroma when roasted; consequently this spice is found in most curry powders, and spicy vegetable and pulse dishes. Also in pickles and chutneys, spiced vinegar, and in *halva*, a sesame-based sweetmeat.

GARAM MASALA
There are many versions of this spice mixture used in Indian and Middle Eastern cuisines and its exact composition is often kept a secret by cooks. Common components are cumin, cloves, cinnamon, cardamom, nutmeg and pepper. For powerful flavour-boost, add the mixture in the last minutes of cooking.

GINGER, fresh
Zingiber officinale
Asian cuisine is not the same without ginger, the root of which is finely chopped or grated, and together with onion and garlic is the basis of many a stir-fry or curry. Look for firm and shiny ginger, avoiding the gnarly.

JUNIPER BERRY
Juniperus communis
Use whole or crushed, especially with game, and in marinades for a gamy flavour. Sauerkraut is much improved by adding a few crushed berries. Also used in English gin and a number of schnapps and brandies.

MIXED DRIED HERBS
Used to flavour savoury dishes, this aromatic mixture consists of basil, marjoram, thyme, parsley and rosemary. May be added directly to the dish during cooking or used indirectly, e.g., in marinades.

GINGER, powdered
Zingiber officinale
Powdered ginger is mostly used in jams, cakes, pies and biscuits, and for flavouring drinks. Also used in savoury dishes, curry mixtures and as a seasoning in ketchup.

LIQUORICE
Glycyrrhiza glabra
The extract from dried and ground liquorice roots is widely used to make the hard or pliable black confectionery some love, others hate, as an expectorant, and to disguise the unpleasant taste of many medicines.

MUSTARD SEED
fam. *Brassica*
White mustard seeds are used in Asian cooking, pickling, in marinades, to flavour sausages, and in 'prepared' mustard. Black seeds are used in spicy dishes and to make oil. Mustard powder is a mixture of both.

HORSERADISH
Armoracia rusticana
The dried root of the horseradish plant is ground into a powder, then mixed with water to make a paste or cream to accompany meat or fish.

MACE
Myristica fragrans
The outer, lacy covering of the nutmeg kernel, flattened and dried in the sun. Available in strips or ground, mostly used in curry mixtures, pickles, as a flavouring for corned beef, soups and sausages.

NUTMEG
Myristica fragrans
Buy whole and grate as needed. Used to flavour soups, vegetables, breads and cakes. A true Bolognese sauce is not complete without grated nutmeg.

PANCH PHORA

An Indian seasoning mix of cumin, black mustard, nigella, fenugreek and fennel seeds. Added to the cooking oil, it imparts a typically Indian flavour to food. Not to be confused with the Chinese Five Spice mix.

PICKLING SPICE

Used in preserved and pickled vegetables, vinegars and chutneys, this mixture consists of dried bay leaves, red chillies, mustard and coriander seeds, allspice, cloves, ginger and mace.

SALT
Sodium chloride
Added to most food, even sweet dishes, to bring out the flavour. Don't add much in the beginning; you can always add more later. VARIETIES: coarse, coarse curing, cooking, fine, rock, sea, table, flavoured, seasoned.

PAPRIKA
Capsicum tetragonum
Hungarian goulash would not exist without this ingredient. Used in soups, sauces, salads, spreads, sausages and salamis, a host of meat, poultry and fish dishes, and in ketchup. Made from finely ground, dried, red capsicum.

POPPY SEED
Papaver somniferum
Used frequently in Indian cooking, primarily as a thickener, this seed from the poppy flower is available in two varieties: black/blue and white. Also used extensively in Middle Eastern and Middle European cuisines.

SANSHO POWDER
Used in Japanese cooking, this powder is made from the dried and ground leaves of the prickly ash and has a peppery, lemon-like flavour. Must be used sparingly.

PEPPER
Piper nigrum
When ripe, pepper berries are red. Black peppercorns are the dried, unripe berry used whole or freshly ground. White peppercorns are riper berries, de-husked and dried. They are hotter and less aromatic than black. Green peppercorns are the fresh, unripe berries.

SAFFRON
Crocus sativus
The dried stigmas of 200,000 mauve, autumn-flowering crocus flowers are needed to obtain 1kg of saffron, so it is not difficult to imagine why it is so costly. Use threads in paella, bouillabaisse, risotto Milanese and saffron cakes. Keep refrigerated.

SICHUAN or **CHINESE PEPPER**
Xanthoxylum piperitum
Like sansho powder, these berries come from the prickly ash and are not related to the peppercorn. They have a distinctive and intense flavour. Buy whole or ground; dry-roast the whole berries for best results.

SESAME SEED
Sesamum indicum
Native to India, the dried fruits of the sesame plant are frequently used to flavour and garnish breads, and to make oil. Available in black and white varieties. Ground sesame seeds are the main ingredient in *tahini* and *halva*.

SUNFLOWER SEED
Helianthus annuus
Native to Peru, the dried seeds of the sunflower plant are extensively used in the manufacture of oil. When roasted, they are eaten as a healthy snack or sprinkled over salads.

VANILLA
Vanilla planifolia
This spice originates from the orchid family. The pods are harvested while immature, so they don't burst. Use to flavour sweet dishes, such as ice creams, puddings, cakes and pies, especially those containing chocolate. Also in liquid form.

STAR ANISE
Illicium verum
This fruit of an evergreen tree has an aniseed flavour. Buy whole or ground and use to flavour Asian dishes, such as stir-fries, pork, veal and duck, and biryani rice. Also used in liqueurs and to disguise medicinal flavours.

TAMARIND
Tamarindus indica
Available as pulp, paste or assam powder, this substance adds a sour flavour. Used in Indian curries. To use the pulp, soak in hot water, stand 20 minutes, then extract liquid from the pulp. Use paste and powder after dissolving.

WASABI
The root of a native Japanese plant, eaten freshly grated or made into a paste. A green, powdered form is available, which is mixed into a paste with water. Used with sashimi and sushi, this hot condiment is mixed with soy sauce for dipping.

SUMAC
Rhus coriaria
The dried berries of this Mediterranean shrub are ground into a reddish-purplish powder. Available in local Lebanese and Middle Eastern food stores, sumac is used to infuse a dish with lemon flavour, without adding any liquid and is sprinkled on *fattoush*.

TURMERIC
Curcuma longa
Available as a whole root, the dried and ground aromatic rhizome is sometimes referred to as 'Indian saffron', but there is no comparison. Used to colour butter, cheese and mustard. Buy ground and keep in a cool, dark place. Cook a little with rice for a golden colour.

ZA'ATAR
A group of herbs and a Middle Eastern spice blend, containing sumac, sesame seeds and the herb za'atar itself. The fresh herbs are available only around the Mediterranean. Local Lebanese and Middle Eastern shops sell the spice blend, which is sprinkled on bread before baking. Good with barbecued meat.

Spreads, *flavourings,* baking goods & preserves

Surely, one of the most glorious sights is pantry shelves laden with glass jars of crisp pickles and preserves, or rows of richly coloured jams and marmalades. These days, few have the time to indulge in producing such delicious items from scratch, so we are fortunate that supermarkets and delicatessens offer us such a spoilt-for-choice selection of scrumptious items from all over the world. Today, even our oldest sweetening agent, honey, comes from far and wide. Not only can we still enjoy the delicate flavours harvested from our own clover meadows, orchards, and from the heathers of the Scottish Highlands, but also those gathered from fields of French sunflowers, Greek pine forests or Australian Blue Gum trees. The range is exotic and seemingly endless.

When honey began to be replaced by sugar as a sweetening agent in the Middle Ages, nobody could have imagined the various forms it would eventually take, developed to suit every purpose and occasion. Flavoursome natural brown sugars are still with us, while fine caster and icing sugars are indispensable to cooks, and rough brown and white cubes adorn smart café tables.

Flavourings and seasonings may not be necessary for a nutritionally balanced diet, but they liven up what might be otherwise dull, unimaginative food. In most households, breakfast is not complete without marmalade on the table; dinner requires the tantalising tang of mustards and sauces; chocolate has legions of fans; and without rich fruit chutney, ploughman's lunch would simply not exist. Salsa has become the taste of the town. Easy to make, this condiment may actually be good for us, made with vegetables and fruit, and embellished with chilli, lemon or lime juice, garlic and herbs.

THICK-CUT ORANGE MARMALADE
Made from the thickly cut rind (pith included) of oranges. Other citrus fruit, such as lemon, lime or grapefruit is also used for marmalade, although originally it was made with quinces.

ORANGE MARMALADE
Made from the thinly cut rind (without the pith) of the Seville orange. Pectin is usually not necessary to make most citrus marmalade, as citrus contains natural pectin, especially in the pith and the pips. These are included in the cooking process in a muslin bag.

THICK-CUT DARK MARMALADE
Made from thickly cut rind of citrus fruit, usually orange, lemon, lime or grapefruit, with the pith left on. Dark marmalade is made with brown sugar.

LIME MARMALADE
Made from thinly cut rind of limes. To make marmalade at home, the fruit should be fresh and not over-ripe. Any wax should be removed from the skin by rinsing the fruit in warm water before slicing thinly.

LEMON CURD
A smooth spread, usually made from lemons, butter and eggs. Not to be confused with lemon butter, which does not contain butter at all. Use on sandwiches and to fill pastries.

REDCURRANT JELLY
A clear, set gel, made from strained redcurrant juice, glucose syrup, pectin and citric acid. Particularly good with poultry and game, or as a sweet spread for croissants.

RASPBERRY JAM
A sweet spread made from sugar, glucose syrup, raspberries, pectin and food acids. A jam is made from cooked, small or sliced fruits and should be soft enough to spread, without being runny.

APRICOT CONSERVE
Made with cooked, whole or large pieces of apricots, with sugar, glucose syrup, pectin and food acid added. A conserve is spoonable and may be served as a sauce with dessert.

STRAWBERRY CONSERVE
Made with cooked, whole or large pieces of strawberries, with sugar, glucose syrup, pectin and food acid added. Conserve may also contain nuts.

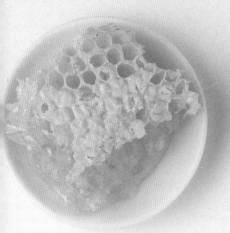

HONEYCOMB
The sweet, clear liquid, made
by bees from flower nectar,
still in the chewy, waxy comb.
The comb is also edible.

CLOVER HONEY
Paler honey is usually made by the bees enjoying
a diet of field flowers which produce a soft,
delicate flavour. Use on sandwiches, to sweeten
drinks and baked goods, and in savoury dishes
such as honey-glazed chicken wings.

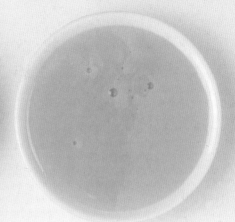

CREAMED CLOVER HONEY
A blend of pure honey, whipped
with superfine candied honey.
Good for sandwiches.

STRAWBERRY JELLY
A sweet, clear, set gel, made from
sugar, strawberry concentrate, glucose
syrup, pectin and citric acid. Particularly
good for children's sandwiches as it
contains no pips or lumps.

PEANUT BUTTER
Made from peanuts, vegetable oils,
sugar and salt. There is a choice of
smooth, crunchy and super crunchy. No-
salt and no-sugar varieties are also
available. Use as a sandwich spread and
to make satay sauce.

ORANGE-BLOSSOM HONEY
Like lavender honey and all of
those gathered from various blossoms,
it is richly flavoured and an excellent
addition when making cakes, desserts
and confectionery.

FRENCH SUNFLOWER HONEY
A bright yellow, thick honey with
a sweet but muted taste and a positive
floral aroma. Good for cooking.

GREEK PINE HONEY
Dark, thick and runny, with a
distinct pine fragrance. Its robust flavour
makes it an ideal inclusion in spicy cakes
and desserts.

HEATHER HONEY
Often from Scotland, it is a pale golden
colour, with the distinctive herbaceous
flavour of heather.

CASTER SUGAR
Finer than granulated sugar, it dissolves more quickly and is mostly used in cooking. Recommended for creamed mixtures, whisked sponges and meringues.

SUGAR CUBES
Compressed cubes of granulated sugar. Use to sweeten hot beverages. The cubes dissolve readily in hot liquid.

GRANULATED SUGAR
An inexpensive, widely used, refined white sugar. A general-purpose sweetener used in beverages and in baking and preserves.

ICING SUGAR
A finely ground, white sugar, often mixed with starch to prevent lumping (icing sugar mixture). Use for icing cakes and biscuits, for dusting cakes, puddings and sweetmeats, and in other mixtures where granulation is not desirable.

DEMERARA SUGAR
Raw brown sugar coated with a little molasses for colour and flavour. Use in coffee or, for a crunchy topping, sprinkle on cakes and desserts before baking.

DARK BROWN SUGAR
Made by mingling clarified molasses syrup with white sugar, providing colour, moisture and flavour. Soft and compact, recipe measurement is usually given for 'firmly packed' brown sugar.

LIGHT BROWN SUGAR
Less moist and slightly harder than dark brown sugar but made in the same manner. This sugar has a higher percentage of white sugar to the molasses syrup than has the dark brown.

RAW SUGAR
Made from clarified cane juice with a high sucrose content. Use as refined sugar, wherever the brown colour does not interfere visually with the finished dish. May be sprinkled on baked goods for a crunchy topping.

FRUCTOSE
Also known as **fruit sugar**, a sugar mostly found in fruit and honey as well as in certain vegetables. It is a major component in ordinary sugar. When used in cold foods, fructose is slightly sweeter than sugar.

ROCK CANDY
Large, brown crystals, very good in hot coffee as the sugar dissolves slowly, gradually taking away the taste of bitterness in the coffee.

DUTCH ROCK CANDY
Large pieces of refined white sugar used to enhance the flavour of hot chocolate, coffee and tea. The sugar dissolves slowly in liquid, gradually sweetening the drink.

COFFEE CRYSTALS
Typically large, sometimes irregular shaped crystals of sugar with caramel. It dissolves slowly to enhance the flavour of coffee.

LOW-JOULE SWEETENER
A granular artificial sweetener. Used by those with a sugar intolerance or to replace sugar in most recipes.

ROUGH BROWN SUGAR CUBES
Made from natural, unrefined cane sugar for use in coffee and other hot drinks. Rough white sugar cubes are also available.

ROSE-HIP SYRUP
A natural syrup made from the pulp of rose-hips. Dilute with water to drink or use as a dessert topping.

BLACKCURRANT SYRUP
A natural syrup made from the juice of blackcurrants and sugar. Use as a dessert topping or dilute with water to drink.

GRENADINE
A sweet, non-alcoholic syrup made from sugar and pomegranate juice. Frequently used as a red colouring in cocktails and confectionery and to sweeten desserts.

MAPLE SYRUP
The sap of North American and Canadian maple trees. A very sweet but relatively thin syrup with red-brown colour and an incomparable flavour. Excellent drizzled over pancakes and as a substitute for molasses or treacle in baking.

27

RICE SYRUP
A liquid extract made from rice. Used as a natural sweetener for cooking, baking and desserts. Ideal on ice cream.

GOLDEN SYRUP
Made from sugar liquors obtained from the cane sugar refining process. These are blended, partially inverted and evaporated to produce the viscous syrup. Gives colour and moistness to cakes. Excellent drizzled on ice cream and pancakes.

TREACLE
A slightly sweeter and standardized form of cane molasses. Rich in colour and flavour, it is ideal for moist fruit cakes, gingerbread, and treacle toffee. Its high mineral content makes it a useful dietary supplement.

SUGAR SYRUP
Made from equal quantities of sugar and water, this syrup may be used when a smooth, non-grainy texture is required, such as in ice cream and confectionery.

POMEGRANATE MOLASSES
Not to be confused with grenadine, which also has a pomegranate base, this thick, tangy syrup is frequently used in Middle Eastern cooking with beans, meats and fish. May be diluted with water for drinks or sorbets.

GLUCOSE SYRUP
Originally produced from sweetcorn and sometimes known as **corn syrup**, in Europe it is more commonly made from wheat or potato starch. A pale, viscous syrup commonly used in baking, preserves and soft drinks.

BLACK MOLASSES
The end product from the sugar refining process. Cane molasses has a pleasant, bitter-sweet flavour and aroma, and is widely used in sauces, confectionery such as liquorice, and in rich fruit cakes.

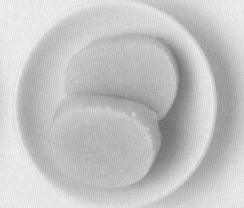

MARZIPAN
Made from ground almonds or almond paste, egg whites and sugar. Used as a filling for pastries or, as a firm mixture, marzipan can be modelled into all manner of decorative and edible shapes.

COOKING CHOCOLATE
A blend of cocoa, chocolate liquor and cocoa butter, with a lower sugar content than 'eating' chocolate, which makes it suitable for addition to sweet recipes. Available in pure and compounded varieties, each in dark, milk or white.

ORANGE ESSENCE
A highly concentrated extract from the orange, mixed with alcohol. Use in sweet cookery and creams, ice creams, confectionery, cakes, biscuits and puddings.

VANILLA ESSENCE
Extracted from the vanilla pod, mixed with alcohol, and used extensively in sweet cookery and creams, ice cream, confectionery, cakes, biscuits and puddings.

ALMOND ESSENCE
Extracted from the bitter or Chinese almond and mixed with alcohol. Use very sparingly, as the flavour is powerful.

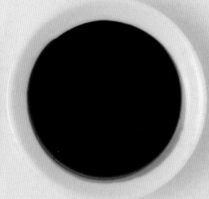

ORANGE WATER
Distilled from the blossom of the Seville tree or bitter oranges. Used extensively in Middle Eastern cooking, particularly in desserts, such as ice cream, cakes and confections, like Turkish Delight.

ROSE WATER
Distilled from rose petals, this fragrant liquid is used extensively in Middle Eastern cooking, particularly in desserts, such as ice cream, cakes and confections, like Turkish Delight.

PARISIAN ESSENCE
Used for adding a rich brown colour to gravies, soups, broths, beef tea, dark fruit cakes and puddings.

COCHINEAL
A red food colouring made from the female *Dactylopius coccus* insects after they are fertilized and before the complete development of the eggs. They are briefly baked or plunged into boiling water, dried and then crushed.

FOOD COLOURING
Edible dyes made with water and alcohol. Use very sparingly at first, then add drop by drop to achieve the required depth of colour. Use to colour icing, ice creams and confections, such as coconut ice.

BITTERS
Bitters is an aromatic mixture of cloves, cinnamon, quinine, nutmeg, rum, dried fruits, plants, flowers and various herbal and root extracts. These days used to spike up drinks and to give a perky lift to desserts.

VERJUICE
This is the unfermented acid juice of unripened white grapes. Use as you would red wine vinegar or lemon juice to flavour when cooking scallops, trout, veal or quail, to pot roast chicken pieces and to deglaze.

GENTLEMAN'S RELISH
Patum Peperium is an anchovy relish, made to the original recipe of 1828. Often sold in porcelain jars, it has a strong, sharp flavour and should be spread sparingly on buttered toast or on crackers as canapés.

CONCENTRATED YEAST EXTRACT
A combination or several yeasts – onion, celery and salt. This healthy spread is rich in B-complex vitamins, in particular, thiamine, riboflavin, niacin and folacin. Use on bread or toast or to make a hot drink.

STOCK CUBES
Dehydrated beef, chicken, fish or vegetables combined with yeast extract, salt, sugar, herbs and spices. Use in stock, soups and sauces.

ROCK SALT
Coarse textured salt in crystallized form obtained from underground deposits.

SEA SALT
Natural salt crystals made from the evaporation of sea water. Considered to be the best salt, this comes as fine, coarse or flaky crystals. Excellent for fish dishes and for seasoning new potatoes or chips.

LIQUID STOCK
Manufactured from slowly simmered chicken, beef, fish or vegetables, glucose and salt. Once opened, may be refrigerated or frozen. A convenient substitute for home-made stock.

STUFFING MIX
Add water to this ready-made mix of breadcrumbs and dried herbs – parsley, sage, rosemary, thyme and marjoram – and use for stuffing roast chicken or turkey, in meatloaves and rissoles. Use dry as a coating for cutlets, schnitzels and chicken pieces.

BREADCRUMBS
Indispensable in the kitchen cupboard, ready-made dry breadcrumbs used for coating a variety of foods before frying and for adding to meat loaves and rissoles.

GARLIC SALT
A mixture of pure ground, dehydrated garlic and salt. Use in vegetable juices, dressings, pasta sauces, salad, casseroles and soup.

CELERY SALT
A mixture of salt and ground celery seeds with the characteristic, slightly bitter flavour of celery. Use to improve the flavour of grills, salad, roasts, barbecues, stuffing, eggs, sauces and vegetables.

ONION SALT
A mixture of salt, ground dehydrated onion and herbs. Use with grills, roasts, barbecues, salad, vegetable dishes and juices, French dressing and egg dishes.

KITCHEN SALT
A fairly coarse salt, best kept in a cool, dry place, such as a salt crock. Use to enhance the flavour of many foods; even in sweet dishes a pinch is often added.

PINK PEPPERCORN
Not a true peppercorn at all, but the dried berries of a rose plant, which is grown in Madagascar. Slightly sweet and pungent, these berries pickled in brine are a good addition to salad, meat and fish.

BLACK PEPPERCORN
The black peppercorn is picked when the berry is not quite ripe, dried until it shrivels and the skin turns from brown to black. Pickled in brine, these soft peppercorns add a spicy, hot flavour.

ANCHOVY PASTE
Not to be confused with Gentleman's Relish, (See page 34), a thick, salty paste made from anchovies, salt and soya bean oil. Use sparingly to give a delicate fishy taste to pies and sauces.

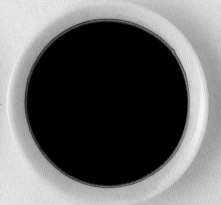

LIQUID CHLOROPHYLL
A concentrated green liquid made from alfalfa, flavoured with oil of mint. Used as a colouring, or it can be taken as a food supplement.

MONOSODIUM GLUTAMATE
Also known as **MSG** or **aji-no-moto**, it is a salty powder, used as a flavour-enhancer, though it has no taste itself. In many processed foods, MSG occurs naturally in some foods.

FOCACCIA & PIZZA FLOUR
Unbleached flour, milled to a special protein level (11.5–12.5 per cent). Eminently suitable for baking focaccia and pizza.

GELATIN
A thickening agent derived from beef and veal bones, cartilage, tendons and other tissue, or from pig skin. When combined with hot water and cooled, the mixture will set into a jelly. Also available as leaf gelatin, which is preferred by professional chefs.

EGG REPLACEMENT
Made from potato starch, tapioca flour, methylcellulose, calcium carbonate and citric acid, this product is completely free of lactose, cholesterol, eggs or derivatives. Used to make cakes, biscuits, pancakes and waffles.

BICARBONATE OF SODA
Also known as **baking soda** or **sodium bicarbonate**, an important component of baking powder. Store in a cool, dry, dark place. Mixed with acid ingredients, such as buttermilk, yoghurt or cream of tartar, it will act as a leavener.

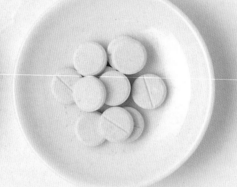

JUNKET TABLET
Junket tablets will set a pudding made with warm milk. Very light to digest, good convalescent food.

DEXTROSE
Also known as **grape sugar**, a form of sugar, it may be used as a sweetener for drinks and puddings, and to make confectionery.

CREAM OF TARTAR
Found in baking powder mixtures. Keep in a cool, dry, dark place. Combine 1 tspn of cream of tartar with 1/2 tspn of bicarbonate of soda to make 1 1/2 tspn baking powder.

MALT EXTRACT
A thick, sticky syrup, made from germinated barley grains. This extract consists mainly of maltose and is used in breads and cakes to keep them moist. Sometimes used as a spread.

TARTARIC ACID
An acid derived from many plants and the lees of wine. Used to make mineral beverages, syrups and digestive powders. In wine production, it is added when the product lacks acidity.

GRANULATED MAPLE SUGAR
Sugar crystallized from the syrup
of the maple tree. Its sweet, aromatic
flavour marries well with desserts
and pancakes.

CHESTNUT PURÉE
Cooked chestnuts pressed smooth, and
available in both sweetened or
unsweetened forms. The former is for
stuffings, while the latter is for
Mont Blancs and other sweet
chestnut desserts.

MARRON GLACÉ
Whole, peeled chestnuts preserved
in sugar and glazed with sugar syrup.
Serve as a *petit four* or use on
"special occasion" cakes.

CHINESE STEM GINGER
Chunks of stem ginger
preserved in its syrup. Use in cakes,
fillings, and stuffings – both sweet
and savoury.

MINCEMEAT
A mix of dried fruits, brown sugar
and suet, sometimes with glamorous
additions such as port, used for
Christmas mince pies.

DRIED CAPE GOOSEBERRIES
Similar to raisins, with a sweet-sour
taste, they can be used in cakes,
muesli and puddings, or simply
for decoration.

GLACÉ FRUIT
Mixed fruit that has been candied
and glazed with sugar syrup for
preservation. Use in baking and for
decorating cakes.

GLACÉ CHERRIES
Cherries that have been candied and
glazed with sugar syrup to preserve them.
Use in baking and for dessert and
cake decoration.

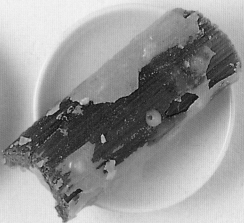

CRYSTALLIZED ANGELICA
The thick stem of the angelica herb that
has been candied and coated in
granulated sugar. Use in cakes and for
decorating trifles and baked goods.

PROVENÇALE MUSTARD
Mustard made with garlic, red capsicum, mustard seeds, white wine, oil, herbs, spices and citric acid. This tangy, smooth mustard is good with cold meats and cheese.

HERB MUSTARD
Made with herbs and garlic, whole mustard seeds, wine vinegar, salt, sugar, parsley, coriander, spices and food acid. Good with cold meat and cheese.

DIJON MUSTARD
Made with mustard seeds, vinegar, salt and citric acid, this popular, smooth mustard is available in many varieties. Frequently used as a flavour base for making mayonnaise.

GERMAN MUSTARD
Made with mustard seeds, salt, spices and food acid, this is a sweetish, smooth mustard, good with sausages and cheese.

HOT ENGLISH MUSTARD
Made with mustard seeds, malt vinegar, salt, food acid, spices, vegetable oil and lecithin, this is a hot, sharp smooth mustard.

AMERICAN MUSTARD
Made with mustard seeds, sugar, salt, food acid and spices, this smooth, sweet mustard is good with hot and cold meats and cheese.

TOMATO MUSTARD
Made with sun-ripened tomatoes, whole mustard seeds, wine vinegar, sugar, salt, food acid and spices.

WHOLEGRAIN MUSTARD
Made with whole mustard seeds, wine vinegar, salt, sugar, food acid and herbs and spices, this is a mild mustard.

FRENCH MUSTARD
Made with mustard seeds, malt vinegar, salt, food acid, sugar, caramel and herbs and spices, this is a smooth, sweet mustard.

SUN-DRIED TOMATO PASTE
Made from sun-dried tomatoes, oil,
garlic, basil, salt, pine nuts, colouring,
sugar and spice. Use in pasta sauces,
pizza and casseroles.

BLACK OLIVE PASTE
Made from black olives and olive oil. Use
in pasta sauces, pizza, casseroles and on
crackers as *hors d'oeuvres*.

PESTO
Made from basil, pine nuts, oil, garlic,
vinegar, herbs and spices. Use as a pasta
sauce or with grilled vegetables.

**DIJON MUSTARD
WITH BLACKCURRANT**
A fruity variation of the classic recipe.
Good served with game.

**COARSE GRAIN MUSTARD
WITH CHILLI**
Rough-textured mustard made with whole
mustard seeds and flavoured with chilli.
Serve with cold meats.

TOMATO PASTE
Made from five times its own weight
of ripe, juicy tomatoes, thick tomato paste
is used in pasta sauces, soups, stews
and casseroles.

**DIJON MUSTARD
WITH TARRAGON**
The classic French mustard from
the Dijon area can be flavoured with a
variety of herbs. This is good with cold
meats, especially chicken.

SAMBAL OELEK
Made from red chillies which give sambal
oelek its distinctively bright colouring.
Usually the seeds are included, as well as
salt and vinegar; served as a side dish and
used to spice up curry meals.

TAHINI
Made from ground sesame seeds, a smooth
paste with a high calcium content,
particularly when the seeds are not husked.
It is used in Middle Eastern cuisines. Use
with salads, in *hummus* and *baba ganoush*,
as a sauce and in cakes.

BLACK BEAN SAUCE
Made from fermented soya beans, this sauce may be thick, and contain beans, or smooth and thin. Widely used in Malaysian and South-East Asian cooking. Store bottle in the fridge once it is open.

SWEET BEAN PASTE
A thick, sweetened paste made from dried beans, and used for Chinese and Japanese desserts, such as moon cakes and steamed buns.

CHILLI SAUCE
A range of hot sauces, although the heat of the chillies may vary greatly, so test carefully. May also contain ginger or garlic and/or oil. These sauces do not generally need refrigeration, even after opening.

RED PEPPER SAUCE
A thin, hot, pepper sauce made from the bright orange-red Tabasco chilli. There are many imitations, but this is probably the most popular — and the best — chilli sauce in the world.

SATAY SAUCE
A peanut-based sauce, mainly used to serve with satays — small pieces of meat, fish or poultry, marinated in a spicy mixture and cooked on the barbecue or grill. The ready-bought sauce may be thinned with water or coconut milk.

TERIYAKI SAUCE
Consisting mainly of soy sauce, mirin, rice vinegar, sugar, ginger and garlic, this is used as a dipping sauce for raw vegetables and fried food, or spooned over rice and noodle dishes. May be used as a marinade for meat, chicken or fish.

MINT SAUCE
Finely chopped fresh mint in a mixture of white wine vinegar and sugar. Serve with lamb.

APPLE SAUCE
Made from apples and sugar, this sauce is particularly good with pork, hot meat dishes, such as shepherd's pie, and cold meats. A chunky variety is also available.

CRANBERRY SAUCE
An American tradition, this sweet-sour sauce with whole berries is particularly good when eaten with turkey, or any roast poultry or game for that matter. Keep refrigerated once opened.

MUSTARD SAUCE
A mildly flavoured sauce,
made with mustard, vinegar and spices.
Excellent with steaks.

BARBECUE SAUCE
A rich sauce which varies depending on
the brand. It is usually made with vinegar,
mustard, tomato paste, salt, sugar, garlic,
chillies, paprika, pepper, Tabasco and
Worcestershire sauce. Use in cooking or
as a sauce with cooked meat.

FISH GRAVY
Essentially the same as fish sauce, but
mainly comes from China, Hong Kong
and the Philippines. It is made from small,
fermented fish or prawns and used
extensively in Thai and Vietnamese food.

TOMATO SAUCE
Also known as **ketchup**, this
popular sauce is made from tomatoes,
vinegar, sugar, herbs and spices.
Frequently served with hot dogs, on
hamburgers and with hot chips.

SWEET AND SOUR SAUCE
A Chinese sauce, made with vinegar,
sugar, soy sauce, garlic and pickled,
finely shredded vegetables. Serve with
Chinese dishes.

WORCESTERSHIRE SAUCE
Made from myriad ingredients, such as
mushrooms, walnuts, vinegar, salt, soy
sauce, sugar, tamarind, peppers, spices,
garlic, caramel and anchovies. Use in
cooking, sprinkled over cooked food and
in a Bloody Mary.

PLUM SAUCE
Made from plums, vinegar, sugar,
onions, wine and spices, this
sauce is frequently served with
poultry or pork.

SOY SAUCE
Made in various Asian countries, there
may be minor differences according to
the country of origin. Used to impart a
salty flavour to dishes. May be used in
Western cooking as a salt substitute.

TARTARE SAUCE
A mayonnaise-based sauce, with the
addition of finely chopped capers,
gherkins, onions, parsley and vinegar.
Goes well with fried fish, vegetables, or
cold meats.

SWEET SPICED GHERKIN
Miniature cucumbers preserved with
sugar, salt, food acid, spices and
colouring. Eat as a snack, with salad,
terrine, cold meat or cheese.

PICKLED ONION
Small onions pickled in vinegar,
white sugar, salt, food acid, colouring and
spices. Good with cold meat or
cheese, particularly with
ploughman's lunch.

COCKTAIL ONION
These small, pickled, tangy onions come
in a range of colours: green, yellow, red.
Serve with cheese, eggs and ham, and
chopped in cold sauces.

GIARDINIERA
A mixture of vegetables, such as
cauliflower, carrot, onion, sweet pepper,
pickled cucumbers and olives,
preserved in salt, food acid, sugar and
preservative. Serve as an appetizer.

PICKLED CHILLI
Mild chillies preserved in salt, food
acid, preservative and mineral salt.
Serve as an appetizer.

PICKLED NASTURTIUM BUD
These are the flower-buds of
the nasturtium plant, pickled in vinegar
and widely used as a substitute
for capers. Often used with garlic,
lemon and olives.

STUFFED GREEN OLIVE
Green olives stuffed with minced
pimento and preserved with salt, food
acid and vegetable gums. Serve
as an appetizer.

SLICED BLACK OLIVE
Fully ripened olives sliced and preserved
with salt, food acid and ferrous gluconate.
Use in stews, risotto, pizza, pasta sauces
and salads.

KALAMATA OLIVE
A Greek olive, usually slit down
one side, preserved with salt and
citric acid or in olive oil.
Use as an appetizer, in stews,
casseroles and salads.

CORN RELISH
A sweet, mild-flavoured relish made with corn, celery, onion, sugar, vinegar and spices. Serve with cold meats, cheese and in sandwich fillings.

GHERKIN RELISH
A sweet relish made with gherkin, sugar, vinegar and spices. Serve with cold meats, cheese and in sandwich fillings.

PICCALILLI
Also known as **mustard pickle**. Made with vinegar, cauliflower, gherkin, onion, mustard, sugar, turmeric, colourings, wheatflour, salt, spices and garlic. A crisp, chunky condiment, which goes well with cold meats and cheese.

TOMATO CHUTNEY
Made from tomato, onion, sugar, salt and spices. Use with cold meats and cheese.

SWEET PICKLE
A superior dark chutney made from various vegetables, sugar, vinegar, dates, salt, apples, lemon juice, colouring, spices, food acid and garlic. Use with cold meats and cheese.

MANGO PICKLE
Made with green mangoes, vinegar, oil, onion and spices. Hot, spicy and tangy. Good with curry meals.

MANGO CHUTNEY
A sweet chutney made with mangoes and mixed spices. Perfect to serve with curries, with cold meats and cheese.

LIME PICKLE
Made with limes, vinegar, oil, salt, mustard seeds, sugar, paprika, onion, turmeric, fenugreek, chilli and citric acid. Hot, spicy and tangy; good with curry meals.

SWEET FRUIT CHUTNEY
Made with apples, sugar, tomatoes, onion, golden syrup, salt, food acid, citrus peel, currants, raisins, sultanas, and spices. Good with cold meats and cheese.

MEDIUM-HOT PICKLED PEPPER
Medium-hot peppers, pickled in vinegar, salt and spices. Refrigerate after opening. Serve with cold meats and cheese.

SAUERKRAUT
German for 'pickled cabbage'. Shredded cabbage is combined with salt and spices and left to ferment. Available fresh or in jars and cans. Rinse before using to remove some of the salt.

PRESERVED LEMON
A Moroccan speciality, quartered fresh lemons are packed tightly with salt in a jar and topped with lemon juice. Refrigerate, making sure lemons are covered. Before use, rinse, discard flesh and finely shred or chop the skin.

PICKLED GARLIC
Whole, small garlic bulbs pickled in vinegar. An essential element in the Thai crisp-rice noodle dish, *mee grob*.

PICKLED WALNUT
The whole walnut, including the shell, pickled in vinegar and spices. Good in hearty, winter casseroles.

PICKLED GINGER
Ginger, shredded and preserved in vinegar, dill, garlic and spices. Use with sandwiches, salads and cheese.

DILL PICKLE
Cucumbers, pickled in vinegar, dill, garlic and spices. Use with sandwiches, salads and cheese.

PICKLED CELERY ROOT
Shredded celery root (celeriac) pickled in vinegar. Crisp and fresh, use as a salad, dressed with vinaigrette. Refrigerate, making sure the celery root is always covered with liquid.

PRESERVED VINE LEAF
Frequently used in Greek and Middle Eastern cuisines to make *dolmas*. Should be rinsed before using to remove the salty flavour. If using fresh vine leaves, simmer in water for 10 minutes to make pliable.

MALT VINEGAR
Brewed from malt and fermented spirit. Use in salad dressings.

BALSAMIC VINEGAR
A rich, dark, rather sweet Italian vinegar, aged over many years in wooden vats. Don't use indiscriminately. Add just a few drops to a dressing or sprinkled over food. If not available, add a small amount of dark brown sugar to red wine vinegar.

CIDER VINEGAR
Made from freshly crushed, whole mature apples and stored in wooden vats, the natural aging process produces a mellow vinegar. Use in dressings.

RASPBERRY VINEGAR
A wine vinegar with natural raspberry flavour. Use in salad dressings or sprinkled over fresh fruit.

HERB VINEGAR
Fresh herbs are infused in white wine vinegar. Crush the leaves slightly before infusing to release the essential oils. Use in salad dressing and mayonnaise or to deglaze the pan when cooking meats.

WINE VINEGAR
Both red and white wine vinegars are available, as well as champagne and sherry. Red wine vinegar is used in salad dressings and in meat cookery to deglaze. Use white wine vinegar in mayonnaise and hollandaise.

WHITE VINEGAR
Brewed from fermented spirit, white vinegar is used for pickling, and apart from cooking, as an antiseptic and to treat insect bites and stings.

SHERRY VINEGAR
Traditionally made from fino sherry in the region of Jerez de la Frontera in south-west Spain, it is delicious in dressings and is a good alternative to balsamic vinegar.

MAYONNAISE
This uncooked mixture is an emulsion of egg, oil and vinegar or lemon juice. Constant whisking, adding the oil slowly, suspends the egg, oil and vinegar particles, making the mixture satiny soft.

43

Oils,
margarines & fats

There are few ingredients which have received as much publicity in recent times as fats and oils, and we can be forgiven for feeling at least a little confused by the bombardment of information.

But when you get down to it, the message is not so difficult. The first thing to recognize is that fats are a natural part of many foods and a necessary part of a good diet. Fats in our diet contribute to shiny hair and fresh, supple skin. Besides that, fats carry flavour and the difference couldn't be more clearly illustrated than by two pieces of prime beef, the first subtly marbled with fat, the second totally lean. The first has a magnificent flavour, the latter comes a very definite second in the taste stakes.

On the other hand, an excess of fat in the diet is never a good thing, no matter whether it is saturated, mono-unsaturated or polyunsaturated. Regardless of the type of fat — butter, oil or margarine — all forms have about the same high kilojoule content.

Saturated fats are potentially the most harmful to our health, and are present in meats and dairy products, but also in some vegetable products, such as palm, palm kernel and coconut oils, as well as many convenience foods.

Mono-unsaturated fats are the good guys, because they can have a beneficial effect on blood cholesterol levels by reducing the 'bad' low-density lipoprotein (LDL) cholesterol, while raising the 'good' high-density lipoprotein (HDL) cholesterol. These fats are found in olive, canola, mustard seed and peanut oils, as well as in olives, chicken, eggs, fish and nuts, such as cashew and macadamia. The much-touted, healthy Mediterranean diet consists of little meat, but a lot of fish, grains and vegetables. Olive oil, in particular, is a major source of antioxidants.

Polyunsaturated fats are found in vegetable oils, such as sunflower, safflower and soya bean oils, and polyunsaturated margarines, as well as certain nuts, seeds and fish.

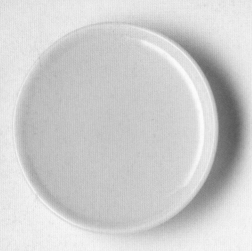

SUNFLOWER OIL
Pressed from the seeds of the sunflower,
it is a light oil excellent for frying and for
salad dressings. Extra virgin sunflower oil
is now available.

PUMPKIN SEED OIL
Extracted from pumpkin seeds, this has a
distinctive nutty taste. Good in dressings
for chunky salads.

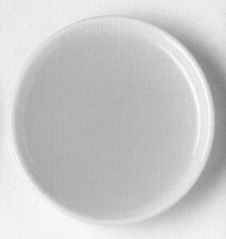

GRAPESEED OIL
Made from grape pips, this light, golden
oil adds flavour to salad dressings and
can also be used for frying.

ALMOND OIL
A delicate, pale salad oil made from
almond kernels, it has a characteristic
almond aroma and taste, and is usually
fairly expensive.

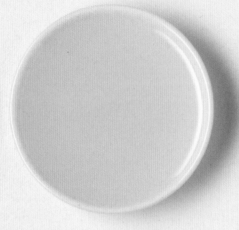

GROUNDNUT OIL
Made from peanuts, and often used in
place of olive oil, it is a good all-purpose
oil for cooking and dressings, and is
particularly good in Asian dishes prepared
in the wok.

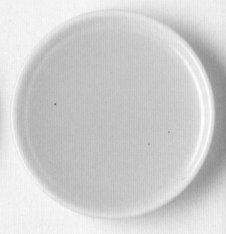

WALNUT OIL
Made from pressed walnuts, it has a
strong, nutty flavour and is excellent in
salad dressings, or for drizzling over
broccoli. Usually bought in small
quantities as it's expensive and doesn't
keep well.

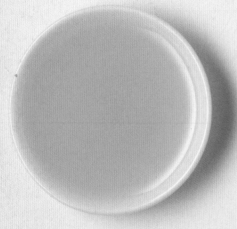

PORCINI OIL
Extra virgin olive oil infused with
porcini. It has a seductive wild mushroom
flavour and is delicious drizzled on pasta
and rice dishes.

TRUFFLE OIL
An infusion of black truffle in extra virgin olive
oil. Use to dress pastas, cold rice dishes, or in
mashed potato.

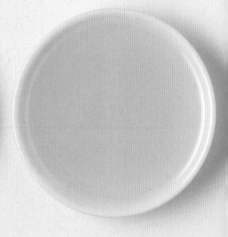

HAZELNUT OIL
Made from pressed hazelnuts, it has a
toasty, nutty flavour and is excellent for
leafy salads which need a lift.

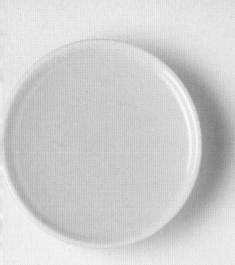

SAFFLOWER OIL
The safflower plant, with its red, orange or yellow flowers, is also known as **Mexican saffron** and is used to produce a light oil high in polyunsaturates. Available refined or unrefined, it is good for dressings and for use in light mayonnaise.

CORN OIL
Made from maize kernels, it is an inexpensive oil, good for crisp, deep frying. The unrefined oil has a definite corn flavour, while the refined oil is rather bland.

VEGETABLE OIL
Made from a blend of vegetable products, this pale, fairly tasteless oil is inexpensive and is best reserved for frying.

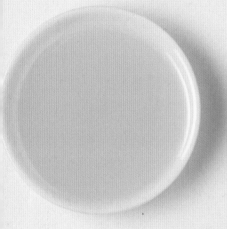

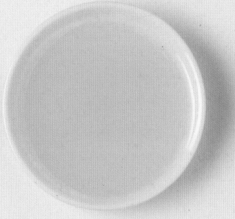

ORANGE OIL
Olive oil infused with orange. Good with a salad of chicory and walnut, or a cold duck salad with frisée.

LEMON OIL
Olive oil, piquantly infused with whole lemons. Good for marinades, dipping crusty bread, drizzled over fish, or stirred into fresh pasta or an asparagus, courgette or prawn risotto.

GRAPEFRUIT OIL
Olive oil infused with grapefruit. Use in fresh green salads.

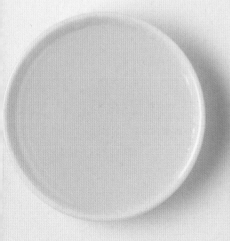

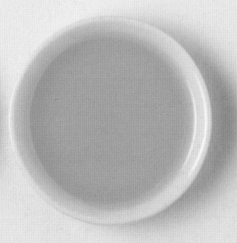

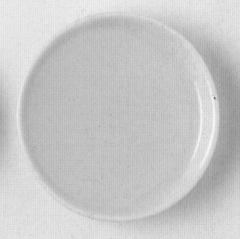

SOYA BEAN OIL
Copious amounts of oil are sourced from the soya bean and used in oil blends and margarines. It is a good deep-frying oil because of its high smoking point.

EXTRA VIRGIN OLIVE OIL
The best of oils, it is derived from the first pressing of fresh olives. The colour is rich and green, and the flavour unmatchable, with a little less acidity than virgin olive oil. Rich in antioxidants, and with a perfect balance of scent and taste, it is used on salads and cold dishes.

LIGHT OLIVE OIL
A blend of olive oils, producing a blander flavour. Good for cooking and for salad dressings.

HERB OIL
Herb oils are infused with one herb or a combination of herbs, spices and condiments. Garlic and chillies are often added. Make your own by placing herbs in a bottle of oil, olive usually. Gently heat or leave in a warm place.

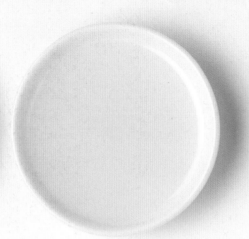

CANOLA OIL
A refined rape-seed oil developed in Canada. High in mono-unsaturated fats, very low in saturates, with a good amount of omega-6 and omega-3 polyunsaturates.

MUSTARD-SEED OIL
Mustard-seed oil is high in mono- and polyunsaturated fats, very low in saturates, and high in omega-3, with traces of omega-6. It does not have a mustard flavour.

OLIVE OIL
Of all the oils, this is the highest in mono-unsaturated fats, with a small amount of saturated fats and omega-6. Use for salad dressings.

SESAME OIL
With about equal amounts of poly- and mono-unsaturated fats and a small amount of saturated fat, this oil should be used sparingly as the taste is powerful.

CREAMED VEGETABLE OIL
A ready-prepared butter or margarine alternative made from polyunsaturated blend vegetable oil. Use in baking, substituting millilitres for grams, and when melted shortening is called for, as in stir-fries, and for greasing tins and pans or brushing filo pastry

AVOCADO OIL
This refined oil is high in mono-unsaturated fats and is used mainly for dressings, vinaigrettes and mayonnaise, but also as a flavour-seal when grilling or roasting white meat and fish.

PISTACHIO OIL
High in mono-unsaturated fats. Use to add the distinctive taste and aroma of pistachio nuts to vinaigrettes, marinades and nut-based salads.

OLIVE OIL SPREAD
A blend of olive oil and margarine, with a delicate olive flavour, suitable for the table and cooking.

SUET
The white fat that surrounds ox kidneys is available in packs, minced and ready to use, or whole from your butcher. It is used in steamed pudding, suet pastry and Christmas puddings.

LARD
This rendered pork fat is a mixture of poly- and mono-unsaturated fats. Once widely used in pastries and doughs or for shallow and deep-frying. A little added to pastry mixtures gives a crisp result.

DRIPPING
Leftover fat and juices from a roasted joint of beef, lamb or pork. Available from butchers, it sets solid when cold and can be used to roast potatoes and make gravies.

COPHA
Derived from the coconut, this is a mainly saturated fat. Melted and mixed with other ingredients, copha will set when cool. Used to make ever-popular chocolate crackles and coconut ice.

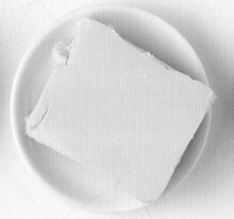

COOKING MARGARINE
Cooking margarine has slightly more mono-unsaturated fats than saturated fats.

SUNFLOWER MARGARINE
Made from sunflower oil, this margarine is predominantly polyunsaturated. Use on bread and toast, in cooking and baking.

CANOLA SPREAD
Made with canola oil, this spread is predominantly mono-unsaturated, with small amounts of saturated fats, omega-6 and omega-3. Use on bread and toast, in cooking and baking.

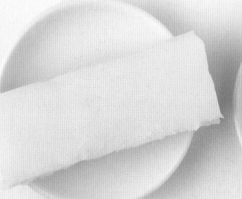

SOLIDIFIED COOKING OIL
This is a shortening, a blend of animal and vegetable oil. It contains higher melting fats and salt levels than margarine. Will maintain a constant heat level. Very good for deep-frying and making pastries.

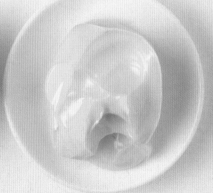

SOYA SPREAD
Made from soya bean oil, this spread is predominantly polyunsaturated, with a fair amount of mono-unsaturates, omega-3 and a small amount of saturated fats. Use on bread and toast, in cooking and baking.

Dairy & farm produce

When asked to picture the typical countryside, one immediately thinks of dairy cattle contentedly grazing on the rolling hills and in the lush, green valleys, as they have done for hundreds of years. In the old days, the white-tiled farm-house dairy was relied upon to produce wonderful, flavoursome butter, rich, thick cream and cheese, as well as fresh milk. There would also be hens roaming around the yard providing a daily supply of eggs.

There are still traditional producers who carry on these time-honoured methods, but increasingly, our dairy produce comes from commercial operations from all over the world. Today the richness and variety of farm produce, whether we live in the country or the city, is truly wonderful.

Even in times gone by, it would be hard to imagine a household without milk, which is so richly endowed with calcium, so important for strong bones and healthy teeth. However, today milk comes in many forms.

The range of creams also has to be seen to be believed. Even single cream now comes in thick or pouring consistencies as well as its regular state.

Butters differ in flavour, depending on their country of origin. Unsalted butters from Denmark are popular for everyday use, while British regional butters are at a premium, but are well worth the cost. From northern France, the excellent unsalted *beurre crû* is a luxury butter for enriching sauces and, using as it comes, on crusty bread.

The world of cheese is vast with regionals, international champions and farmhouse-produced cheeses widely available. When buying cheese, try to go to a specialist cheese shop, where attendants are knowledgeable and can give you advice on ripeness, flavour and texture, and will introduce you to new varieties. There's enough choice to keep you happily exploring for a lifetime.

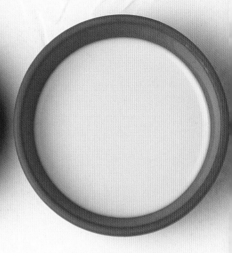

COW'S MILK
When pasteurized, it is heat-treated, whole milk with 3.9 to over 5 per cent fat. When homogenized, the cream is evenly distributed throughout. Long-life milk is ultra heat-treated homogenized milk that does not need refrigeration until opened.

SEMI-SKIMMED MILK
This is a reduced fat milk containing only 1.1 per cent of fat. UHT semi-skimmed milk is also available.

EVAPORATED MILK
This milk is condensed to 40 per cent of its original volume. Store indefinitely, but once opened, refrigerate and use quickly. May be reconstituted by adding three parts water to two parts evaporated milk.

POWDERED MILK
Made up with water, it is usually low-fat, and a good store cupboard standby.

SKIMMED MILK
Ideal for those on a weight-reduction programme, this is whole milk with almost all the fat removed. UHT skimmed milk is also available.

CONDENSED MILK
More concentrated than evaporated milk, condensed milk is very sweet, with added sugar. Store indefinitely. Does not need refrigeration once opened. Reconstitute to sweet milk, adding twice the volume of milk to water.

FLAVOURED MILK
Available pasteurized, sterilized or UHT as whole, semi-skimmed or skimmed milk. Flavoured with a variety of fruit tastes, chocolate or coffee, it can be drunk as is, or made into milk shakes.

BUTTERMILK
Made from pasteurized skimmed milk, it is a low-fat, thick milk with a slightly acidic flavour. Good for baking.

GOAT'S MILK
Nutritionally similar to full-fat cow's milk, although it is slightly sweeter and whiter. Refrigerate and check the best-before date. Good for drinking.

FRESH SINGLE CREAM
A pouring-consistency cream. it is also available in UHT form. It contains 18 per cent fat and is not suitable for whipping. Good on desserts and fruit.

EXTRA THICK SINGLE CREAM
Thicker than single cream and spoonable, it contains 18 per cent fat and is not suitable for whipping. It is good on desserts and fruit.

NATURAL YOGHURT
Made from either cow's or sheep's milk, it can contain living bacteria, and must be refrigerated and consumed by the 'use by' date. Available in a number of styles, it can contain up to 10.5 per cent fat.

SOURED CREAM
Made from homogenized milk with cultures added to give a slightly acidic flavour. Good in stews such as Hungarian goulash, soups, sauces and dips.

CLOTTED CREAM
Originating from Devon, Cornwall and Somerset, this is a high butterfat (55 per cent) cream which is essential for strawberry cream teas. It is also delicious in cakes and with berries.

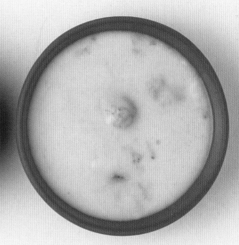

FLAVOURED YOGHURT
Flavoured yoghurt is available in full-fat and low-fat varieties, and in many different flavours. The extra sugar added usually makes it higher in calories (kilojoules) than plain yoghurt.

DOUBLE CREAM
A rich pouring cream which whips well given its 48 per cent fat content. Also available in extra thick, homogenized to produce a sturdy spooning cream. **Whipping cream** (35–40 per cent fat) will whisk to double the volume.

CRÈME FRAÎCHE
French double cream fermented enough to give a slightly sour flavour. Excellent with fresh fruit desserts, in pancakes, sauces and soups. A low-fat variety is also available.

DRINKING YOGHURT
Made from yoghurt with added milk and fruit juice. It is available either fresh or in UHT form.

BUTTER
Made by whipping cream until the butterfat separates. Usually salt is added for better keeping quality. Refrigerate and check best-before date. Use on bread and toast, in cooking and baking. Mainly saturated fat and very high in calories.

FRESH DUCK'S EGG
Larger than a hen's egg, with a stronger flavour and slightly oily taste. Not suitable for boiling as it needs a long time to cook to destroy harmful bacteria, but it is good in baking.

PICKLED EGG
A fresh hen's egg is hard-boiled and pickled in a mixture of vinegar and salt. Raw onion rings may be added for extra flavour. Serve as a snack or as an accompaniment to cold meats or ploughman's lunch.

UNSALTED BUTTER
Made by whipping cream until the butterfat separates. Sometimes a culture is added for a lightly sour flavour. Refrigerate and check best-before date. Has the same saturated fat and calorie content as salted butter.

PRESERVED DUCK'S EGG
The yolk is rich, thick and yellow/orange in colour. Use in Chinese pastries or boil for 10 minutes; the texture is mealy, like cooked dried beans. Store in the fridge for months; but, once the shell is cracked, use within a day.

GHEE
Unsalted butter which has been clarified, i.e. the milk solids have been removed. Ghee can be heated to high temperatures without burning. Refrigerate for long periods.

100-YEAR-OLD EGG
Also known as **1000-year-old egg**, this is a duck's egg covered with a paste of leaves, wood ash, lime, salt and water, and cured in a sealed jar for about 15 days, then rested for a month. Serve as an appetizer.

EMU'S EGG
About 10–12 times the size of a hen's egg, with a
similar nutritional make-up, these eggs are good for
making omelettes.

OSTRICH'S EGG
Larger than an emu's egg, with a thick shell. Use in the
same way as hen's eggs, in making scrambled eggs
and in baking cakes.

HEN'S EGG
White and brown hen's eggs are nutritionally identical, the
shell colour merely indicates the variety of hen which laid
the egg. Yolk colour may be more intense from a free-
range hen than from a battery hen, depending on what it
has eaten. Boil, poach, bake, fry, scramble or pickle.

QUAIL'S EGG
About a third of the size of a hen's egg, these
thin-shelled eggs are usually cooked for
about three minutes and shelled. Good in
salad, aspic, pickled in mild vinegar, or fried,
for mini bacon and eggs *hors d'œuvre*.

SICILIAN BUTTERCUP HEN'S EGG

SHAVER HEN'S EGG

BRAHMA HEN'S EGG

ORPINGTON HEN'S EGG

WELLSUMMER HEN'S EGG

BANTAM'S EGG

56

MARAN HEN'S EGG

GUINEA FOWL'S EGG

INDIAN RUNNER DUCK'S EGG

CAMPBELL DUCK'S EGG

LAVENDER ARCANA HEN'S EGG

BLUE DUCK'S EGG

WATSONIA
A mild-flavoured, creamy textured, Australian cheese made from cow's milk.

BEGA BROWN WAX
A sharp-flavoured, mid-range, Australian cheddar, made from cow's milk.

FARMERS UNION VINTAGE
A soft-textured, Australian, cow's milk cheese with a moderately sharp flavour.

KING ISLAND BLACK WAX MATURED
A sharp-flavoured, Tasmanian, cow's milk cheese with crumbly texture, matured for 18 months.

PYENGANA CLOTH CHEDDAR
A cloth-bound, Australian, cow's milk cheddar, with a sharp, lingering flavour.

EPICURE
A New Zealand, cheddar-style cheese, with sharp flavour and crumbly texture. Made from cow's milk.

KING ISLAND SURPRISE BAY
A drier-style, Tasmanian cheddar, made from cow's milk. It has a sharp flavour and crumbly texture. Milder than Black Wax Matured.

58

SOUTH CAPE VINTAGE
A full-bodied, flavoursome, Australian cheddar, made from cow's milk.

WENSLEYDALE
A semi-hard, English cheese made from cow's milk. It has a flaky texture and sweetish aftertaste.

RED LEICESTER
A hard, English cheese made from cow's milk. Grainy, yet moist texture with hard rind and a full, rich flavour.

RACLETTE
This famous Swiss melting cheese made from cow's milk gives its name to a traditional cheese dish. A whole cheese is melted and blistered over the fire, then scraped on to hot plates. It is traditionally served with gherkins, boiled potatoes and onion salad.

FONTINA
A creamy cheese from the Italian Aosta Valley, made from full-cream cow's milk. With a pronounced flavour and soft texture, this is an excellent melting cheese.

SAGE DERBY
Hard, rindless, uncooked, cow's milk cheese, very like cheddar. Has fresh sage leaves rubbed in.

59

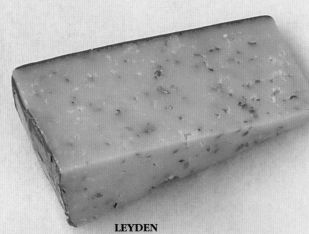

LEYDEN
A close-textured, Dutch cheese with hard rind, made from part-skimmed cow's milk, with added cumin and/or caraway seeds and spices.

HAVARTI
Similar in flavour and texture to Esrom, this cow's milk cheese is less pungent. Tiny, irregular holes and small cracks are typical. A good melting cheese.

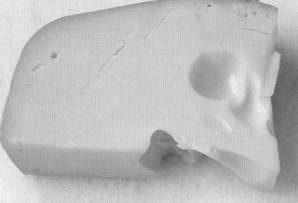

MAASDAM
A relatively new, hard, Dutch cheese, with large holes, mild flavour and nutty aftertaste. Made with cow's milk. A good substitute for Emmental.

GOUDA
A semi-hard, Dutch cheese with mild flavour. Made with cow's milk. When mature, the cheese becomes more piquant.

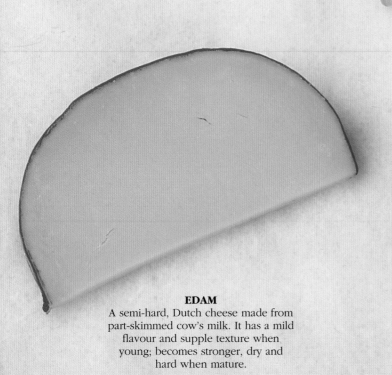

EDAM
A semi-hard, Dutch cheese made from part-skimmed cow's milk. It has a mild flavour and supple texture when young; becomes stronger, dry and hard when mature.

KASHKAVAL
A hard cheese from Hungary with aromatic, salty flavour and a dry, supple rind. Made from ewe's milk.

KASERI
A Greek cheese, semi-hard
with salty flavour, similar
to Provolone. Made
from ewe's milk.

JARLSBERG
A hard, Norwegian cheese made
from cow's milk. It has a soft
texture, large holes and sweet
flavour. A good substitute
for Emmental.

AUSTRALIAN EMMENTAL
Made in New South Wales,
a cow's milk cheese
similar to
Swiss Emmental.

AMBROSIA
A soft-textured,
Italian cheese, made
from cow's milk;
distinguished by tiny holes
permeating the
cheese. Has a mild but
distinctive flavour.

TILSIT
A semi-hard cheese made in several
northern European countries from
cow's milk, typically has a few cracks,
medium-sized holes and a
distinctive flavour.

ESROM
A Danish, semi-hard
cheese with small holes
and a spicy, pungent
flavour. Made from
cow's milk.

61

MOZZARELLA
Originally made only from buffalo milk, but now mostly from cow's milk (when it should be called *fior di latte*), this cream cheese has an elastic, stringy quality.

PROVOLONE
Typically a long, cylindrical shape, bound with string, this is a semi-soft to hard, salty flavoured, Italian cheese made from cow's milk. Ranges from semi-strong to strong.

CREAM CHEESE
A fresh cheese made from whole cow's milk or whole milk and cream. It has a high fat content, but there are low-fat varieties.

BOCCONCINI
Small balls of fresh mozzarella, preserved in whey. Some enterprising smaller manufacturers are making the buffalo milk variety again.

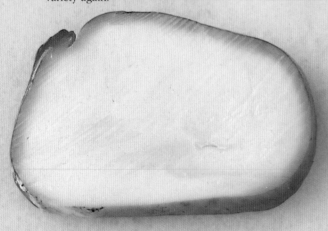

SMOKED MOZZARELLA
A cheese with all the qualities of mozzarella, but with a distinctly smoky flavour.

MATURE STRACCHINO
This Italian cheese develops a distinctive crust and has a soft centre and mild flavour. Made with cow's milk.

BAKED RICOTTA
Fresh ricotta baked in a tin and served in slices. Egg whites, paprika or other flavourings and oil are often added.

FETTA
A traditional Greek-style cheese made from the milk of goat, sheep or cow. It has a soft-to-firm or crumbly texture, depending on method of manufacture. Salty flavour and frequently sold in a brine solution.

NEUFCHÂTEL
A soft, fresh, unripened, low-fat cream cheese with refreshing taste. Made from cow's milk.

BOURSIN
A French, soft, cream cheese with garlic and herbs added as flavouring. Made from cow's milk.

CREAMED COTTAGE CHEESE
A low-fat cheese. Small, white, tender particles that have been washed repeatedly, and a light cream dressing added. Made from cow's milk.

COTTAGE CHEESE
A low-fat cheese which comes in a fairly solid mass, with a paste-like consistency and mildly acidic flavour. Made from cow's milk.

RICOTTA
A cream cheese traditionally made from whey but now mostly from skimmed cow's milk. Very low in calories. Pure white with a soft texture and barely discernible sour flavour.

MASCARPONE
A cream cheese made from pure cow's cream. May replace cream in recipes, for example in desserts and pasta sauces.

QUARK
An unsalted, slightly acidic type of cottage cheese made with skimmed milk.

63

FIORE SARDO
A Sardinian cheese, made from ewe's
milk. It has a hard texture and tangy
flavour which becomes stronger as
the cheese ages, at which stage
it is used for grating.

OSSAI IRATY
A firm, sheep's milk
cheese with a hard rind,
smooth, slightly holey
texture and nutty flavour.
Originates in the Pyrénées.

HALOUMI
A stringy, salty,
goat's cheese of Middle
Eastern descent, with chewy
texture and mild flavour. Frequently
grilled or fried in oil.

KEFALOTYRI
Usually made from a mixture of raw,
unpasteurized sheep's and goat's milk. It
has a firm texture and salty flavour. Used
in cooking and for grating.

ASH LOG
The ash is traditionally the
ash of vine leaves. A fresh-to-
semi-mature or mature cheese with
full-bodied flavour. Made with goat's milk.

KERVELLA
A magnificent, fresh cheese with sharp
flavour and slightly grainy texture. Made
with goat's milk.

SHEEP'S MILK RICOTTA
Ricotta cheese with a pronounced
tangy flavour.

MANCHEGO
A Spanish, sheep's milk
cheese, made from whole
milk of sheep that graze at
La Mancha. Full-bodied
flavour, this is a hard variety,
frequently used for grating.

SHEEP'S MILK BLUE
A powerful, firm-textured cheese in
which the blue culture matures the
cheese from the inside out.

YUULONG LAVENDER
Australian cheese, with small
fragments of lavender and a
distinct lavender flavour.
Made from sheep's milk.

FRESH GOAT PYRAMID
A soft-textured, tangy flavoured, goat's
milk cheese.

FRESH GOAT CURD
The fresh curd has a far milder
flavour than the cheese.

CROTTIN
A firm, matured, goat's milk
cheese, with distinctive rind and
pungent flavour.

KING ISLAND ADMIRALTY
A Tasmanian, cow's milk cheese, Stilton-style with a high moisture content and strong flavour.

DOLCELATTE
A soft, creamy textured cow's milk, blue vein. This Italian cheese is a milder version of Gorgonzola.

GORGONZOLA
A green-marbled, cow's milk cheese with a creamy, soft texture and buttery flavour. Serve at room temperature.

GIPPSLAND BLUE
Very distinctive, creamy textured, blue-veined, Australian, cow's milk cheese with strong, full-bodied flavour.

STILTON
A semi-hard, English, blue-veined, cow's milk cheese, with a slightly creamy, yet crumbly, texture and a rich, complex flavour.

BLUE CASTELLO
Very creamy textured, Danish blue-veined, cheese with full-bodied flavour. Made with cow's milk.

DEEP BLUE
A traditional cow's milk blue cheese from Tasmania. It has an earthy aroma, a pleasant taste and a firm but crumbly texture.

BLUE BRIE
A mild, creamy textured, blue-veined, cow's milk cheese with the typical white mould of Brie.

DANISH BLUE
A semi-hard, blue-veined cheese with a creamy, buttery flavour and slight tang. Made with cow's milk.

KING ISLAND BASS STRAIT
A drier type of blue-veined, cow's milk cheese from Tasmania. Firm texture and full flavour.

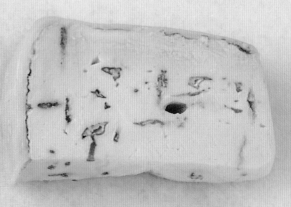

SHADOWS OF BLUE
A mild, soft-textured, blue-veined cheese, with a stronger flavour than Blue Brie. Made with cow's milk.

**TARRAWINGEE
WASHED RIND**
Semi-soft texture and
delicate flavour. An Australian cheese
made with ewe's milk.

**MUNGABAREENA
WASHED RIND**
Pungent-smelling,
strong-flavoured cheese
with a Brie-like texture
and hint of eucalyptus.
Made with cow's milk.

**TOP PADDOCK WASHED
RIND**
Semi-firm, mild, Australian
cheese, with typical orange
rind. Made with cow's milk.

LIMBURGER
Semi-hard, full-flavoured, strong-smelling
cheese, made in Germany, Belgium and
Alsace. Made with cow's milk.

TOP PADDOCK WINE WASHED
Semi-firm, Australian cheese, washed
with a fine cabernet. It has a typically
sticky rind and a strong smell when
mature. Made with cow's milk.

**CAMEMBERT
(FACTORY MADE)**
The more commonly found
version of the original French,
cow's milk cheese.

**JINDI TRIPLE
CREAM**
An Australian,
Brie-style
cheese, very
creamy and rich
in flavour.

BRIE
A soft, French, cow's milk
cheese with a pronounced,
sweet smell when ripe.

TALEGGIO
An Italian, soft cheese with
mild flavour and soft rind.
Excellent for melting.

PORT SALUT
A semi-soft, French, cow's milk cheese with
soft texture and bland flavour.

ST NECTAIRE
A semi-firm, double-pressed,
French cheese with a musty
smell and nutty flavour. Made
from raw cow's milk and
matured in damp cellars.

GRANA PADANO
An admirable substitute for Reggiano Parmigiano. Made from semi-skimmed cow's milk, this medium-fat, hard, Italian cheese is best eaten with fruit or grated.

GRATED PARMESAN
Ideally, Parmesan should be bought in a piece and grated just before serving. Otherwise the cheese loses its flavour and dries out quickly.

GRUYÈRE
A nutty flavoured, hard, smooth, pale yellow, Swiss cheese used in the preparation of *gratins* and fondues, as well as eaten on its own. Made from cow's milk.

ASIAGO
Originating in the Italian Alpine region, this semi-hard cheese with tiny to mid-size holes has a mild, tangy taste when young. The texture becomes hard and the flavour intensifies with age; at this stage the cheese is mostly used for grating.

MIMOLETTE VIEILLE
A firm, reddish, slightly holey, cow's milk cheese with a full-bodied flavour. Originally made in Holland and now in France.

PECORINO ROMANO
A cooked, hard cheese from Sardinia and Rome made from full-fat, sheep's milk. Usually well matured. A good grating cheese which is sharper in flavour than Parmesan.

REGGIANO PARMIGIANO
The undisputed king of Italian cheeses, this fine-flavoured cheese only from Parma, Reggio Emila and Modena is mainly used for grating, but, especially when young, it also makes a fine ending to a meal, eaten with fruit. Made from cow's milk.

PECORINO VIEILLE
A popular sheep's milk cheese from Italy's central and southern regions where, when young, it is typically eaten with uncooked young broad beans or with a crunchy pear. When older, it is mostly used for grating.

71

TEIFI
A hard, full-fat,
unpasteurized cow's
milk cheese from Wales;
it has a characteristic
peppery taste.

**KIRKHAM'S
LANCASHIRE**
A superlative farmhouse
cheese made from
unpasteurized cow's
milk from the Kirkham's
herd in Lancashire.
Ranking amongst the best
in Britain, this white,
crumbly cheese is
matured for 4 to 6 months
and has a mellow,
subtle taste.

MONTGOMERY'S CHEDDAR
A medium-textured cheese with a smooth,
fruity flavour, made from home-produced
and pasteurized cow's milk and matured for
up to 18 months. Cheddar is ideal for
ploughman's lunch as well as cooking, toasting
and for sauces.

KEEN'S CHEDDAR
A classic Somerset cheddar from a small
producer, using unpasteurized cow's milk from
its own herd. This firm-bodied cheese is
matured for between 10 and 18 months, and has
a sharp, nutty flavour.

GABRIEL
From Cork in Ireland, this is a Swiss mountain-style cheese similar to gruyère. Made from unpasteurized cow's milk, it has a dense, dry, hard texture, and a tough rind. The taste is full, with a zing on the palate.

CHESHIRE
Also known as **Chester** in Europe, this is the oldest of British cheeses with some farmhouse versions still made from unpasteurized cow's milk. It is crumbly with a fresh taste and a salty tang, and can be red, blue with subtle veining, or white, the latter having a slightly sharper taste. Red and white are good melting cheeses.

DOUBLE GLOUCESTER
A hard cheese made from whole cow's milk, with farmhouse versions sometimes still made from unpasteurized milk. Eaten at around 4 - 6 months, this cheese is firm, but with a subtle, closed texture. The taste has notes of nuttiness and citrus.

SINGLE GLOUCESTER
Made from skimmed cow's milk which gives it a mild, light, soft texture, this cheese should be enjoyed in its youth.

SPENWOOD
From Berkshire, this modern farmhouse, hard, sheep's milk cheese is creamy on the palate with a hint of natural sweetness.

73

WIGMORE
A Berkshire cheese made from
unpasteurized sheep's milk, and one of
the few remaining washed rind cheeses
made in Britain. Semi-soft with a giving
texture, it has a rich taste reminiscent
of cashews.

EMLETT
An unpasteurized sheep's milk cheese
which comes in small, stubby rounds. The
crusted rind is Penicillium. It has a
characteristic yeasty, mushroomy aroma
and, on the tongue, a soft texture which
softens more as it ages.

MILLEENS
An Irish unpasteurized
cow's milk cheese from
the west Cork region. It
is semi-soft, dotted with
small holes, and has a
good savoury taste with
notes of herbs in the
background.

BONCHESTER
Scottish farmhouse cheese
made from unpasteurized
Jersey cow's milk. It is rich
and buttery with a
seductive soft and creamy
consistency.

MRS SEATER'S ORKNEY
Nationally famous Scottish island cheese which is similar to Cheddar. Made from unpasteurized cow's milk, it is crumbly with an acid bite, and needs to be eaten young.

DUCKETTS CAERPHILLY
One of the traditional British territorials, this is the best of the Caerphilly. Made from unpasteurized cow's milk, it is moist and crumbly with a subtle, slightly sour taste. As it ripens rapidly, Caerphilly is ready for eating after just two weeks.

CASHEL BLUE
Made by the family Grubb who were thrown out of England for religious reasons in the 17th century. They ended up in Tipperary and became famous millers and butter makers. In the mid 1980s, their descendants developed Cashel Blue, the first Irish blue cheese. Moist and creamy, backed up with a sharp, salty bite.

LLANGLOFFLAN
A Welsh farmhouse cheese from Pembrokeshire, made from the unpasteurized milk of Jersey and Swiss Brown cows. Crumbly with a sensational creamy taste, this cheese has fruity, herbaceous and peppery notes. There is also a red version flavoured with chives and garlic.

75

AMI DU CHAMBERTIN

A small, round, unpasteurized cow's milk cheese from Burgundy, it is washed in *Marc de Bourgogne*. It has a robust and salty, slightly pungent flavour.

MARIOLLES

Made in Flanders, this is a strong, spicy, square cheese with a rind washed, many times, in brine. It should be ripened for up to 4 months and is delicious on a cheese board or cooked in a pie or flan.

LANGRES

A farmhouse unpasteurized cow's milk cheese with a washed rind. It comes from the Champagne region, and has a characteristic depression in the top due to the turning of the curds. Mostly used on cheeseboards, but it melts well for dipping.

VACHERIN MONT D'OR

Vacherin is traditionally made in winter by the French and the Swiss producers of Comté. Bound with pine bark, it is a flat cheese with a creamy texture and an earthy, mushroomy taste.

SAINT-NECTAIRE

From the Auvergne region, this is a semi-soft, full-fat, farmhouse cheese made from unpasteurized cow's milk. Featuring a hard rind with a greyish crust, it is smooth and rich with herbaceous notes.

CAMEMBERT DE NORMANDIE

This is the traditional Camembert made from unpasteurized cow's milk. The more common factory-made Camemberts are usually made from pasteurised milk. It has a soft, white, bloomy rind and a creamy texture when ripe.

BRIE DE MEAUX
From the Île-de-France, where it has been made since 774AD, this is the traditional, unpasteurized, farmhouse cheese. It has a soft, bloomy, white rind, and a smooth, rich, creamy texture when ripe. Both aroma and taste have a hint of wild mushroom.

CRAYEUX DE RONCQ
A square cow's milk cheese which is washed in the local beer, it has a pungent and salty flavour.

MUNSTER
Traditionally or creamery made in Alsace, this is a smooth, yellow cheese with a thin, orange rind. The distinguishing features are its pungent aroma and mildly acidic, creamy flavour, which teams up particularly well with onions and rye bread.

FLEUR DU MAQUIS
An unpasteurized sheep's milk cheese from Corsica. Covered in herbs and fresh, sweet chillies, it is aromatic with a deliciously creamy flavour.

CŒUR POITEVIN
A heart-shaped goat's cheese with a natural crust and a creamy texture.

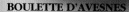

BOULETTE D'AVESNES
The curd of this cone-shaped, fresh cheese is mashed with tarragon, parsley, crushed cloves and paprika. It has a spicy flavour and a firm, but crumbly, moist texture.

BANON À LA FEUILLE
From Provence, it can be made from goat's, sheep's or cow's milk, or a mix. To help age and flavour the cheese, it is traditionally wrapped in chestnut leaves and tied with raffia.

TOMME
Tommes are traditional mountain cheeses produced in winter. They can be made from sheep's, cow's or goat's milk, and are recognisable by their thick crust and semi-hard texture dotted with tiny holes.

SAINT-MARCELLIN
From the Rhône, this cheese can be made from either unpasteurized goat's or cow's milk. Produced as a small, round disc with a wrinkly crust, it is soft and meltingly creamy. Although usually a table cheese, it is also good for cooking.

LIVAROT
From Normandy, a semi-soft, unpasteurized cow's milk cheese with an orangey crust traditionally wrapped in reeds or paper. It has a strong, pungent flavour and a gently rubbery texture. Good for snacks.

BONDE EN GATINE
A small, log-shaped goat's cheese rolled in ash, it features a crumbly texture and a fruity tang.

CROTTIN DE CHAVIGNOL
From the Loire, a winter, unpasteurized goat's milk cheese which hardens on ageing. Dubbed with a name that means "horse droppings", its white interior has a crumbly texture and a full flavour. Excellent for grilling.

BLEU D'AUVERGNE
Traditional farmhouse or creamery made cow's milk blue cheese which is moist and crumbly with a lively, herbaceous, fresh, spicy taste. Good in salads.

BLEU DE GEX
Blue cheese from the Jura, sometimes known as **Bleu de Haut Jura**. A traditional farmhouse or co-op, unpasteurized cow's milk blue cheese which comes in a large wheel. The taste is pungent and the texture firm. A good salad cheese.

ROQUEFORT
From the Rouergue and made from unpasteurized sheep's milk. Cheeses have been matured in the limestone caves of the Cambalou Plateau, where the moulds known as *penicillium roquefortii* thrive, for more than 2000 years. This great, aristocratic cheese has a damp crust and a sweet, crumbly creaminess cut through with the delicious, sharp taste of green/blue mould.

FOURME D'AMBERT
A cow's milk blue cheese from the Auvergne. The crust is soft and supple and the cheese is smooth and moist, spiked with blue patches of mould. A strong, sharp, table cheese, also good for leafy salads and dressings.

BEAUFORT D'ESTIVE
A gruyère style of cheese from the Haute Savoie. Always found at ski resorts, it comes in large wheels and melts well to make fondue. Made with the summer milk from cattle which graze on alpine grass and flowers, it has a hard, dark crust and a smooth, close texture. A good grating cheese.

EMMENTAL
Made in Switzerland since 1293, this classic hard cheese is recognisable by its large holes and its nutty fragrance and taste. A good grilling and melting cheese.

SALERS (CANTAL)
From the Auvergne region of France, it is a traditional farmhouse cheese made from unpasteurized milk. Reminiscent of cheddar, it has a thick, dark crust, a firm, creamy texture and a savoury flavour. An excellent cheese for cooking whenever cheddar is needed.

TOMME DE SAVOIE
Tomme de Savoie is made from unpasteurized cow's milk, and has a nutty flavour. Good for grating and grilling.

BREBIS PYRÉNÉES
A large, tub-shaped cheese made from sheep's milk, it has a dark orange crust, a smooth texture and a sweetish, nutty flavour.

TETILLA (D.O.*)
From Galicia, this is one of
the few Spanish cheeses
made from 100 per cent
cow's milk — it can be
either pasteurized or
unpasteurized. It is a mild,
creamy cheese, and is easily
recognisable by its
distinctive breast-like shape.

ZAMORA
From the Castille
Leon region, an
excellent table
cheese made from a
blend on milks.
Also good for
cooking.

MANCHEGO (D.O.*)
Made in La Mancha exclusively from raw or pasteurized
Manchega ewe's milk. It has a firm texture, dotted with tiny holes.
The taste is light and piquant. Good served with crusty bread.

IDIAZÁBAL
Traditional, full-cream, unpasteurized, ewe's milk cheese made by
the farmers and shepherds in the Basque Country and Navarra. It
is pressed or semi-cooked before maturing, and has a distinctive,
strong, smoky flavour. Good for *gratins* or served with fruit.

RONCAL (D.O.*)
A firm-textured, sheep's milk cheese from Navarra. It is
pressed or semi-cooked and left to fully mature. The flavour
is strong, sharp and buttery.

*D.O. = Denomination of Origin, controlled by its regulatory board.

GARROTXA
A white, artisan cheese made from the milk of Murciana and Granadina goats. It has a smooth, creamy texture and a mild, slightly sharp, nutty flavour.

MAHÓN (D.O.*)
Made from the milk of Fresian and Menorquina cows in Menorca, it is a square-shaped cheese which is pressed but not cooked. It has a sharp, milky, slightly acidic, salty flavour and a moist texture.

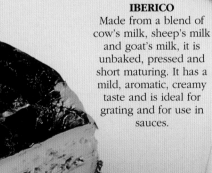

IBERICO
Made from a blend of cow's milk, sheep's milk and goat's milk, it is unbaked, pressed and short maturing. It has a mild, aromatic, creamy taste and is ideal for grating and for use in sauces.

PICOS BLUE
An excellent, semi-soft, blue-veined, cow's milk cheese, aged for a year in mountain caves, then wrapped in maple leaves when mature. It has a rich flavour and a creamy texture. Delicious served with wine, or it can be used in sauces.

MAJORERO
A pressed cheese from Fuerteventura in the Canary Islands. It is made from the milk of the island's own breed of goat, and is sold fresh or cured. It has a firm, buttery texture and a toasted aftertaste.

83

Fruit,
vegetables & fungi

When broad beans and artichokes arrive in the greengrocer's, it is one of the surest signs that spring has arrived. In the same way, the first berries of summer, the crisp apples and pears of autumn, and the root vegetables of winter signal each new season. The cycle of the year, measured as it is by the seasons of fruit and vegetables, keeps us in touch with Mother Nature.

Or, at least, that's the way it used to be. Now it seems just about everything is available at almost any time of the year. Quick and easy access to most parts of the globe means we can enjoy fruits and vegetables that were unheard of in our grandmother's day.

In fact, there is hardly a country not represented on any supermarket's fruit and vegetable counters. Exotic tropical fruits such as papaya and passionfruit have become as familiar as apples and pears. Even seasonal berries such as strawberries have become year-round fruits with imports from Australia, California and Spain.

Despite the wealth of choice, it is still essential to select well when you buy. The golden rule is to purchase in season, when fruit and vegetables are at their peak and, therefore, less expensive. It's also less wasteful to buy tomatoes and bananas, for example, at different stages of ripeness, some to eat straight away and some to ripen at room temperature.

Exotic and tropical fruits should also be ripened at room temperature, before being stored in the fridge. Then there are the more commonplace, such as tomatoes, avocados and pears, which should not be refrigerated until fully ripe, as they will not ripen after chilling. Rinse fruits such as berries only just before using and not when storing. Potatoes should be removed from their plastic bags and stored in a cool, dark, dry place in an open basket, so air can circulate.

Dried beans, peas and lentils, known as pulses and legumes, are a great standby as they can be an important component of a healthy diet, and they store well.

SWISS CHARD
Beta vulgaris
Sometimes confused with spinach, this is also known as **silver beet**. The leaves should be dark green and shiny and the stems white, without signs of bruising. Use the leaves cooked as you would spinach or raw, mixed with other salad greens. Use the stems in soups or stews, or braise them until tender, then bake in a gratin dish with Parmesan cheese.

CURLY ENDIVE
Cichorium endivia
This slightly bitter vegetable can be lightly steamed or boiled, or eaten raw in salads. Rinse well in cold water. Buy specimens with bright, white hearts and crisp, green leaves. Use the more tender, light green leaves for salads.

MESCLUN
A mixture of fresh and tender, young salad leaves. It may consist of various lettuce leaves, baby spinach leaves, lamb's lettuce, rocket, curly and broadleaf endive, nasturtium leaves, snowpea shoots, radicchio and edible flowers.

SPINACH
Spinacia oleracea
A great source of iron, although not to the extent that many people believe. After rinsing several times in cold water, cook in just the water adhering to the leaves. Use in soups, pasta sauces, curries and stews; uncooked, in salads.

LAMB'S LETTUCE
Valerianella locusta
Also known as **mâche** or **corn salad**, it has a nutty flavour and is ideal for winter salads.

MUSTARD SEED SPROUTS
Brassica alba
Crunchy, with a mild, peppery taste, these are grown from white mustard seeds. Often combined with cress in sandwiches.

BABY SPINACH

RED SWISS CHARD
Beta vulgaris spp.
Also known as **ruby chard** or **rhubarb chard**. Prepared and cooked in the same way as Swiss chard.

ROSETTE BOK CHOY
Brassica chinensis var. *rosularis*
Also known as **tatsoi**, this dark-leafed, low-growing vegetable is a variety of bok choy. It has the same flavour and vitamins A and C, but is tougher and requires longer cooking. Use in soups and stir-fries.

ROCKET
Eruca sativa
Also known as **arugula**, the leaves resemble those of the dandelion and have a peppery flavour. Use in pasta, risotto, pesto, salsa, soups and stews, or as a salad leaf, either by itself or in combination with other leaves.

UPLAND CRESS

WATERCRESS
Nasturtium officinale
The slightly peppery leaves are a popular addition to sandwiches, salads, salsas, pesto and soups. Buy crisp bunches with healthy, green leaves. Discard the tough stems. Rich in iron and vitamins and contains many trace elements.

CHICORY
Cichorium intybus
After discarding the tough stems, the leaves are used as a salad ingredient, or cooked as a vegetable side dish. The pleasantly bitter leaves should be briefly blanched before using in a salad or cooked until tender in only the water adhering to them.

LETTUCE
Lactuca sativa
Originally regarded as a weed, the lettuce today is cultivated in many varieties for its edible leaves. Served raw in green and mixed salads, lettuce can be braised, stuffed and puréed, and is often used as a garnish.

RADICCHIO
Cichorium intybus
A variety of chicory and of Italian origin, it ranges from ruby-red to pink to white in colour. The flavour is peppery and pleasantly bitter. Mostly used as a salad vegetable, it is also good in pasta sauces and risotto and, when quartered and grilled, to accompany meat dishes.

GREEN OAK LETTUCE

RADICCHIO

RED OAK LETTUCE

BUTTERHEAD LETTUCE

GREEN LOLLO

MIGNONETTE

ICEBERG
LETTUCE

COS LETTUCE

LOLLO ROSSO
LETTUCE

89

DELAWARE
Creamy skin, white flesh.
Roast, bake, microwave, deep-
fry. Good for gratins but not
for mashing.

DESIRÉE
Pink skin, golden flesh.
Boil, roast, bake or mash. Good for
salads, but not for deep-frying.

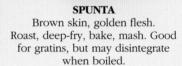

PINK FIR APPLE
Creamy pink skin, waxy flesh.
Boil or bake. Superlative
salad potato.

SPUNTA
Brown skin, golden flesh.
Roast, deep-fry, bake, mash. Good
for gratins, but may disintegrate
when boiled.

CHATS
Also known as **new potatoes**.
Thin, diaphanous skin, sweet flesh.
Boil, roast.

PATRONE
Creamy skin, yellow, waxy
flesh. Boil, sauté, bake. Good
for salads, but not for mashing.

NICOLA
Creamy skin, yellow, waxy
flesh. Boil or use in salads.

SEBAGO
Creamy skin, white flesh.
Boil, bake, fry. Superlative
mashing potato.

POTATO
Solanum tuberosum
Potatoes are divided into two basic types: early crop (or new) and late crop (mature or old).

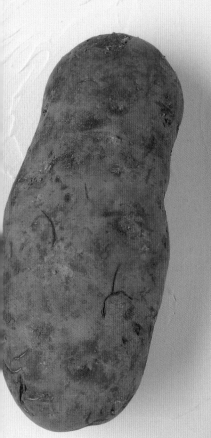

BINTJE
Creamy white skin, yellow,
waxy flesh.
Boil, roast, deep-fry, mash.
Use in salads and for gratins.

PINK EYE
Also known as **southern gold**, **sweet
gold** and **pink gourmet**. Creamy skin
with pink, purple-stained eyes, yellow,
waxy flesh. Boil, deep-fry, use in salads,
but not good for mashing.

RUSSET BURBANK
Also known as **Idaho**. Brown
skin, pale yellow flesh.
Deep-fry or roast.

PURPLE CONGO
Dark purple skin with purple, mealy
flesh, which stays purple when cooked.
Deep-fry or boil.

PONTIAC
Red skin, white, waxy flesh.
Good for most cooking methods, for
gratins, and in salads.

KING EDWARD
Creamy, pink-dappled skin, white flesh.
Mash, deep-fry, roast, boil.

COLIBAN
White, smooth skin, floury flesh.
Bake, mash, steam. May disintegrate when boiled.

KIPFLER
Golden skin, yellow, waxy flesh.
Boil, sauté, bake or use in salads.

ESTIMA
A waxy potato, good for salads. It also keeps its shape in cooking, making it ideal for stews and casseroles.

NADINE
An early variety of waxy potato with firm flesh. Good for potato salads.

JERSEY ROYAL
Considered the king of new potatoes, it has papery skin which can be rubbed off with a thumb and forefinger. It has deep yellow, flavoursome, waxy flesh. Good for boiling.

FRANCINE SALAD
A standard English new potato, good for boiling and serving with butter and chives.

PENTLAND JAVELIN
A waxy potato with firm flesh. Good in salads.

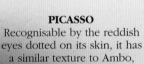

PICASSO
Recognisable by the reddish eyes dotted on its skin, it has a similar texture to Ambo, and is suitable for roasting and boiling.

TRUFFLE POTATO
Also known as **Truffes de Chine** or **Chinese Truffles**, it is distinguished by its black skin and purple and white flesh. Starchy with a lovely, sweet flavour, it should be boiled in its skin to avoid the colour of the flesh leaching out. Peel afterwards as the skin can be tough. Dress with butter or mayonnaise.

MARFONA
A waxy variety for use in salads.

LA RATTE

A small, long and knobbly early variety with firm flesh. It has a superb nutty taste. Good for use in salads and for boiling.

ROMANO

A red-skinned, firm-fleshed, waxy, main crop variety, good for roasting and for making chips.

MARIS BARD

A good size for an early-crop potato. Good for boiling and sautéing.

AMBO

A red-eyed potato bordering on being floury for an early variety. Good for boiling and roasting.

ROSEVAL

A red-skinned variety, good for roasting.

SALAD BLUE

The flesh of this unusual potato is tinged with blue, making it an attractive ingredient for salads.

CHARLOTTE

A midget potato, typically grown in France. It has a set skin which needs to be peeled rather than rubbed off with the fingers. Good for sauté potatoes, but too small for roasting.

BALMORAL

An old crop potato which is a starchy all-rounder.

93

RED SWEET POTATO
Ipomoea batatas
Often confused with yam, it should be prepared and cooked as ordinary potatoes. Do not refrigerate but store in a well-ventilated, cool, dark place. Used in soups, pies and, in the US, as a candied accompaniment to Thanksgiving dinner.

TARO
Colocusia esculenta
Large, starchy, edible tuber with dry-textured flesh and a flavour not unlike sweet potato. Colour of flesh ranges from cream to pink. Bitter when eaten raw. Peel thickly before use but protect your skin with rubber gloves. Cook as potato, such as chips. Can be made into sweet dishes.

YAM
Oxalis crenata
Resembling sweet potato, this pink-skinned, tropical tuber grows up to 15cm (6in) in length. Do not refrigerate, but store in a well-ventilated, cool, dark place. Cook as potato: mash, boil, bake or deep-fry.

WHITE SWEET POTATO
Ipomoea batatas
One of the many varieties of sweet potato available, the white sweet potato has creamy coloured skin and creamy yellow flesh. Use as a potato or pumpkin substitute, as a vegetable side dish, or in soups, scones, biscuits, cakes and pies.

JERUSALEM ARTICHOKE
Helianthus tuberosus
This vegetable is no relation to the globe artichoke, neither does it have anything to do with Jerusalem. The name is thought to be derived from the Italian word for sunflower, *girasole*. Choose tubers which are not too knobbly, as these are difficult to peel. Cook as potatoes. Use in soups, stews and for *gratins*, and raw, very thinly sliced, in salads.

**BABY
BEETROOT**

TURNIP
Brassica rapa
Closely related to the
swede, and indeed the
two are often confused.
This is a versatile
vegetable which can be
mashed, cooked whole or
in pieces, baked alongside
a roast, or sliced thinly
and eaten raw in salads.
Don't discard the green
tops; these can be cooked
as you would spinach.

BEETROOT
Beta vulgaris
In prehistoric times, beetroot was cultivated for its leaves only, but
these days the bulb, with its high sugar content, is the more valuable
part. The most famous application is in *borscht*, although beetroot is
frequently used as a vegetable and in salads. Cook without trimming,
so the colour does not 'bleed'.

PURPLE-TOP TURNIP

TOKYO TURNIP

PARSNIP
Pastinaca sativa
Shaped like a carrot, with a herb-like flavour,
this root vegetable has proven beneficial in
cold winters thanks to its high starch content.
Buy small- to medium-sized roots, as the large
ones have a woody core. Use in soups,
mashed as a vegetable side dish, in stews,
and raw, very thinly sliced or grated for a
winter salad.

CARROT
Daucus carota
Choose bright orange, shiny specimens; avoid those with soft spots or cracks or those which are limp. In spring, look for baby carrots with their green tops intact. These do not need peeling or scraping, whereas older ones do. Serve cooked or raw in salads.

SALSIFY
Tragopogon porrifolius
Both black and white salsify are available. White-skinned salsify is also called **oyster plant** because of its glossy appearance and delicate flavour once cooked. The black-skinned root, closely related to the white, is called **Scorzonera** (*Scorzonera hispanica*). Both can be boiled or sautéed. The skin is removed easily once cooked.

CELERIAC
Apium graveolens var. *rapaceum*
This tuberous root, also know as **turnip-rooted celery**, has brown gnarly skin, white fibrous flesh and a mild, celery flavour. The plant is especially grown for its root and is not the same as green celery, which is grown for its stalks. The French bistro preparation, *rémoulade*, is a mixture of mayonnaise and grated celeriac. Celeriac is also good in soups, stews and gratins.

SWEDE
Brassica napus
Also known as **rutabaga**, these are very popular in Scotland, where they accompany haggis: they are mashed with potatoes, and become 'tatties and neeps'. Like most root vegetables, they are often used in wintertime, in warming soups, stews or mashes.

RADISH
Raphanus sativus
An edible root, the radish belongs to
the mustard family, as does daikon.
Its flesh is crisp, juicy and white,
while shape and skin colour vary.
There can be a great variation in
strength, so taste before adding it to
salads. Look for bright, shiny globes,
with fresh green tops. Use the
globes, as well as the green leaves,
in salads. Also good for sandwiches
and crudités, and braised for a
vegetable accompaniment.

WHITE RADISH

DAIKON
Raphanus sativus
Also known as
Japanese radish or
mooli; has a sweet,
fresh flavour. Widely
used in both Japanese
and Chinese cooking;
raw in salads; as an
accompaniment to
sashimi, and cooked
in soups and stews.
Look for white,
unblemished skin.
Avoid overly large
ones, which tend to
be fibrous.

RED RADISH

ASPARAGUS
Asparagus officinalis
Shoots of a feathery plant, native to Eurasia.
Choose green or white, firm, crisp stalks of an
even thickness, with tightly closed tips. Young
asparagus needs to have only the woody stem
snapped off; older asparagus may need
peeling. Cook for the shortest possible time
for good colour and texture.

GLOBE ARTICHOKE
Cynara cardunculus
The globe artichoke is the
unopened flower-bud of a thistle-
like plant belonging to the daisy
family. Choose those with glossy
green, purple or bronze leaves,
heavy for their size. Cook whole
and eat the fleshy base of the
leaves (petals) until the prize part –
the heart – is reached, or trim the
leaves, halve or quarter lengthwise
and remove the fuzzy centre, or
choke, before gently braising.

FENNEL
Foeniculum vulgare var. *azoricum*
Often wrongly labelled anise, and indeed, it has a
very pronounced aniseed flavour. The aromatic,
fleshy bulb is cooked or used raw in salads, the
feathery fronds are used as a herb, and the seeds
are used in Mediterranean and Indian cuisines.
Pieces of raw fennel are frequently served
at the end of a meal in Italy to
cleanse the palate.

CELERY
Apium graveolens var. *dulce*
Celery has come to be appreciated for
its flavour and crunchiness. There are two distinct
types. One is bleached white and the other is dark to light
green in colour. Frequently present as a flavouring in stock, especially with
game and fish, it is also good braised, in soups and stews, or raw in salads.

CHICORY
Chichorium intybus
Also known as **Belgian endive** or by its Flemish name **witloof**,
this vegetable has a delicate bitter flavour. Roll the lightly cooked heads
in ham and cover in béchamel sauce for a delicious winter dish, or
serve as a cooked vegetable or raw in salads.

COURGETTE
Cucurbita pepo
Zucchini
Also known as
zucchini. The
courgette comes in
a variety of colours,
ranging from green
to grey, and yellow
and nearly black. Its
bland taste is
improved by garlic,
tomato and herbs.

CUCUMBER
Cucumis
sativus
cultivars
Although we
tend to think
of the
cucumber in
salad and
with crudités,
it is
surprisingly
good when
braised and
served as a
vegetable,
especially
with fish and
seafood
dishes. Look
for glossy,
crisp, bright
green
vegetables.
The feathery
herb, dill, is
its natural
companion.

LEBANESE CUCUMBER

RIDGE CUCUMBER

HOT-HOUSE CUCUMBER

100

CUSTARD MARROW
Cucurbita pepo
Also known as **pattypan
squash**, the colour varies from
pale to bright green through to
pale or deep shades of yellow.
Best eaten young, boiled
or baked whole.

**YELLOW CUSTARD
MARROW**

ACORN SQUASH
Cucurbita pepo
An American variety found in autumn. It
has a thick, green skin and yellow, sweet-
flavoured flesh. It is delicious halved,
stuffed and baked, or it can be boiled or
steamed. It is easier to remove the tough
skin after cooking.

**GREEN CUSTARD
MARROW**

BITTER MELON
Momordica charantia
This wrinkled, cucumber-like vegetable is eaten while still
unripe. With bitter tasting flesh, which improves when
cooked, the bitter melon features in South-east Asian dishes,
such as cooked salads, stir-fries and, made into a tart pickle,
it is popular in India.

101

GOLDEN NUGGET SQUASH
Cucurbita pepo

JAP SQUASH

KABOCHA SQUASH

SQUASH
Cucurbita maxima
Also known as **pumpkin** elsewhere, it has many varieties and differs from summer squash, such as cucumber and zucchini, in that it has a hard, inedible skin. Choose one that is heavy for its size and buy uncut if possible as, once cut, it does not store well. Use in soups, casseroles, pies and as a vegetable; baked, mashed or dry-roasted.

BUTTERNUT SQUASH

103

RED GLOBE ONION
Hotter than the red onion,
but with better keeping qualities.
It can be eaten raw or cooked.

GARLIC
Allium sativum
Like the onion, this vegetable
belongs to the lily family, along
with the green and spring onion,
leek, chive and shallot. With its
assertive, pungent flavour, garlic
is equally adored and despised.
To peel a clove of garlic, place it
on a chopping board and press
down hard with your hand on the
flat blade of a large knife.

SPANISH ONION
Large and copper-brown in
colour, it is mild and sweet in
flavour, making it ideal for use
in salads. It can also be fried
or baked.

SPRING ONION
This is an immature onion with an
unformed bulb. Mild in flavour they can
be used in antipasto and cheese plates,
soups, salads and stir-fries.

BABY LEEK

ONION
Allium cepa

Onions are indispensable in our day-to-day cooking. There are dry onions and green onions. Dry onions are left in the ground to mature and have a tougher, outer skin for longer storage. Green onions are merely young and immature. There are many varieties and many ways to use them.

PICKLING ONION
It can be any variety of early harvested dry onion.

RED ONION
Known to Americans as the **Spanish onion**, it is mild and sweet in flavour and is delicious eaten raw in salads and antipasto.

SHALLOT or ESCHALOT
Allium ascalonicum

A small bulb with a sweeter, lighter, more delicate flavour than an onion. There are a number of varieties including grey, pink and brown. Most easily obtained in spring and summer, shallots are often required in dishes from France.

WHITE ONION
Milder than the brown onion. Use for all-purpose cooking and raw in salads. Stores well.

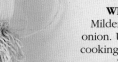

LEEK
Allium porrum

Of the same family, but milder in flavour than *Allium cepa* species, the leek is a cold-weather vegetable, good in soups and stews, pasta sauces and risotto. May replace onion when a less pronounced onion flavour is desired. Always rinse well to make sure no grit remains between the leaves.

GREEN ONION
Also known as **scallion**, these are ideal for pickling when they are young. They can also be eaten raw and used in a similar fashion to spring onions.

DAIKON SPROUTS

MUNG BEANSPROUTS

PEA
Pisum sativum spp.
Peas are the seeds contained in the pea pod. Choose fairly large, bright green pods and taste pea for sweetness. *Petit pois* are picked before developing fully and are considered to be the finest flavoured peas. Cook peas in a small amount of boiling water for about 4 – 8 minutes.

SPROUTS
Phaseolus aureus
Buy sprouts that are crisp and fresh-looking, avoiding those with brown tips. Use as soon as possible. Cook briefly. To gro your own sprouts, place a handful of dried seeds (preferably m in a jar, secure a piece of muslin over the opening with a rubber band and rinse the seeds several times a day with wa water. Lay the jar on its side out of direct sunlight, and the see will sprout in about six days.

ALFALFA SPROUTS

SUGAR-SNAP PEA
Similar to *mangetout*, but the peas inside the edible pod have matured. Best steamed, lightly boiled or used in stir-fries.

SOYA BEANSPROUTS

MANGETOUT
Also known as **snow pea**. The pod, which contains immature seeds, can be eaten whole. Steam, lightly boil, stir-fry or use raw in salads.

BABY CORN
Imported from Asia, it lacks great flavour but adds colour and texture to stir-fries.

SWEET CORN
Zea mays
Also known as **Indian corn** or **maize**. This seed of a grass grows in an 'ear' surrounded by a green husk. Always buy corn with the husk intact, as the sugar in the kernels transforms into starch the moment the husk is removed. Cook briefly in boiling water (about 6 – 8 minutes) or barbecue with the husk on.

OKRA
Hibiscus esculentus
Also known as **ladyfinger** or **gumbo**, this vegetable belongs to the hibiscus family. It is particularly popular in Creole and Cajun cooking. Okra has a glutinous texture and is a natural thickener. The viscosity can be minimized by soaking for 30 minutes in vinegar, diluted with water.

FRENCH BEAN

STRINGLESS GREEN BEAN

GREEN BEAN
Phaseolus vulgaris
There are many varieties of the 'green' bean. Colour varies from pale green or yellow to dark green. The actual bean is cooked and eaten in the pod. Avoid limp and dull looking specimens. These days, most beans are stringless and only need to be 'topped and tailed'.

WING BEAN
Psophocarpus tetragonolobus
This exotic looking bean, which grows profusely in tropical countries, is not related to the *Phaseolus* family. The immature seeds within the young pods taste like garden peas. The Wing bean has nutritional values and properties similar to the soya bean, and is popular in Asian cuisines.

WAX or YELLOW BEAN

RUNNER BEAN

SNAKE BEAN
Vigna unguiculata
Also known as the **Chinese bean**. This very long, narrow, dark green variety is cooked as you would a green bean. Tie in a knot to serve.

BROAD BEAN
Vicia faba
Popular since pre-historic times, broad beans became a staple for the poor around the Mediterranean, although upper class Greeks and Romans rejected them, thinking they caused confusion. The large pod with its soft, furry lining can be eaten only when very young and fresh. Usually the beans have to be podded, and when a little older, these in turn, need to be shelled.

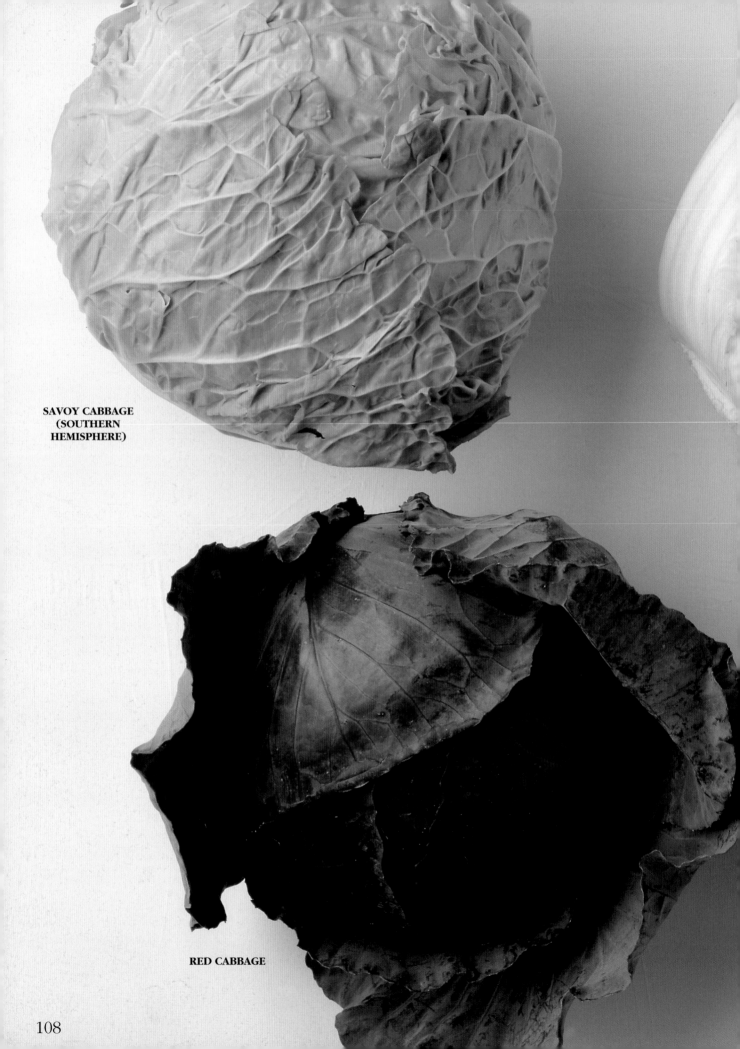

**SAVOY CABBAGE
(SOUTHERN
HEMISPHERE)**

RED CABBAGE

108

CABBAGE
Brassica oleracea var. *capitata*
Related to broccoli, cauliflower,
kohlrabi and Brussels sprouts.
Choose heads which are heavy for
their size, with crisp, shiny, outer
leaves. Eat raw in salads. Cook only
for a minimum time in a covered
saucepan and drain very well.

CHINESE CABBAGE

GREEN CABBAGE

109

SAVOY CABBAGE
Crinkly textured, dark green, mild-flavoured cabbage available through the winter months. Should be eaten soon after purchase, and can be stir-fried, steamed or stuffed.

WHITE CABBAGE
Sometimes called **Dutch cabbage**, the tightly packed, crunchy leaves are perfect for eating raw in coleslaw and other cabbage salads. It is also used in sauerkraut. This cabbage keeps well.

KALE, CURLY KALE
Brassica oleracea acephala
Loose-leafed with sturdy stems and frilly
leaves, there are many varieties of kale,
including those with silver or purple
leaves. Best cooked in stocks and broths.

111

CAULIFLOWER
Brassica oleracea var. *botrytis*
Closely related to broccoli; look for bright white, tight flower heads, when choosing this vegetable. Avoid those with bruising or open flowers. Especially good in winter. Serve cooked on its own or in soups and stews, raw in salads or as crudité. Try serving individual baby cauliflowers smothered in a cheese sauce as a simple starter.

BROCCOLI
Brassica oleracea var. *italica*
Broccoli is regarded as one of the most health-giving vegetables. Look for fresh, green, tight heads, without any yellow discoloration. Do not discard the stems; these may be peeled and sliced and cooked along with the florets.

112

KOHLRABI
Brassica oleracea var. *gonglyoides*
Often confused with a root vegetable, this is actually a swollen stem. To cook, trim the stalks and cook whole in the skin, or peel and use in soups and stews. The cooked, diced vegetable can be used in salads.

BRUSSELS SPROUTS
Brassica oleracea var. *gemmifera*
A winter vegetable, these baby cabbages form along the stem at the base of the leaves of yet another member of the *Brassica* family. For the best flavour, choose sprouts that are small, firm and bright green. Cook lightly. Use in soups and stews. Shredded, they can be added raw to salads.

113

RAPE (Southern Hemisphere)
Brassica campestris
This vegetable, with its relatively mild flavour, may be used in stir-fries or even in pasta sauces. The smaller leaves may be used whole in salads; the larger leaves first need to be shredded.

CHRYSANTHEMUM GREENS
There are several varieties of this green, including shungiku and tung hao. Tender leaves may be used in salads; coarser leaves must be blanched before using. Cook briefly as soon as possible after buying to prevent bitterness.

SHUNGIKU

TUNG HAO

MIZUNA
A Japanese green with delicate, mustard-flavoured, crisp leaves and white stalks. When young, serve in salads. When older, mizuna is good in stir-fries.

114

GAI LARN
Brassica alboglabra
Also known as **Chinese broccoli** or **Chinese kale**, these greens are most prized for their stems. To cook, discard the large, coarse leaves, cut the stems into 5cm (2in) pieces and boil in salted water until crisp-tender. Serve with oyster sauce.

BOK CHOY or CHINESE CHARD
Also known as **pak choy**, this Chinese, white, cabbage vegetable has a mild, cabbage flavour. Both the leaves and the stems are frequently used in stir-fries and soups, but it can also be eaten as a vegetable or raw in a salad.

bok choy.

choy sum

CHOY SUM
Brassica campestris
Also known as **flowering cabbage**, this popular Chinese green is often seen with yellow flowers. The flowering stems are tender and are cooked along with the leaves. Frequently served boiled, stir-fried or steamed, by themselves or in vegetable mixtures.

BABY CHOY SUM

SWEET PEPPER
Capsicum annuum
Also known as **capsicum**, it can be eaten both raw and cooked.
In its raw state it is an excellent source of vitamin C, 20g (3/4oz) providing a
person's vitamin C needs for a day. There are red, yellow, orange, brown, purple
and lime-green varieties. Choose glossy ones, which are heavy for their weight,
without blemishes or soft spots. Sweet peppers continue to ripen after picking. The
ripe, red variety tastes sweeter and is less pungent than when green and still
immature. The spice, paprika, is dried and ground sweet pepper.

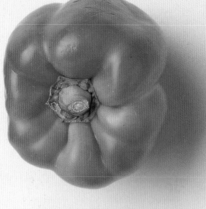

ORANGE PEPPER
Also known as **orange bell
pepper**, thick-fleshed and sweet.
Use in salads, salsas, casseroles,
pasta and rice dishes. To remove
skin, grill until charred, then 'sweat'
for 20 minutes. Mild.

RED PEPPER
Also known as **red bell pepper** or
sweet red pepper. Thick-fleshed, very
sweet. Use in salads, salsas, casseroles,
pasta and rice dishes. To remove skin,
grill until charred, then 'sweat' for 20
minutes. Mild.

YELLOW BANANA PEPPER
Medium-fleshed, slightly sweet chilli
with sharp and intense waxy taste.
Use to make yellow *mole* sauces. May
be eaten in salads, salsas, casseroles,
pasta and rice dishes, or stuffed.
Medium hot.

BIRD'S EYE CHILLI
Related to cayenne and Tabasco
chillies, the colour may range
from deep red to cream, yellow
or orange. Thin-fleshed with a
deep, fiery heat, flavour may
range from mild to sweet.
Use in salsas, casseroles
and stir-fries. Hot.

POBLANO CHILLI
One of Mexico's most popular
fresh chillies, this thick-fleshed chilli is
often roasted to intensify its flavour.
Frequently stuffed with other
ingredients (*chiles rellenos*), cooked in
sauces and stews, or blended and
added to sauces and soups.
Medium hot.

GREEN THAI CHILLI
The colour ranges from green to red
with thin skin, fleshy texture and copious
seeds. Used frequently in South-East Asian
dishes, chopped to contribute heat, and
sliced as a garnish on noodle and salad
dishes. When not available, substitute
three serrano chillies for one Thai.
Medium hot.

SERRANO CHILLI
Colour ranges from bright green
to red with thick flesh and a
tangy, biting heat. The red is
slightly sweeter than the green,
and is used frequently as
garnish. Use in salsas, pickled
(*en escabeche*), roasted in
sauces. Medium hot.

116

RED BANANA PEPPER

A thick-fleshed, sweet pepper, similar in flavour to capsicum. May be eaten in salads, salsas, casseroles, pasta and rice dishes, or stuffed. Mild.

YELLOW PEPPER

Thick-fleshed, with very sweet, fruity flavour. Use in salads, casseroles, salsas, and in pasta and rice dishes. May be barbecued or roasted. Mild.

GREEN PEPPER

Thick-fleshed with a tangy, sweet flavour. It is less sweet than red or yellow capsicum, so don't substitute in dishes as the flavours may clash. Use in salads, casseroles and rice dishes or stuffed. Mild.

JALAPEÑO CHILLI

Colour ranges from green when unripe to red when ripe. Thick-fleshed with a fresh flavour, sweeter when ripe. Use in salsas, stews, sauces and dips, pickled (*en escabeche*) or roasted and stuffed with cheese, meat or fish as a nibble with drinks. Medium hot.

HABANERO CHILLI

Probably the hottest chilli available; may be 30-50 times hotter than the jalapeño. Take care when handling or eating this chilli. With tropical flavours, it combines well with tomatoes and dishes which include tropical fruits. Use in salsas, chutneys and marinades, and pickled (*en escabeche*). Fiercely hot.

CAYENNE CHILLI

Thin-fleshed chilli with searing, clear heat and tangy flavour. Use in salsas, sauces and soups, and as a garnish. Fairly hot.

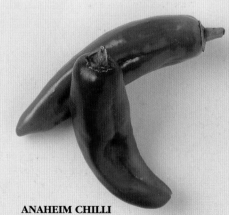

CHILLI

Capsicum frutescens

The small, green unripe or ripe red chilli is used to spice up food, and to make cayenne pepper, chilli pepper, Tabasco sauce and Indonesian sambals.

ANAHEIM CHILLI

Medium-to-thick flesh with bright flavour, rather sweeter when ripe. Roasting improves the flavour. Use in sauces, pickled (*en escabeche*), stuffed (*chiles rellenos*) and as a garnish for noodle dishes, casseroles and soups. Mild to medium.

THAI APPLE EGGPLANT
Solanum ferox

AUBERGINE
Solanum melongena

Also known as **eggplant**, this smooth-skinned, shiny fruit comes in a large variety of colours. Look for unblemished fruit, which are heavy for their size. These days most eggplants do not have bitter juices, but to make sure, the fruit can be sliced, sprinkled with salt and left to stand for 30 minutes to extract them. Rinse and pat dry. OTHER VARIETIES: Black Beauty, Black Enorma, Black Prince, Onita, Short Tom, Small Green, Thai Pea, Variegated, White.

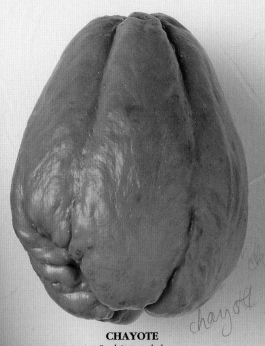

HASS AVOCADO

CHAYOTE
Sechium edule
Our growing awareness of foreign cuisines has sparked a new interest in this pear-shaped, bland, easily digestible food. Peel chayotes under cold water, as the sticky substance they exude is otherwise hard to remove from your hands. Chayotes can be used in the same way as small squash.

AVOCADO
Persea americana
Pear-shaped or round, the avocado has skin that may be grained or smooth and shiny. In colour, it is dark green or purplish brown with flesh of a buttery consistency. This fruit is unique, as it contains fat of the mono-unsaturated type but, beware, the calorific content is high. To ripen, place it in a paper bag, together with a banana, and leave at room temperature until the avocado yields slightly when pressed around the neck.

ROUND TOMATO

PLUM TOMATO

VINE-RIPENED TOMATO

TOMATO
Lycopersicon esculentum
The first tomatoes introduced to Europe were yellow; hence the Italians called the fruit *pomodoro* or 'golden apple'. With a high water content, but low in calories, the tomato is rich in vitamins A,B and C. Widely used, cooked or raw, as a vegetable, in salads, in juice or sauces. Best late summer to autumn, there are many varieties to choose from.

YELLOW TOMATO

CHERRY TOMATO

119

BEEFSTEAK TOMATO
Lycopersicon exculentum
These fleshy tomatoes, with full-bodied flavour, are exceptional for salads. Refrigerate once ripe, but remove from the fridge about one hour before eating. Buy tomatoes in different stages of maturity, to ensure a steady supply of ripe ones.

HYDROPONIC TOMATO
Lycopersicon exculentum
Hydroponically grown tomatoes are nutritionally identical to any other tomato, but they tend to lack flavour.

FUERTE AVOCADO
Persea americana
This Mexican strain of avocado, with thin, green skin and creamy to yellow flesh with buttery texture, has a medium-sized stone. When fully ripe, the skin is easily removed from the flesh.

DRIED TOMATO
Dried tomatoes don't need lengthy soaking to reconstitute — simply simmer until tender.

DRIED SWEET PEPPER
Store in a dry, cool, dark place. To reconstitute, soak in hot water for about two hours, then simmer until tender.

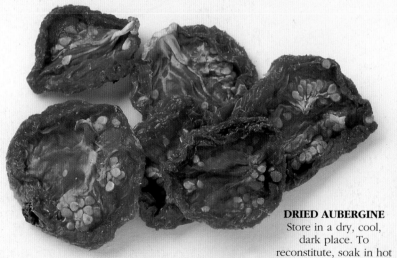

DRIED AUBERGINE
Store in a dry, cool, dark place. To reconstitute, soak in hot water for about two hours, then simmer until tender.

STRAW MUSHROOM
Volvariella volvacea
These delicately flavoured mushrooms are very popular all over Asia, where they are usually available fresh. They grow naturally or the spores are cultivated on paddy-straw. In Britain we frequently find them canned or dried.

CHANTERELLE MUSHROOM
Cantharellus cibarius
With their yellow cap, frilly edges, yellow flesh and fruity aroma, these mushrooms are very popular in Europe as well as in Thailand. Soak in hot water for 20–30 minutes. Strain the soaking water and retain for soup or stock for risotto.

DRIED GOURMET SHIITAKE MUSHROOM (left)
Lentinus edodes
Also known as **Chinese black mushroom**, this fungus is actually more popular when dried than in its natural state, as the flavour becomes stronger. Choose those with thick, fleshy caps, rather than small, thin ones. Soak in hot water for 20–60 minutes, depending on thickness of caps. Strain the soaking water and retain for soups.

DRIED PORCINI MUSHROOM (below)
Boletus edulis
Also known as **cep** or **boletus mushroom**, this fragrant variety is very popular in European cooking, especially French and Italian, as well as Thai cuisines. Soak in hot water for 20–60 minutes, depending on thickness of the caps. Strain the soaking water and retain for soup, or stock for risotto.

DRIED MOREL MUSHROOM (below)
Morchella conica
The hollows in the cone-shaped cap are prone to harbouring grit and small pebbles. Always check very carefully. The dried variety has a strong flavour and aroma. Soak in hot water for 20–30 minutes, strain the soaking water and retain for soup or stock for risotto.

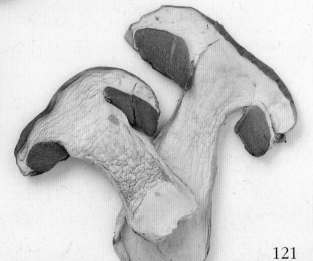

121

OYSTER MUSHROOM

ENOKITAKE MUSHROOM

GOURMET SHIITAKE MUSHROOM

SHIITAKE MUSHROOM

LARGE BUTTON MUSHROOM

NAMEKO MUSHROOM

MUSHROOMS AND FUNGI

There are around 2000 varieties of mushroom eaten throughout the world. The cultivated common button or open, flat mushrooms or the field mushroom, which grows wild, are known as 'the meat for vegetarians'. Mushrooms are richly endowed with minerals, iron and B group vitamins. Due to our increased interest in foreign cuisines, other varieties, such as the shiitake mushroom, first cultivated in Japan more than 2000 years ago, oyster, nameko, shimeji, chestnut, enokitake, Roman and Swiss brown mushrooms, black and white fungi, as well as truffles, are available. Look for dry, fresh and plump-looking specimens. Avoid any which look slimy or shrivelled. Don't wash; wipe with a damp cloth, if necessary. Never peel mushrooms. Eat raw or cook very briefly. Don't discard stems; if not required in a recipe, save for stuffings, soups and stocks.

BUTTON MUSHROOM

TRUFFLES

**ROMAN BROWN
MUSHROOM**

FLAT MUSHROOM

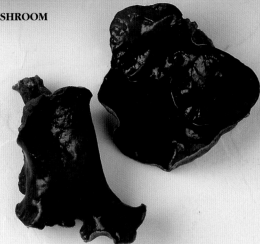

**SWISS BROWN
MUSHROOM**

BLACK FUNGUS

fungus

SHIMEJI MUSHROOM

WHITE FUNGUS

CHESTNUT MUSHROOM

123

HORN OF PLENTY
Craterellus cornucopioides
Also known as the **trompette des morts** it is a forest mushroom found in autumn. Cut lengthways to clean. Its earthy flavour is excellent with eggs and poultry. The dried version adds extra flavour to stews.

PIED BLEU
The farmed version of the **Wood Blewitt** *(Lepista nudum)*. With a delicious flavour and a distinctive blue stalk, it must be cooked before use as it may cause allergic reactions when eaten raw.

PIED DE MOUTON
Hydnum repandum
The name translated means "sheep's foot", but it is also known as **hedgehog fungus**. A forest mushroom found under deciduous trees in late summer and autumn, it has furry gills under the cap, which should be removed by scraping before cooking. Lacking an outstanding flavour, it's best in soups, stews and sauces, or mixed with other mushrooms.

CHANTERELLE
Cantharellus cibarius
Also known as a **girolle** in France, this wild, woodland mushroom is found in autumn. Orange in colour, the firm flesh has a peppery flavour with a hint of apricot. It requires longer cooking than most mushrooms to tenderise it, or it can be eaten raw. Particularly good with eggs, poultry and fish.

PHOLIOTTE
Pholiotte spp.
With a chocolate-coloured cap and a cream stalk, this mushroom is usually sold before the cap opens so that it resembles a walking stick with a knob at the top. The flesh is nutty and good in meat dishes.

CHANTERELLE GRISE
Cantharellus spp.
Found in autumn, a much-sought-after wild mushroom because of its versatility. Its aromatic flavour lends itself well to fish and risotto dishes.

CHANTERELLE YELLOW LEG
Cantharellus infundibuliformis
A woodland mushroom found in autumn. It is distinguished by its dark brown cap and bright yellow stalk. Use as normal chanterelles.

125

DRIED PULSES

Pulses are the edible seeds of leguminous plants, such as beans, peas and lentils. In their dried form, they have been a staple food in the Mediterranean region, Mexico, the Middle East, China, North Africa, Central and South America and India for years. Think of chickpeas, black-eyed peas, lima, soya and red kidney beans and a traditional dish associated with a region springs to mind. They are usually filling, full of flavour and inexpensive.

Pulses are available in a great variety of shapes, sizes and colours and can be stored for long periods. Due to their high-energy value and low-fat content, they are becoming increasingly popular in the western world.

In India, where the population is largely vegetarian, dhal provides an excellent source of fibre and protein. Technically, dhal is a dried split pea but covers all dried peas and beans.

Unlike other pulses, lentils do not require soaking and, compared to other pulses, require only a very short cooking time. Once cooked, they may be securely packaged and stored in the refrigerator for up to five days or in the freezer for three months at the maximum.

The bulk increases by about 2-3 times after cooking and this depends on their ultimate use; use the minimum-indicated cooking time for salads, medium time for a side dish and stews and the longest time for soups and lentil purées.

Buy pulses at outlets which have a quick turnover: local Asian, Greek or Middle Eastern food stores, health food stores, and most grocery and fruit supermarkets are a good source of supply.

STORING
Store pulses in a cool, dry place in a covered container and consume them within a reasonable time (about six months). Older beans become very hard and take a long time to cook.

COOKING
● Sort through the beans, peas or lentils and pick out any damaged seeds and small stones. Rinse to remove grit.
● Soak pulses overnight. There are a few exceptions, namely adzuki beans, black-eyed beans and mung beans, which have a thin skin and need only a short soak, and most lentils and dhals, which don't need soaking at all. Overnight soaking is preferable if you like to keep the beans whole, without the skin splitting. If this is not important, there is a quick-soaking method. Cover the beans in a pan with plenty of cold water, bring to a boil and allow to cook 1-2 minutes. Remove from the heat, cover the pan and stand for one hour. Drain and proceed with the recipe.
● To cook, cover the soaked beans with plenty of cold water, slowly bring to a boil, then simmer until tender. Do not add salt during cooking; this hardens the skin and lengthens the cooking time.
● When cooking beans for a salad, cook them for a slightly shorter time than for a soup or stew. Test by tasting.
● Feel free to substitute one type of pulse for another, but take timing into account.

ADZUKI BEAN
Phaseolus angularis
Also known as **aduki**, **adsuki** or **asuki**. Small, reddish-brown, oval bean with nutty, light flavour and fairly thin skin.
Cooking time: 30-45 minutes.

BLACK KIDNEY BEAN
Phaseolus vulgaris
Also known as **frijoles negros**, **black turtle bean**, **Spanish** or **Mexican black bean** and **lablab**. Medium-sized, oval bean with an earthy, sweet flavour.
Cooking time: about 60 minutes.

CANNELLINI BEAN
Phaseolus vulgaris
Mild-flavoured and fluffy when cooked, this bean is popular in Italy, in particular, Tuscany, where Florence is known as the city of *mangia fagioli* (bean-eaters).
Cooking time: about 40 minutes.

CHICKPEA
Cicer arietinum
Also known as **ceci** and **garbanzo**. Medium-sized pea with a little pointed top. Robust and nutty flavoured, the chickpea holds its shape well with cooking. Cooking time: about 60 minutes.

LUPIN
Lupinus luteus
A flat, bitter pulse, this bean needs prolonged soaking in salted water, and cooking for several hours to eliminate alkaloids. Once cooked, soak in cold, salted water. Large lupins need soaking for up to seven days, changing the water twice daily.

MUNG BEAN
Phaseolus aureus
Also known as **green gram** or **moong dhal**. Available unhulled, hulled and split. Mild in flavour, the small, green bean can be eaten with butter or spices or ground into flour. Widely used for sprouting.
Cooking time: 25-40 minutes.

BLACK-EYED BEAN
Vigna sinensis
lso known as **black-eyed Suzies**, **black-eyed
ea** and **southern pea**. Medium-sized, kidney-
haped bean with subtle, sweet flavour. Very
in skinned, these beans do not need soaking.
Cooking time: 40-60 minutes.

BORLOTTI BEAN
Phaseolus vulgaris
Also known as **cranberry bean** or
Roman bean. A brown bean, with
wine-coloured dappling. Sweet flavoured,
the colouring fades with cooking.
Cooking time: about 40 minutes.

BROAD BEAN
Vicia faba
Also known as **fava**, **feves**, **Windsor beans** and
horse beans. Oval-shaped with thick skin. Nutty
flavour and creamy texture, especially favoured
in Middle Eastern and Mediterranean cuisines.
Cooking time: about 40 minutes.

FUL MEDAMI
Lathyvus sativus
Also known as **Egyptian brown bean**,
this thinner-skinned variety of the
broad bean (the size of a small, black
bean) has a nutty flavour.
Cooking time: 45-60 minutes.

FLAGEOLET
Phaseolus vulgaris
Small green beans with a subtle flavour.
The French serve them with roast leg of
lamb with garlic. Available fresh on the
Continent, and dried or canned in the UK.
Cooking time: about 40 minutes.

LIMA BEAN, large
Phaseolus limensis
Also known as **fagioli della nonna**, this
large, pillowy bean has a creamy texture
and delicate flavour. To prevent skin
slipping off, bring to a boil very slowly.
Cooking time: about 40 minutes.

NAVY BEAN
Phaseolus vulgaris
Also known as **haricot bean**, this is the
bean in baked beans. A member of the
white bean family, this small, oval variety
is very similar to the great northern bean.
Cooking time: 45-60 minutes.

PINTO BEAN
Phaseolus vulgaris
The pinto (lit. 'painted') bean with its
earthy flavour and mealy texture is a close
relative of the red kidney bean.
The mottled skin fades to a pink
colour when cooked.
Cooking time: 45-60 minutes.

RED KIDNEY BEAN
Phaseolus vulgaris
Also known as **Mexican bean** and
haricot rouge, this medium-sized,
elongated bean ranges in colour from
deep red to a lighter pink. Creamy texture
and full-bodied flavour when cooked.
Cooking time: 45-60 minutes.

The soya bean is one of the richest natural foods, with a large amount of protein, oil, vitamins A and B, and potassium, calcium, magnesium, zinc and iron. As soya beans contain trypsin inhibitors, which prevent the body absorbing the protein, eating uncooked beans is not recommended.

Fresh soya beans, at the time of writing, are not as popular as the dried item, but nevertheless are appearing on the market in increasing quantities. The soya bean is even appearing on the menus of fashionable restaurants.

Frozen soya beans (above) are widely available in local Asian food stores. They may be cooked and served in the same manner as frozen peas or broad beans, as a side dish, or in soup and pasta sauces, although they take longer to soften.

Dried soya beans need lengthy soaking and cooking, necessary to destroy the trypsin inhibitors. As a consequence, Asian countries have used the soya bean to develop more easily digestible products. These include:

● **tofu (below)**, curdled soy drink made into a cheese-like substance, which may be soft, firm or fried.

● **tempeh**, which is sturdier than tofu, made from fermented beans.

● **miso**, fermented bean paste, used in soups, sauces and as flavouring.

● **soy sauce**, made from fermented soya beans and a roasted grain.

● **shoyu**, fermented and aged soya bean product, mellower than soy sauce.

● **tamari**, a wheat-free, fermented soy sauce, stronger in flavour than shoyu.

● **soya flour**, high in protein and low in carbohydrates, mixed with other flours for baked goods.

● **soy drink**, a non-dairy substitute, high in protein, cholesterol-free, low in fat and calcium: usually calcium is added; also used to make tofu.

● **soya bean oil**, used to make margarine and, when highly refined, in cooking oils.

● **soya beanshoots** take about 3-5 days to appear. Blanch or cook for better digestibility.

BEAN SOUP MIX
A ready-made mixture of small beans and lentils, such as red kidney, pinto, great northern, small lima and borlotti beans, red and brown lentils and split peas. Soak for six hours or overnight in cold water before using.

SOYA BEAN
Glycine max
Also known as **soy bean** or **soy pea**. The whole bean is not very easy to digest. Hence the soya bean has spawned a huge industry of related food items, such as soy sauce, shoyu, tamari, miso and tofu. Cooking time: 60 minutes

GREEN/BROWN LENTIL
Lens esculenta
Flat, lens-shaped, green to brown colour. Full-flavoured.
*Cooking times: 20, 40 or 60 minutes.

WHOLE RED LENTIL
Lens esculenta
These salmon-coloured, whole lentils cook very quickly and care should be taken not to cook them into a mush. The colour will fade to yellow with cooking.
*Cooking times: 6, 10 or 20 minutes.

CHANNA
Pisum sativum
These are Indian yellow split peas, smaller than the normal yellow split pea, with a nutty flavour. In southern Indian recipes, this dhal is roasted and ground and used as a spice.
Cooking time: 40-60 minutes.

BLACK URAD
Phaseolus mungo
Also known as **black gram**, these small, mild-flavoured beans are creamy coloured inside. When soaked and ground, used as a fermenting agent in Indian pancakes (*dosas*), and in pappadams and curries.
Cooking time: 40-60 minutes.

WHOLE DRIED PEA
Pisum sativum
Also known as **blue pea** or **field pea**, this greenish-coloured pea with an earthy flavour disintegrates when cooked, thus is best for thickening soups and stews.
Cooking time: about 50 minutes.

SPLIT GREEN PEA
Pisum sativum
A variety of the common garden pea, these peas are peeled and split in half. They do not keep their shape in cooking. Best used for soups and stews.
Cooking time: 45-60 minutes.

SPLIT YELLOW PEA
Pisum sativum
Except for the colour, identical to the split green pea.
Cooking time: 45-60 minutes.

LA LENTILLE VERTE DU PUY
Lens esculenta
uch smaller and plumper than brown or green
entils. Slate-coloured with exceptional texture
d a slightly peppery flavour, they are expensive
but worth it for special occasions.
*Cooking times: 20, 30 or 60 minutes.

SPLIT RED LENTIL
Lens esculenta
Also known as **masur dhal**, these thin discs have a subtle, spicy flavour suited to soups and purées. Like whole red lentils, colour fades to yellow with cooking.
Cooking time: 20 minutes.

LENTIL SOUP MIX
A ready-made mixture of lentils, pulses and grains, such as brown and red lentils, split green and yellow peas, brown rice, pearl barley and cracked buckwheat. May be used without prior soaking.

WHITE URAD
Phaseolus mungo
These are black urad beans which are hulled.
Cooking time: 40-60 minutes.

TOOR
Cajanus cajan
Also known as **toovar** or **pigeon pea**, this is a hulled, yellow-coloured split pea with an earthy flavour.
Cooking time: 40-60 minutes.

YELLOW MUNG
Phaseolus aureus
Also known as **moong dhal** or **green gram**, these are split green mung beans.
Cooking time 40-60 minutes.

*Use minimum indicated cooking time for salads, medium for a side dish and stews, and longest for soups and lentil purées.

RED DELICIOUS
Originally from America, a deep red apple with a soft and appealing sweet taste.

WHITE TRANSPARENT
A Russian apple with a refreshing, slightly tart taste. Best used in purées, sauces and pies.

JACQUIN
From France, a firm-skinned apple with crisp, white flesh.

FRENCH BRAEBURN
Originally from New Zealand, this apple is fragrant, firm, crisp and refreshing.

BRAMLEY'S SEEDLING
A cooking apple, it is uneven in shape and high in acidity. Its crisp, juicy flesh softens to a purée during cooking. Excellent for apple sauce.

COLONEL YATE
Grown in the UK, a large eating apple with fresh-tasting, sweet, juicy flesh.

130

McINTOSH
From Canada and now widely
planted throughout America
and northern Europe, it has
juicy, sweet flesh and a subtly
flavoured, crisp skin.

TENTATION
A cross between a Golden Delicious
and a Grifer, this French apple has a
superb flavour and an incredibly
crunchy texture.

KAISER WILHELM
A German apple, discovered by a teacher
in the 1800s. Originally grown for its
abundant juice, it has a sweet flavour.

COX'S ORANGE PIPPIN
An English apple,
originally grown by
Richard Cox from Slough,
it has creamy, crunchy
flesh, with notes of spice,
honey and nuts.

HARRY PRING
Developed in the UK by
Harry Pring in 1914, it has a
crisp, savoury flavour and
soft flesh.

GALA
An eating apple from New Zealand, it
has rich, honeyed, perfumed, juicy flesh.

BROWN'S SEEDLING
UK-grown, it is rich and
sweet and gives a yellow
purée when cooked.

CRAB APPLE
Tiny, extremely tart, English apple not
suitable for eating. Used to make jelly
to serve with meat.

131

GOLDEN DELICIOUS APPLE

Distinguished by five bumps around the eye. Juicy with mild, sweet flavour. A good eating apple, also good for pies and tarts.

PINK LADY APPLE

A fairly new, fragrant variety; a cross between Golden Delicious and Lady Williams, with a flavour reminiscent of Golden Delicious. A good eating apple.

GRANNY SMITH APPLE

Firm and juicy; the flavour ranges from sweet to tart. A good eating apple, but also good for cooking, juice, canning and drying. Best apple for sauce.

FIRMGOLD APPLE

A cross between Golden Delicious and Red Delicious. Creamy green when ready to eat, with sweet, crunchy flesh. A good eating apple, but suitable for cooking.

APPLE

Malus communis

A summer fruit, the apple stays fresh-tasting and firm for weeks. It is also a good source of vitamins and minerals. When buying apples, look for those with a glossy, unblemished skin; they will keep their texture for long periods, especially when refrigerated.

FUJI APPLE

Despite a crisp texture and sweet flavour, it is not as juicy as some. Keeps its shape and texture when cooked.

NEW ZEALAND BRAEBURN APPLE
Probably a cross between Lady Hamilton and Granny Smith. Very firm, crisp and juicy, with pale cream flesh and a sweet, sub-acid flavour. A good eating apple.

EMPIRE APPLE
Dark red, crisp and juicy, it is a dual-purpose apple for both cooking and eating.

BEURRE BOSC PEAR
The colour ranges from greenish-brown to a dark cinnamon brown. It has a delicate texture, is juicy, with aromatic flavour. Good for cooking, such as poaching in wine or baking with savoury dishes.

NASHI PEAR
Pyrus pyriformis
A variety of **Asian pear**, this crisp, juicy fruit looks like an apple, but tastes like a pear. Slice thinly and serve with cheese, in fruit or a savoury salad. Choose fruit heavy for its size, with unblemished skin. Keeps well at room temperature for several weeks; after that store in fridge.

CORELLA PEAR
A crisp, tropically flavoured, small pear with hardly any core, so it consists mostly of flesh. May be eaten hard or soft. A good eating pear with cheese or in salads.

PEAR
Pyrus communis
This juicy fruit, a member of the rose family, is picked when fully developed, and after that ripens from the inside out. Choose plump fruit with unblemished skin, ripen at room temperature, then refrigerate. Eat by itself, with cheese, in fruit salad, baked or poached, cooked in puddings, crumbles, tarts, pies and cakes or purée for sorbet.

PACKHAM'S TRIUMPH PEAR
A sweet and subtle flavour and white juicy flesh; the skin may remain green when ripe or may change to light yellow.

WILLIAMS'
A delicious smooth-skinned pear with a sweet, musk flavour.

COMICE
A large and sometimes knobbly variety from France. Considered one of the best pears, it was originally named Doyenné du Comice in 1849. It has delicious, scented, juicy flesh.

RED ANJOU
Grown in Oregon, USA, this variety has an excellent flavour and succulent, butter-coloured flesh.

ANJOU
Green with small brown spots, this variety has sweet, juicy flesh.

BLANQUILLA
A juicy, sweet-flavoured, green pear from Spain.

CONFERENCE
A popular English pear which acquired its name in 1855, after being awarded the 'First Class' certificate at a pear conference in Chiswick. It has tender, juicy flesh and a delicious flavour.

ROCHA
A Portuguese pear with a crisp skin and fragrant, soft, juicy flesh. Excellent for desserts, tarts, crumbles and pies. Keeps well for up to 7 days in a fruit bowl.

134

LIMONERA
Early, Italian pear which ripens to have a full, sweet flavour.

GUYOT
A French pear with a crunchy, juicy texture.

FORELLE
A late, South African pear considered to be one of the best in the world. It is golden with a rosy blush. Even when eaten hard, the flesh is refreshing and juicy.

135

LEMON
Citrus limon
Choose shiny, firm fruit which is heavy for its size and rinse in warm water to remove any insecticide. Use the rind finely grated or cut into thin strips when poaching fruit or making syrups. Use the juice to enhance the flavour of chicken, fish, custards, soups, drinks and marinades. Juice squeezed over raw vegetables and fruit prevents them turning brown.

LIME
Citrus aurantifolia
Choose firm, shiny, fruit which is heavy for its size. Unlike lemons, a green skin indicates ripeness. May be used as you would a lemon, and in many Asian dishes, particularly in preparation of Thai food. Also popular in Mexican and Tahitian cuisines. Juice may be frozen. VARIETIES: Tahitian, West Indian.

CLEMENTINE
Citrus spp.
A hybrid of the tangerine and the North African wild orange, it has an easy-to-peel, thin skin, and an almost seedless, sweet and juicy flesh.

TANGERINE
Citrus reticulata
Related to the orange, its flavour is more delicate. Choose fruit which feels heavy for its size, with unblemished, tight-fitting, glossy skin. Eat by itself in segments, use in fruit salad, tarts, pies and cakes or for making marmalade. Dried tangerine peel is used in Chinese cookery.

BLOOD ORANGE

ORANGE
Citrus sinensis
Greatly valued for its high vitamin C content, this fruit has travelled the world protecting sailors from scurvy. To this day and probably in perpetuity, much enjoyed as a juice at breakfast time; the fruit is enjoyed as is, in salads, with meats and in desserts such as soufflés, and to make marmalade. There are three main varieties: navel, Seville and Valencia.

NAVEL ORANGE

CUMQUAT
Fortunella japonica
Looking like a miniature orange, the fruit is often grown in tubs for decorative purposes. Choose firm, unblemished fruit and refrigerate. Especially good when cooked to offset rich meats and game. May be preserved and served with ice cream and to make marmalade. When fully ripe, the fruit may be eaten fresh.

POMELO
Citrus grandis
This large, grapefruit look-alike should be heavy for its size, with glossy, unblemished skin. Store at room temperature. Eat by itself, with breakfast cereal, in fruit salad or savoury salads.

TANGELO
Citrus tangelo
A hybrid of the grapefruit and the tangerine. Eat in segments or add to fruit salads and savoury salads. Squeeze the juice for a drink, or use in marinades, salad dressings or jelly.

138

UGLI FRUIT
Citrus spp.
A cross between a grapefruit, a
tangerine and a Seville orange.
Slightly smaller than a
grapefruit, it has a yellow-green,
pitted skin and sweet flesh.

PINK GRAPEFRUIT

GRAPEFRUIT
Citrus paradisi
Varieties have yellow, pink or red flesh. Good for breakfast, halved
and eaten as is or with a little sugar, in cocktails, salads,
marmalade or simply juiced. Yellow-fleshed grapefruit may range
from tart to sweet, pink flesh tends to be sweeter. Choose heavy,
unblemished fruit, without soft spots.

YELLOW GRAPEFRUIT

139

WATERMELON
Cucumis citrullus
This large, green-skinned melon contains sweet, juicy, pink-to-deep-red flesh with copious black seeds. The white flesh surrounding the pink may be pickled and eaten with curries and cold meats. Watermelons do not ripen further once picked, so choose sweet-smelling specimens, which give slightly when pressed at the blossom end. Once cut, refrigerate. Eat by itself, in fruit salad or purée for drinks, sorbet and mousse.

CANTALOUPE

MELON
Cucumis melo
The two main groups of dessert melon are the musk, or netted melon, *Cucumis melo* var. *reticulatus,* and the winter melon, *Cucumis melo* var. *inordorus.* The first group is so called because of its musk-scented aroma and includes the hard-rind, netted melons, such as cantaloupe, also called **rockmelon**. The second group is non-odorous and smooth-skinned; honeydew melons, for instance, belong to this group.

YELLOW HONEYDEW

HONEYDEW

GALIA
Small and round with netted skin, it has white, sweet, juicy flesh when ripe. Serve chilled by itself or include in fruit salads.

ROUGH-SKINNED CANTALOUPE
Small and round with rough, netted skin, its flesh is orange and fragrant with a delicious, ripe, honeyed taste. A summer fruit which should be served chilled by itself or included in fruit salads.

ISRAELI GALIA
A larger variety of Galia melon, often with slightly darker flesh.

OGEN
First cultivated in Israel, this is a small, round melon with smooth, motley skin and segment markings. The flesh is green and sweet. Allow one melon per person, and serve with the top cut off and the seeds scooped out.

PIEL DE SAPO
Also known as **frog melon**. A green-skinned, oval melon with sweet and juicy, white flesh.

CHARENTAIS
A small melon with pale, green, smooth skin and deeper green segment markings. It has sweet, exotic-tasting, orange flesh and a heady fragrance. Excellent as a first course served with Parma ham.

143

GLEN PROSEN
Rubus idaeus
A mid-season, very firm
raspberry used mostly
for cooking.

GLEN MOY
Rubus idaeus
An early, firm-textured
raspberry with a full flavour.

CHILLIWACK
Rubus idaeus
A summer raspberry
with a sweet,
fruity flavour.

LEO
Rubus idaeus
A late season, large,
round, orange-red
raspberry with an
intense taste.

JULIA
Rubus idaeus
A large, good-quality,
mid-season raspberry
packed with flavour.
Use for desserts.

COMMON RASPBERRY
Rubus idaeus
Small, sweet and juicy for
desserts, and particularly
good for stuffing grouse.

GOLDEN RASPBERRY
Rubus idaeus
The yellow version
of the common
raspberry.

WHITECURRANT
Ribes sativum
White cousin of the
redcurrant, it has a sweet,
sharp taste. Excellent for
tarts and other desserts.

REDCURRANT
Ribes sativum
A tart berry good
for jellies.

CRANBERRY
Vaccinium oxycoccos
A sharp berry which must
be cooked with sugar to
make it palatable.

BLACKCURRANT JUMBO
Ribes nigrum
A large variety of blackcurrant.

BLACKCURRANT
Ribes nigrum
An acidic berry good for pie fillings
and, lightly poached in sugar syrup,
for summer pudding.

BLUEBERRY
Vaccinium spp.
A sweet berry
good for preserves
and muffins.

ELSANTA
Fragaria virginiana
A popular, sweet strawberry.

FRAIS DE BOIS
Fragaria virginiana
Also known as **alpine strawberry**.
Tiny with an intense taste.

MARA DE BOIS
Fragaria virginiana
A wild/cultivated cross variety.

TAYBERRY
Rubus var.
A cross between a
blackberry and a
raspberry, it has a rich,
aromatic taste.

LOGANBERRY
Rubus loganbaccus
Another
blackberry/raspberry
cross with a tangy
flavour. Ideal for berry
desserts and jam.

SUNBERRY
Rubus var.
A raspberry hybrid
with an excellent,
full flavour.

BOYSENBERRY
Rubus var.
A cross between a
youngberry and a raspberry,
it is a large berry with a juicy,
raspberry flavour.

SILVANBERRY
Rubus fruticosus
An early-ripening
blackberry, it
is large and juicy
with a good
aroma.

RED LOGANBERRY
Rubus loganbaccus
A small
blackberry/raspberry
cross. Ideal
for jam.

LOCH NESS
Rubus fruticosus
A large, firm
blackberry.

KING'S ACRE
Rubus var.
A large, long, oval
raspberry/
blackberry hybrid
with a sweet
flavour. A good
dessert fruit.

WALDO
Rubus fruticosus
An intensely
glossy, well
flavoured,
cultivated
blackberry.

BEDFORD GIANT
Rubus fruticosus
The most widely
cultivated
blackberry, it is an
all-rounder, good for
cooking and eating.

ADRIENNE
Rubus fruticosus
An early, spine-
free blackberry
with an incredibly
rich flavour.

BRAMBLE
*Rubus
fruticosus*
A wild
blackberry,
good for
making jam.

RED GOOSEBERRY
Ribes grossularia
A sweet variety of gooseberry.

LEVELLER
Ribes grossularia
A large, common gooseberry which is
almost hairless.

GOOSEBERRY
Ribes grossularia
Sharp flavoured and green when immature; may
sweeten and change colour when ripe.

145

FLAT or DIRECTOR
A French variety with white or yellow flesh and a sweet, almond-like flavour.

FRENCH JUMBO
A very large, peach-sized variety with deep orange flesh and a sunset blush. This is a dessert apricot, but it is also good served in fruit salads.

PEACH
Prunus persica

APRICOT
Prunus armeniaca

ORANGE RED
A small, sweet dessert apricot.

SPRING BELLE
With orange flesh, it has an intense flavour.

MONIQUE
A pale yellow, firm-fleshed apricot best suited for cooked desserts.

ROYAL GEM
An orange-fleshed table peach, good in fruit salads, crumbles and tarts.

BERGERONS
A small eating variety with a rosy blush to its skin.

ITALIAN SNOW QUEEN
It has delicious, white flesh which is tinged pink when really ripe.

SPRING RED
A juicy, honey-flavoured, early variety.

NECTARINE
Prunus persica var. *nectarina*

HADEN
Standard mango with a concentrated honey flavour.

BIG TOP
A large, yellow-fleshed nectarine from Mediterranean countries.

PAKISTANI HONEY
Yellow-fleshed with a sweet honey flavour.

FLAVOUR GOLD
A juicy and sweet, golden-fleshed nectarine from the Continent.

DATE
Phoenix dactylifera
Plump and brown, fresh dates have a delicious, smooth, creamy texture.

MANGO
Mangifera indica

TOMMY ATKINS
A large mango with a luscious, exotic flavour.

CALIFORNIAN MEDJOOL
A sweet and juicy, common seedless date variety.

PLUM
Prunus

VICTORIA
A delicious, golden-fleshed eating plum, it is also perfect for pies and puddings.

BLACK DIAMOND
A round, firm-fleshed, black plum with juicy amber-coloured flesh.

GREENGAGE
An old English fruit of the plum family. It is pale green with golden/green, juicy, sweet flesh.

HERMAN
A small, black juicy plum with sweet, yellow flesh.

GAVIOTA
From Spain, it changes from gold to orange with a red blush when fully ripe. The soft, succulent flesh has lots of juice and a good, fruity flavour.

TRAGEDY
A mauve plum with sweet, sharp flesh.

BLACK PRINCE
A small, black plum with green, firm-textured flesh.

EARLY LAXTON BROGDALE
An English, red plum with yellow flesh. Because of its high acidity, it is best used in cooked recipes.

WHITE
Pale yellow with a red blush. Excellent for a fruit bowl.

STELLA
A large, rich-flavoured, extremely succulent, English cherry.

SANTA ROSA
A Spanish variety with dark red skin which becomes progressively rosy as it ripens, and orange flesh. Sweet and lusciously juicy.

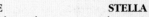

CHERRY
Prunus

HAY
A soft-textured, sweet, golden plum.

PICOTA
A Spanish variety which is good for cooking.

GAUCHER
A firm-fleshed, juicy, English cherry with a fruit flavour balanced with acidity.

BREADFRUIT
Artocarpus communis
A large, pulpy fruit
usually roasted as a
vegetable in
Caribbean dishes.

PLANTAIN
Musa paradisiaca
A firm, starchy, not-so-
sweet member of the
banana family used
for cooking. Cook like
a vegetable in
Caribbean dishes.

POMEGRANATE
Punica granatum
The thick, mostly pink to red, leathery skin envelopes
'chambers' with pithy walls, containing seeds surrounded
by sacks of red, sweet, juicy pulp. Store pomegranates at
room temperature; they make a beautiful display. Use the
seeds in fruit salads, mixed green salads, chicken, fish and
rice dishes, especially in Eastern Mediterranean cuisines.

DURIAN
Durio zibethinus
An Asian fruit with a questionable, almost off-putting aroma. The flesh is sweet and pineappley and is often used in cooking.

Loquat

LOQUAT
Eriobotrya japonica
Also known as **Japanese medlar**, has yellow- to orange-coloured skin. The flesh is crisp, white to soft yellow, fragrant but slightly acidic. Choose firm fruit, attached to the branch, if possible. Refrigerate. Peel the skin and eat fresh, or use to make jelly.

RED ISRAELI LYCHEE
Litchi chinensis
A deeply perfumed, translucent fruit which originated in China.

THAI LYCHEE
Litchi chinensis
A variety with a seductive fragrance and a slightly tropical taste.

RAMBUTAN
Nephelium lappaceum
Also known as the **hairy lychee**, to which it is closely related, the flesh has a grape-like flavour. Choose highly coloured fruit and store in the fridge for about one week. Eat by itself, in fruit or fish salad, in Asian dishes or with cheese.

149

MANGOSTEEN
Garcinia mangostana
A Malaysian fruit with a thick skin which encloses the sweet, white, refreshingly luscious fruit. Although it resembles a lychee, it is not related. Good in fruit salads or as a garnish for ice-cream.

CAPE GOOSEBERRY
From the shrub *Physalis peruviana*, it is of the same family as the Chinese lanterns used in decorative flower arrangements. Surrounded by a papery husk, which folds back, is a small, golden berry which has a sweet, sharp taste. It is often coated in fondant as an after-dinner sweet, or used to decorate desserts.

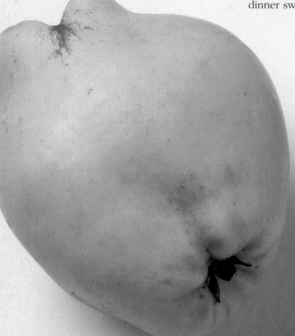

SALAK
Salacca edulis
A member of the palm family and related to the coconut, this is a small, plum-sized fruit with a scaly skin. It is also known as **snake fruit**. The firm, white flesh is in three segments with a seed in each. The taste is sharp and nutty.

QUINCE
Cydonia oblongo
Related to the apple and the pear, it is a native of Asia. The hard, bitter, raw flesh is inedible. Once the fruit is washed, peeled and cored, it can be used to make excellent jam. It is also often used in Moroccan dishes such as lamb stew.

PERSIMMON
Diospyros
Persimmons originated in Japan and should only be eaten when fully ripe, otherwise they have a sour, astringent taste. The **Sharon Fruit** is a seedless, non-astringent version of the persimmon, and was developed in Israel. It can be eaten whilst still firm, like an apple.

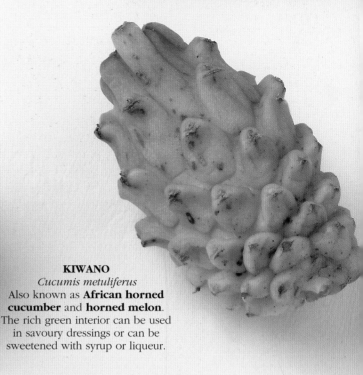

GRANADILLA
Passiflora edulis
A variety of **passionfruit**, named as
such by the Spanish because it looks
like a small pomegranate. Halve, scoop
out the seeds and use for topping
cheesecakes or other desserts. The skin
should be discarded.

KIWANO
Cucumis metuliferus
Also known as **African horned
cucumber** and **horned melon**.
The rich green interior can be used
in savoury dressings or can be
sweetened with syrup or liqueur.

PRICKLY PEAR
Opuntia ficus indica
Originally from South America and brought to Europe by
Christopher Columbus. It now grows around the Mediterranean
and other temperate regions. A member of the cactus family, it
should be handled with care because of the sharp prickles. Buy
when orange to red in colour, and firm. Peel off skin and serve
orange flesh in fruit salads and trifles.

PITAHAYA
Hylocereus guatemalensis
The fruit of a cactus originally from
tropical woodlands of South America.
Use in the same manner as prickly pear.

151

SUGAR BANANA

LADY FINGER BANANA

CAVENDISH BANANA

BANANA
Musa paradisiaca
Bananas grow in 'hands'; the bananas themselves are called 'fingers'. Choose firm, yellow fruit; a few brown specks indicate complete ripeness. Green bananas will ripen at room temperature. When fully ripe, bananas can be stored in the fridge or freezer; the skin will turn dark, but the flesh remains unaffected. The **plantain** is a green cooking banana used in a savoury manner rather than sweet.

GUAVA
Psidium guajava
This is a member of the custard apple family; the green skin turns yellow when fully ripe, and the creamy to salmon-coloured flesh is fragrant and juicy. Mostly used for juicing and making jelly. Choose firm, unblemished fruit; refrigerate when ripe.

TAMARILLO
Cyphomandra betacea
Also known as a **tree tomato**, this smooth, egg-shaped, maroon-coloured fruit has tangy flesh and seeds. Choose large, firm, glossy fruit with unblemished skin and store in the fridge. Eat from the skin with a spoon, or peel, and add to fruit salad, tarts and puddings, mousse, soufflé, ice cream, sorbet or drinks. Use to make chutney, jam and jelly. When poached, the tamarillo is good to eat with rich meats.

SAPODILLA
Manilkara zapota
This green-skinned fruit with yellow, sweet flesh must be fully ripe before eating. Choose firm, unblemished fruit, ripen at room temperature until soft, then refrigerate. Eat from the skin with a spoon, add to fruit salad or purée to make ice cream or sauce.

STAR-APPLE
Chrysophyllum cainito
A relative of sapodilla and sapote, the star-apple has skin which may vary from yellow to pink to dark purple, with white star-shaped flesh. Choose fruit with firm, unblemished skin, ripen at room temperature, then refrigerate. Serve with cheese, or eat with a spoon from the skin, add to fruit salad or purée for ice cream, sorbet, drinks or sauces.

152

PEPINO
Solanum muricatum
With a flavour reminiscent of both melon and pear, this juicy fruit has a soft, yellow green skin with purple streaks and pale yellow flesh. The fruit will continue to ripen after being picked. When fully ripe, the skin turns creamy and the fruit is sweetly perfumed. Select unblemished, glossy fruit and refrigerate once ripe. Eat by itself, in fruit salad, with cheese, in savoury dishes, or purée for sorbet or drinks.

CARAMBOLA
Averrhoa carambola
Also known as **five corner fruit** or **star fruit**, this originates from the East. Even when green, the fruit is edible and the star-shaped slices are a great addition to fruit salad. Buy unblemished fruit and refrigerate.

FIG
Ficus carica
The colours of this multi-seeded member of the mulberry family vary from white to green to brown to purple to black. Serve with prosciutto, cheese, in fruit salad, poached or caramelized or with ice cream. Choose sweet-smelling, soft fruit with unblemished skin. Refrigerate.

SAPOTE
Diospyros digyna
Also known as **chocolate-pudding fruit**, the white or green skin turns dark brown when fully ripe and the flesh varies from red to black. Eat from the skin with a spoon, purée for ice cream, mousse or sauces.

KIWI FRUIT
Actinidia chinensis
The brown, downy skin reveals bright green, juicy flesh with a large number of tiny, black seeds. Choose firm fruit, which will ripen at room temperature. Once ripe, store in the fridge. Good eaten as is, from the skin with a spoon, or with ice cream, cheesecake, pavlova, in fruit salad or with cheese.

BANANA PASSIONFRUIT

PANAMA PASSIONFRUIT

PURPLE GRANADILLA

PASSIONFRUIT
Passiflora spp.
Some varieties are also called **granadilla**, which means 'little pomegranate'; the name passionfruit refers to the vine-growing flowers, used by the Spanish Jesuit missionaries to explain the passion and crucifixion of Christ. The hard, leathery skin varies from green to yellow to brown. The edible seeds are contained in a yellowy pulp, which is both tart and sweet.

JACKFRUIT
Artocarpus heterophyllus
The large fruit, with hard, knobbly skin, contains flesh which can be eaten as a fruit when ripe or cooked as a vegetable when unripe. The fruit is ripe when the skin changes from green to yellow. Store in a cool place when whole, but refrigerate once cut. The numerous, large seeds may be boiled and roasted like chestnuts.

PINEAPPLE
Ananas comosus
The pineapple does not ripen any further once picked, so choose sweetly fragrant fruit, with fresh-looking green leaves. Some green varieties are fully ripe. Refrigerate and use as soon as possible. Cut skin off by standing pineapple on its cut base and cutting downwards, following the curve of the fruit. Serve by itself, in fruit salad and Chinese dishes; grill and serve with meats; bake in cakes, pies, tarts; purée for sorbet and drinks.

154

PAPAYA
Carica papaya
Also called **pawpaw**; a yellow skin usually indicates ripeness, although some species remain green. The flesh varies from yellow to pink to orange. Choose unblemished, sweet-smelling fruit. Green papaya is used in chutney and curries, especially in Thai cuisine. Papaya contains the enzyme papain, which helps tenderize meat, but prevents the fruit from setting in gelatin.

CUSTARD APPLE
Annona cherimola
The bumpy, green skin encloses creamy flesh with an excellent fruity flavour, sometimes compared to a cross between strawberries and pineapple. The fruit may be halved and the flesh eaten out of the skin with a spoon, or diced in fruit salad, used in tarts, cakes or ice cream. Buy unblemished fruit and refrigerate when ripe.

SOLO PAPAYA

155

RHUBARB
Rheum rhaponticum
Really a vegetable, but most often
used as a fruit, rhubarb is related to
sorrel, and is grown for its stems
alone. Choose crisp, firm stalks and
remove the leaves. Refrigerate and
use within four days. Cut into
manageable lengths and stew or
poach until tender. Use for mousse,
fools, ice cream or sorbet, in tarts or
pies and puddings.

JABOTICABA
Myrciaria
Also known as **Brazilian tree grape**,
it looks like a large, black grape or
very round black olive. The tart-
flavoured skin hides fragrant, lychee-
flavoured flesh. Choose firm, glossy,
unblemished fruit. Refrigerate. Eat by
itself, in fruit salad or with cheese.

156

WALTHAMCROSS GRAPES

BLACK MUSCAT

GRAPE
Vitis vinifera

One of the oldest known cultivated fruits, the grape is grown for the table and for making wine. The colour may vary from palest green to light mauve to deep purple and black, depending on variety. Taste before buying, as grapes do not ripen any further once picked. Refrigerate fresh grapes without rinsing. Rinse just before serving. A pair of grape scissors on the table means guests can cut off as much as they like without disfiguring the bunch. Apart from being eaten fresh, either by themselves or with dessert cheese, in fruit salad or savoury salads, in sauces or to garnish platters, the most important and popular use of grapes is in making wines. Dried grapes, such as sultanas, currants and raisins, are a great pantry standby for baking, and dried muscatels on the branch are a good addition with dessert cheese.

157

MESSINA BLACK SEEDLESS
Good with soft cheeses.

MESSINA GREEN SEEDLESS
Good served with goat's cheese, in fresh
fruit salads or in Sole Veronique.

THOMPSON SEEDLESS
A sweet and juicy, common variety. Can be
eaten both fresh or dried.

SUGRANE
From Spain, a seedless grape with a
tough skin and a slightly tart taste.
Use in pies.

DAN-BEN HANNAH ISRAELI
A black, seeded grape with a tannic skin
and a sweet, juicy flavour.

FLAME
A sweet, red, seedless, standard
table grape.

APPLE
Store up to six months. Eat as a snack or use in baking. To reconstitute, soak in boiling water for 30 minutes or in cold water overnight. Use in muesli, cakes and stuffings for pork or poultry, or simmer until tender and purée for sauce.

APRICOT
Store up to 12 months. A pleasantly tart flavour. To reconstitute, soak for 30 minutes in boiling water or in cold water overnight. Serve in fruit salad, muesli, pilaf, stuffing, purée as a sauce, use in baking or as a flavouring for ice cream.

BANANA
Store up to 12 months. Eat as a snack. Soak in boiling water for 30 minutes and use in baking. The dried fruit may be milled and the resulting flour used for baking or in puddings.

CRANBERRY
Store up to 12 months.
Soak in boiling water for 30 minutes and use in sauces, stuffing, desserts and baking.

CURRANT
Store up to 12 months.
Small, seedless, dried grapes. Use in pilaf, dolmades and desserts. May be macerated in liqueur before being used in baking.

DATE
Store up to six months.
May be dry, semi-dry or soft. Eat as a snack, stuffed with cheese or marzipan, as a dessert with cheese, or use in baking.

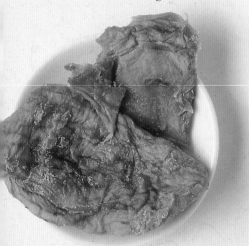

MANGO
Store up to six months.
Soak in boiling water for 30 minutes or overnight in cold water. Use in cakes, ice cream and desserts, purée for a sauce for savoury dishes or desserts, or use as a flavouring for soufflés and ice cream.

MIXED FRUIT
Store up to 12 months.
A mixture of dried fruits, such as raisins, sultanas and citrus peel. Best in baking.

MUSCATEL
Store up to 12 months. A dried, dark-skinned, succulent grape, usually seedless. Frequently available in clusters, a welcome addition with cheese for dessert. Also good with pork and quail, in pilaf and stuffings.

BLUEBERRY
Store up to six months. The dried berry may be soaked for 30 minutes in boiling water and used in baking muffins and cakes, puréed as a sauce for savoury dishes or desserts, or used as a flavouring for soufflés and ice cream.

CHERRY
Store up to six months. The dried cherry may be soaked for 30 minutes in boiling water and used in baking muffins and cakes, puréed as a sauce for savoury dishes or desserts, or used as a flavouring for soufflés and ice cream.

CITRUS PEEL
Store up to 12 months. The dried peel of citrus fruit — mostly oranges and lemons — is used in baking, for instance, in Christmas cake.

FIG
Store up to 12 months. Stew gently in water for about 20 minutes until tender. Serve for breakfast or with cheese and sweet wine after dinner. Soak in wine for a dessert.

GINGER
Store up to 12 months. Fresh ginger, cubed and crystallized in sugar syrup. Use in rich fruit cakes or butter cakes. Especially good with pear.

KIWI FRUIT
Also called **Chinese gooseberry**. Store up to six months. To reconstitute, soak in boiling water for 30 minutes or overnight in cold water. Use in baking, purée as a sauce for savoury dishes or desserts, or use to flavour soufflés and ice cream.

PAPAYA
Store up to six months. To reconstitute, soak in boiling water for 30 minutes or overnight in cold water. Use in baking, purée as a sauce for savoury dishes or desserts, or use as a flavouring for soufflés and ice cream.

PEACH
Store up to 12 months. Eat as a snack; include in muesli. Soak in boiling water for 30 minutes or in cold water overnight. Stew gently until tender. Use in Middle Eastern meat recipes, puréed as a sauce, or as a flavouring.

PEAR
Store up to six months. Eat as a snack; include in muesli. Soak in boiling water for 30 minutes or in cold water overnight. Stew gently in water until tender. Use in dried fruit salad, in stuffing, puréed or as a flavouring.

PINEAPPLE
Store up to 12 months.
Eat as a snack. To reconstitute, soak in
boiling water for 30 minutes or in cold
water overnight. Use in rich fruit cakes or
purée as a sauce.

PLUM
Store up to six months.
Eat as a snack. To reconstitute, soak in
boiling water for 30 minutes or in cold
water overnight. Serve in fruit salad or
purée as a sauce.

PRUNE
Store up to six months.
This is a dried sugar plum. Stew gently
and eat for breakfast. Eat with pork and
game, purée as a sauce for desserts or use
as a base for soufflé and ice cream.

ALMOND, in shell
Prunus dulcis
Store whole almonds in a cool, dry, dark
place to retain maximum flavour.
Almonds grow on trees, native to
southern Europe. There are bitter and
sweet varieties. Eat as a snack.

ALMOND, kernel
Prunus dulcis
Store in a cool, dark, dry place, refrigerate
or freeze. Eat as a snack. Used in savoury
dishes, particularly Middle Eastern, in
baking and confectionery.

ALMOND, ground
Prunus dulcis
Store in freezer. Ground, blanched
almonds. Use in baking, added to pastry,
in confectionery, such as praline and
marzipan, or to make almond butter.

BRAZIL NUT, in shell
Bertholettia excelsa
Store in a cool, dark, dry place. From a
South American forest tree, the nut is a
seed surrounded by a hard shell and
grows in clusters inside a large coconut-
like shell. Rich, creamy texture.

BRAZIL NUT, kernel
Bertholettia excelsa
Store in fridge or freezer.
The shelled nuts can be served with
dessert and cheese, and used in rich fruit
cakes, such as panforte.

CASHEW NUT, raw
Anacardium occidentale
Store in a cool, dark, dry place, refrigerate
or freeze. Native to Brazil, this nut now
grows primarily in India. It is widely used
in Eastern and Asiatic cuisines. A mildly
sweet flavour and soft texture.

ROCKMELON
Store up to six months.
Eat as a snack; include in muesli. To reconstitute, soak in boiling water for 30 minutes or in cold water overnight. Use in sweet dishes or purée as a flavouring for soufflé and ice cream.

RAISIN
Store up to 12 months.
Large, succulent and mostly seedless, dried grapes. Use in baking and desserts. May be macerated in liqueur before using in baking.

SULTANA
Store up to 12 months.
A dried grape with pale-coloured skin.
Eat as a snack, use in baking, add to muesli, salads, pilaf, curries, stuffings and casseroles.

ALMOND, flaked
Prunus dulcis
The blanched nut shaved into paper-thin slices. Store in fridge or freezer. Use to decorate cakes before baking or toast until golden and aromatic and sprinkle on baked cakes, vegetables, rice dishes etc.

ALMOND, blanched
Prunus dulcis
Store in fridge or freezer.
The brown skin is removed by covering with boiling water for a few minutes. Drain, dry and the skin will slip off easily. Use in baking or to make almond butter.

ALMOND, slivered
Prunus dulcis
Store in fridge or freezer.
The blanched nut which has been fairly thickly sliced. Use in cakes, in both sweet and savoury salads, stuffing, rice and pasta dishes.

CHESTNUT
Castanea mollissima
A starchy nut with low-fat content and good dietary fibre. When fresh, store in the fridge. Use in soups, stuffing, with vegetables or purée for desserts, such as soufflé or ice cream.

COCONUT
Cocos nucifera
Store in the fridge. The fruit of a tropical palm, the flesh may be eaten fresh or dried. The milk makes a refreshing drink and is used in many Asiatic cuisines. Coconut oil is high in cholesterol.

COCONUT, flaked
Cocos nucifera
Store in a well-sealed jar in a cool, dark, dry place. Use in baking and desserts and in many Indian dishes.

163

HAZELNUT, in shell
Corylus avellana
Also known as a **filbert**, the hazelnut grows worldwide. It is very popular in baking and in savoury dishes. Also used to make hazelnut oil and butter.

HAZELNUT, in skin
Corylus avellana
Store in fridge or freezer. To remove skin, roast nuts in a medium oven for 10 minutes or until fragrant. Rub in a clean tea towel until skin comes off. Use whole in rich fruit cakes and chopped in sweet and savoury dishes.

HAZELNUT, ground
Corylus avellana
Store in freezer. Use in cakes, such as tortes, in biscuits, confectionery and desserts, such as soufflé and ice cream, in pastry and to make praline.

PEANUT, raw
Arachis hypogaea
Store in fridge or freezer. Skin usually slips off easily; otherwise blanch briefly. Use to make peanut butter. Roast raw peanuts in a moderate oven for 10 minutes or until fragrant.

PEANUT, roasted
Arachis hypogaea
Store in fridge or freezer. Chop and add to salads, sauces (such as satay) and poultry, meat, fish, pasta, and rice; also to cakes and biscuits.

PECAN NUT, in shell
Carya illinoinensis
The kernel of the fruit of the hickory tree, the pecan resembles the walnut and can be used in the same way, although both have their own flavour; pecan is the more delicate. Use in savoury or sweet dishes.

PISTACHIO NUT, salted
Pistacia vera
Native to Syria, but now cultivated worldwide. The pistachio is a small, green kernel in a cream-coloured shell, with a natural opening on one side.

PISTACHIO NUT, roasted
Pistacia vera
Store in freezer. Use in desserts, such as cakes, ice cream and soufflé, add to pastry and used to make praline.

PISTACHIO NUT, ground
Pistacia vera
Store in freezer. The blanched pistachio nut is used in desserts, such as cakes, ice cream and soufflé, added to pastry and used to make praline.

MACADAMIA NUT, shelled
Macadamia integrifolia
Store in fridge or freezer.
Eat as a snack or chop and use in salads, cakes, biscuits and desserts, such as ice cream and tarts.

MACADAMIA NUT, ground
Macadamia integrifolia
Store in freezer.
Use in cakes, biscuits and desserts, such as ice cream, in pastry and to make praline.

PEANUT, in shell
Arachis hypogaea
Store in a cool, dark, dry place. The peanut, also known as **groundnut**, grows in pairs in brittle shells, which makes it an ideal snack. Adaptable to savoury and sweet dishes.

PECAN, shelled
Carya illinoinensis
Store in fridge or freezer. Eat as a snack, use whole in pecan pies and fruit cakes or chopped in cakes and biscuits.

PECAN, ground
Carya illinoinensis
Store in freezer.
Use in pastry, biscuits, ice cream and to make praline.

PINE NUT
Pinaceae
This nut grows inside cones on pine trees. It has a sweet flavour and soft texture. When roasted, use to sprinkle on salads, in pilaf and with pasta. An essential element in pesto sauce.

WALNUT, in shell
Juglans
Store in a cool, dark, dry place. American walnuts have a dark shell and skin surrounding white flesh with a strong flavour, whereas the European variety is milder. Used to make oil.

WALNUT, shelled
Juglans
Walnuts are good as a snack, or with cheese and port after dinner. Halved or chopped, they can be added to salads, rich fruit cakes, pasta sauces, biscuits and stuffings.

WALNUT, ground
Juglans
Store in freezer.
Use in biscuits, tarts, to make praline or add to pastry.

Flours, grains, cereals & pasta

Banished to the proverbial desert island, most people would remain happily ensconced for quite some time, given a constant supply of good, fresh bread, together with some cheese and, perhaps, the occasional glass of red wine.

'Our daily bread' signifies so much more than sliced loaves in plastic bags; to Western minds, bread is the staff of life and, in the sense of the Lord's Prayer, it is life itself.

In many countries, bread is revered and sacred; it is said that when crumbs are dropped on the floor in Italy, they should be picked up with the eyelashes. In Spain, bread dropped on the floor is kissed before it's put back on the table. Bread never needs to be wasted: consider making bread salads, such as Italian *panzanella* or Lebanese *fattoush*; keep some chunks to dip into melted cheese for fondue, or some thick slices to float on robust soups.

Not so many years ago, in Western households, rice was simply rice. Now, we are more sophisticated in our food choices and buy Arborio rice to make risotto, Jasmine rice to serve with Thai dishes and Basmati to accompany Indian curries. Different varieties of rice take varying lengths of time to cook.

With pasta, too, we have seen many changes. There are now more than 700 different pasta shapes, from the familiar spaghetti to shells, ears and butterflies — the list goes on. Many fresh pasta shops have sprung up, where you can buy all manner of filled and unfilled pasta, often coloured and flavoured. Better shops stock imported, artisan-made pasta. Once you've tasted it, you'll be converted. Dried pasta keeps for months in the larder, while fresh pasta should be used immediately or frozen for later use.

Asian noodles, couscous and polenta, as well as a wide variety of grains, such as barley and bulgur wheat, are all enjoying increasing popularity.

BROWN LONG-GRAIN RICE
Very nutritious. The inedible outer husk is removed, but the bran layer is still intact. Suitable for pilaf and rice salad, this rice has a fluffy texture when cooked.

BROWN SHORT-GRAIN RICE
Very nutritious. The inedible outer husk is removed, leaving the bran layer still intact. Grains tend to cling together, when cooked. Suitable for puddings.

WHITE LONG-GRAIN RICE
The polished whole grain, this rice has a fluffy texture when cooked. Suitable for pilaf and rice salad.

WHITE SHORT-GRAIN RICE
The grains tend to cling together when cooked, making it suitable for puddings.

WHITE GLUTINOUS RICE
A stickier version of short-grain rice, also known as **sticky rice**. Widely used in Asia for desserts and sweets, this is also the rice used for Japanese sushi.

BASMATI RICE
A long-grain rice with aromatic flavour, which develops with storage. Grains stay firm and separate when cooked. Suitable for pilaf and rice salad.

JASMINE RICE
A soft, delicately aromatic, long-grain rice used in Asian recipes, pilaf and rice salad.

BROWN AND WILD RICE MIXTURE
This combination has extra nutty flavour. Attractive to the eye, it is suitable as a side dish or in rice salad. The two varieties take the same time to cook.

ARBORIO RICE
Especially for risotto, this large-grain rice releases its starch during constant stirring with stock. Originally only grown in the Po Valley, in Italy, it is now widely available

CARNAROLI, super fino
Especially for risotto, this large-grain
rice releases its starch during constant
stirring with stock.

VIALONE NANO, semi fino
Slightly smaller than Carnaroli, this rice is
especially for risotto, releasing its starch
during constant stirring with stock.

CALASPARRA
Especially for paella, this rice is
imported from the east coast of Spain.
If not available, substitute Arborio,
Carnaroli or Vialone Nano.

THAI BLACK RICE
The bran coating on this rice is soluble;
thus the colour leaches into the cooking
water. Grassy flavour, chewy texture.
Combine with coconut milk or
desiccated coconut for dessert.

THAI WHITE RICE
A long-grain rice, slightly sticky when
cooked, with a distinctive aroma. In
Thailand, where rice is seen as a symbol
of purity, it is always cooked without salt
or spices and served by itself.

SUSHI RICE
Coated with corn syrup and
cornstarch, this is especially good for
Japanese sushi, as the short-grain
rice becomes sticky when cooked.
Similar to glutinous rice.

RICE BRAN
The outside brown layer of the rice
kernel, containing the bran and a small
part of the germ. High in fibre and a
cholesterol deterrent. Add to baked
goods or meat loaf.

GROUND RICE
A coarser form of rice flour, slightly
toasted. Do not use this on its own for
general cooking or baking, as rice does
not contain gluten. A good thickener.
Also used for making sweets.

RICE FLOUR
Both white and brown rice flour are
available. This silky flour is used as a
thickener, or a substitute flour for those
with wheat or gluten allergies. For general
cooking, mix with other flours. Also used
to make rice noodles.

POHA FLAKES
Rice which has been parboiled, flattened and dried. Use in savoury snacks or to make milk puddings. This is not a breakfast cereal.

RICE FLAKES
These are crisp, dry cereal, made from rice. Use as a breakfast cereal or in baked goods and breads.

WILD RICE
Zizania aquatica
Not technically a rice, but an aquatic grass. The longest grains are the best quality; shorter grains have a similar flavour for a considerably lower price.

CORN MEAL
Zea mays
Also known as **maize meal**. Coarser than polenta, may be reconstituted with water and made into porridge.

CORNFLOUR
Also known as **cornstarch** or **maize flour**, this flour is milled from the starch of corn kernels. It does not contain gluten and, as a thickener, gives a smooth, clear sauce used frequently in Chinese cooking. Mix with other flours for baking.

POLENTA
Polenta is a grainy flour made from yellow or white corn. Bring to a simmer in water and cook to a porridge-like consistency. Eat when soft and hot or allow to cool and cut into slices, which are grilled or fried.

POLENTA, white
Used in the same way as yellow polenta but made from white corn.

POLENTA, instant
Use in the same way as yellow and white polenta but requires less cooking time.

POPCORN
Zea mays everta
A strain of corn, this grain contains kernels which pop when dried and heated. The corn may be popped in a covered pan with a little oil or in a special corn popper.

170

CORNFLAKES
These are crisp, dry cereal made from various types of corn kernels, ground, rolled and toasted. Most brands are enriched with nutrients. Eaten with cold or hot milk.

RYE
Secale cereale
Widely used to make breads. Containing less gluten than wheat, it makes a robust loaf, which takes longer to digest. Also used to make pumpernickel and crisp bread.

RYE FLAKES
Similar to rolled oats, these are steamed and rolled rye groats and may be eaten as porridge for breakfast and sprinkled on loaves before baking.

RYE FLOUR
Available in wholemeal and lighter varieties, this is whole rye, ground to a finer consistency than rye meal. Blend with gluten flours to make bread and crackers.

BARLEY
Hordeum vulgare
Used to make beer, whisky and barley water, it is also good in soups, stews and casseroles.

PEARL BARLEY
Hulled and polished barley grains, mostly added to soups and stews to thicken them and in casseroles.

BARLEY FLAKES
Also known as **rolled barley**. Steamed and flattened barley. Use as a cereal, in baked goods, or as a thickener in soups and stews.

BARLEY FLOUR
Finely ground, hulled barley with low gluten. Mix with other gluten flours for baking. Also used as a thickener.

ARROWROOT
A starch obtained from the rhizomes of tropical plants. Use in biscuits, puddings. When used as a thickener it leaves sauces and glazes transparent.

171

WHOLEWHEAT
Triticum vulgare
Also known as **wheat berries**. May be cooked to use in salads; do not add salt while cooking.

WHEAT FLAKES
Also known as **rolled wheat**, these are whole wheat grains which are rolled in the same way as oats. Use as cereal or to top loaves before baking.

BULGUR
Wheat grains which are hulled and steamed before cracking, then dried. Popular in Middle Eastern cuisine especially vegetarian dishes, such as *tabbouleh*.

WHEATGERM
The wheat grain in its embryonic state. Eat as is, raw or toasted, in baked goods, on cereal, or to crumb fish, chicken or meat. Keep frozen or refrigerated to prevent rancidity.

WHOLEMEAL FLOUR
The bran and germ of the whole wheat grain are present, therefore this flour is subject to rancidity. Only buy small amounts and keep refrigerated, if possible. Plain and self-raising.

WHITE FLOUR
This refined flour retains a lower percentage of the wheat grain than wholemeal flour, but is fortified to restore some lost nutrients. Plain and self-raising for cakes and pastries; strong for bread.

UNBLEACHED FLOUR
Wheat flour which has not been through a bleaching process.

SEMOLINA
Ground endosperm of hard durum wheat, the wheat of choice to make pasta. Also used to make Indian *dosas*, vegetable pilaf and couscous. Good for baking breads and in desserts.

DURUM SEMOLINA FLOUR
This is flour milled from hard durum wheat, the perfect flour for making pasta.

MOROCCAN COUSCOUS
Made from flour-coated semolina, these tiny pasta pellets are available in an instant variety, which takes about five minutes to prepare. The the Moroccan way takes at least an hour. The instant variety may be cooked the Moroccan way, giving you more couscous for your money.

ISRAELI COUSCOUS
Made in the same way as Moroccan couscous, this variety is the size of peppercorns. Cook the traditional (long, not instant) way as for Moroccan couscous or stir like rice, as for a risotto.

LEBANESE COUSCOUS
Made in the same way as Moroccan couscous, this variety is the size of small peas. Also marketed as **mograbeyeh** or **mougharbiye**. Cook in the traditional (long, not instant) way as for Moroccan couscous, or stir like rice, as for a risotto.

ATTA FLOUR
Made from wheat grain, this slightly coarse flour is used to make chapatis and other baked products. Available as plain white and coarse brown atta flour.

BUCKWHEAT
Fagopyrum esculentum
Buckwheat (whole, but not roasted) is gluten free. Used in pilaf or stuffings.

KASHA
This is roasted buckwheat. Particularly popular in Russia, it is nutty, with a slightly grassy flavour and chewy texture.

BUCKWHEAT FLOUR
Available in light and dark varieties, the dark version has tiny black specks due to a large percentage of finely milled hull particles being present. Used to make pizzoccheri pasta, blini, noodles, or mixed with other flours for baked goods.

TRITICALE
Triticum secale
A cross between wheat and rye, triticale is the first human-engineered grain. Used in breakfast cereals, breads, soups, cakes and pancakes. The nutty flavour is a mix of wheat and rye.

QUINOA
Pronounced keen-wa, quinoa is a protein-rich ancient grain which originates from the Andes. It is being hailed as the 'supergrain of the future'. Rinse before cooking to remove the bitter flavour and cook as you would rice.

MATZO MEAL

The ground meal from matzo, (unleavened bread) used before Jewish Passover when all yeast and leavened foods are avoided in kosher households. Used instead of flour to thicken sauces and stews and in baked goods.

MATZO, fine

Like matzo meal, but finely ground. Used in preparations such as gefilte fish, matzo balls and pancakes, to thicken soups and as crumbing for fried foods.

SAGO
Metroxylon sagu
Small balls of starch, made from the inner trunk of palm trees. Smaller than tapioca, the product is used in the same manner as a thickener and to set puddings.

SOYA FLOUR

Twice the protein content of wheat flour, and low in carbohydrates, this flour needs to be mixed with other flours for baked goods. Used to make snacks in Japan.

TAPIOCA, pearl
Manihot utilissima
Made from the roots of cassava, this starch may be replaced by arrowroot or cornflour. The little balls are larger than sago and are used for thickening and in desserts.

TAPIOCA, fine
Also known as **cassava flour**.
Use as a thickening agent for soups, fruit fillings in pies and tarts, and glazes. Cornflour or arrowroot are substitutes.

MILLET
Panicum milaceum
Widely used as birdseed. It has a nutty, polenta-like flavour and, when toasted, the fragrance of roasted corn.

MILLET MEAL

Not to be confused with millet flour, this is coarsely ground. Used in baked goods and in cereal. You can grind whole millet yourself in a coffee grinder.

URAD FLOUR

Milled from washed, black gram dhal or urad dhal, which are split urad beans with the black skins removed. Widely used in southern Indian cooking.

174

OATS
Avena sativa
The untreated, hulled oats, with a minimal amount of outer chaff or hull removed. Very nutritious. Soaking overnight shortens the cooking time.

ROLLED OATS
Steamed and flattened oats. For best results, stir into just less than three times their bulk of boiling water, cover and stand for 10 minutes. Also use in biscuits, muesli, bread and meatloaves.

OATMEAL
Small particles of the whole grain, ground into semi-fine-to-fine flakes. Used for porridge, in baked goods, and also in the famous Scottish haggis.

LINSEED
Mostly used in the production of linseed oil and may be added to breads.

LINSEED MEAL
This remains after the oil has been extracted from the whole seed. Nearly completely devoid of fat and a rich source of protein. Although mostly used as animal fodder, it is suitable for human consumption.

POTATO FLOUR
Ground, dried potatoes. The resulting flour is a good thickener for soups and sauces. Very popular in Middle European countries for making cakes and biscuits.

BRAN FLAKES
A breakfast cereal; large flakes made from the coarse outer layers of cereal grains.

WHEAT BRAN
Finely milled outer layers of the wheat grain, removed during the early stages of milling. Sprinkle on breakfast cereal, fruit, yoghurt, and breads and cakes before baking or add to meatloaf mixtures.

BESAN
Also known as **chickpea flour**, this flour is milled from a small variety of chickpeas. Widely used in India, especially for fritters, as a thickener and in sweet preparations.

175

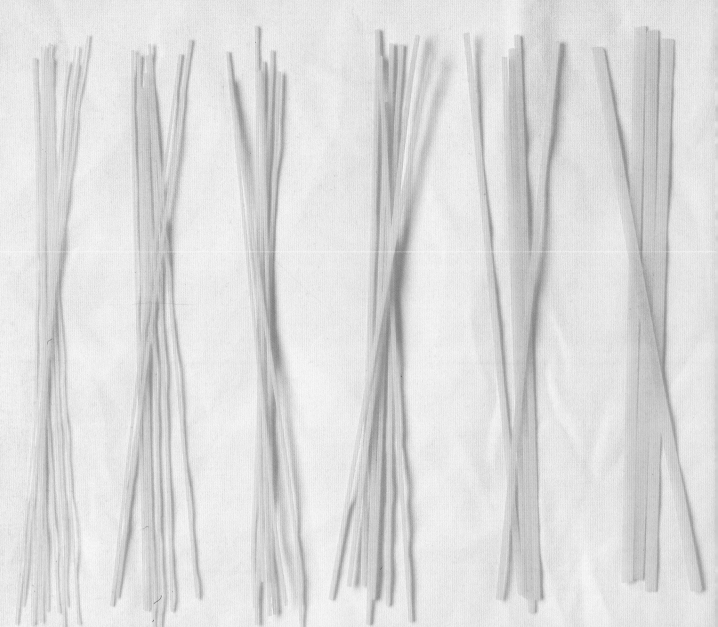

CAPELLINI
Very fine pasta, best with the very lightest of sauces or in broth. Also known as **capelli d'angelo** or **angel hair**.

FEDELINI
Slightly thicker than capellini.

SPAGHETTINI
Thicker than capellini and slightly thinner than spaghetti, this pasta is well suited to lighter sauces.

SPAGHETTI
Probably the most popular pasta. Used with a wide variety of sauces, both thick and chunky, and thin and delicate. Available in various flavours.

LINGUINE
Linguine's flat shape accommodates most sauces. Also available in spinach (*con spinaci*) and wholemeal (*tipo integrale*) flavours. Also known as **tagliatelle** or **bavette**.

FETTUCCELLE
A thicker version of linguine.

TAGLIERINI
Very fine, flat strips of delicate egg pasta, often served in broth or with a very light sauce.

TAGLIOLINI or **LINGUINE FINI**
A thinner version of linguine.

VERMICELLI
A size in between spaghetti and spaghettini.

BUCATINI
This pasta is hollow and ideal for serving with sturdy sauces.

PERCIATELLI
Hollow and ideal for sturdy sauces.

FUSILLI BUCATI LUNGHI
A hollow pasta shaped like a long corkscrew.

ZITA
A long, thick, hollow pasta. Also known as **ziti**.

LASAGNETTE
A ribbon-shaped pasta, also sold in nests (*nidi*), between pappardelle and fettuccine in width.

LAGHANELLE CON SALVIA
Wide strips of hand-made pasta made from durum wheat flour and flavoured with sage. Serve with meat sauces.

FETTUCCINE/TRENETTE
Ribbon-shaped pasta, about 5mm (1/4in) wide, especially good with butter- and cream-based sauces. Available in various flavours.

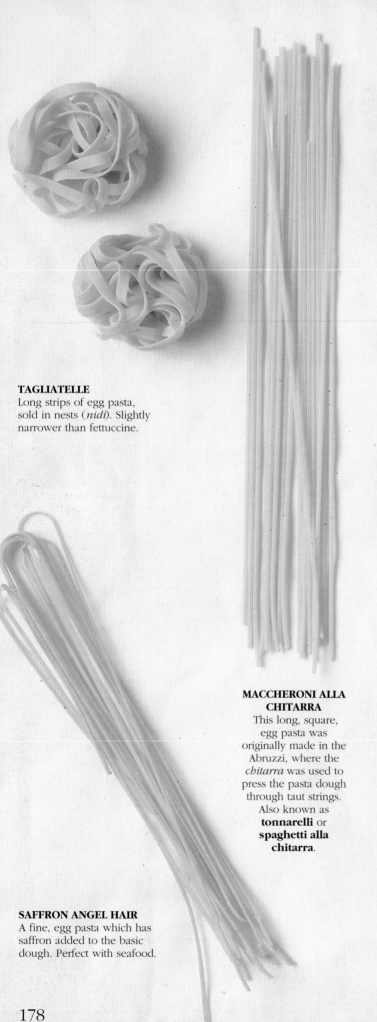

TAGLIATELLE
Long strips of egg pasta, sold in nests (*nidi*). Slightly narrower than fettuccine.

PAPPARDELLE
The widest, ribbon-shaped egg pasta. Often sold in nests (*nidi*). Available straight or crinkle-edged, this pasta is particularly good with robust sauces. Also available in spinach (*con spinaci*) flavour.

SPINACH AND BASIL LINGUINE SQUID INK LINGUINE

MACCHERONI ALLA CHITARRA
This long, square, egg pasta was originally made in the Abruzzi, where the *chitarra* was used to press the pasta dough through taut strings. Also known as **tonnarelli** or **spaghetti alla chitarra**.

SAFFRON ANGEL HAIR
A fine, egg pasta which has saffron added to the basic dough. Perfect with seafood.

LASAGNE
This egg pasta is available in sheets, and is mostly used to make the dish by the same name. Available fresh and dried.

LASAGNE VERDI
Puréed spinach is added to the basic pasta egg dough.

FETTUCCINE/TRENETTE
Ribbon-shaped egg pasta nests (*nidi*), especially good with butter- and cream-based sauces, such as *fettuccine all' Alfredo*. Available in various flavours.

TAGLIOLINI
Very fine strands of egg pasta.

CANNELLONI
An egg pasta shaped into big, hollow tubes, suitable for filling and baking with sauces.

179

CAVATAPPI
Corkscrew-shaped pasta.

CASARECCIA
Also known as **strozzapreti**
(meaning 'priest strangler').

PASTA AL CEPPO
Scroll-shaped pasta.

FARFALLE
Butterfly-shaped pasta. Also available in
spinach (*con spinaci*) flavour.

FARFALLINE
Tiny, butterfly-shaped pasta.

FARFALLONI
Large, butterfly-shaped pasta.

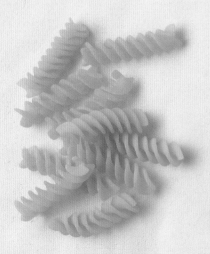

FUSILLI
Spring-shaped pasta. Also available in
spinach (*con spinaci*) and wholemeal
(*tipo integrale*) flavours.

ELICOIDALI
A narrower form of rigatoni, this hollow
pasta takes its name from its spiral
pattern. Also available in wholemeal (*tipo
integrale*) flavour.

MACCHERONI
Short lengths of hollow pasta tubes.

PENNE LISCE
Short, pen-shaped, smooth, hollow pasta.

PENNE RIGATE
Short, pen-shaped, ridged, hollow pasta.
Also available in spinach (*con spinaci*)
and wholemeal (*tipo integrale*) flavours.

MEZZE PENNE RIGATE
Medium, pen-shaped, ridged,
hollow pasta.

PENNONI
Large, pen-shaped, smooth, hollow pasta.

PENNONI RIGATI
Large, pen-shaped, ridged,
hollow pasta.

PENNE MEZZANE
Short, thin, pen-shaped hollow pasta.

GNOCCHI
A cloud-shaped, hollow pasta, not to be
confused with the dumpling made of
potato or flour.

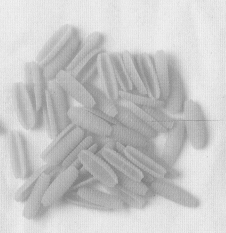

GNOCCHETTI SARDI
Small, Sardinian version of gnocchi.

ROTELLE
Wheel-shaped pasta.

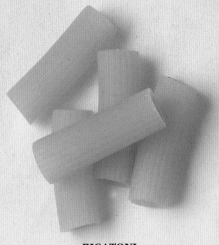

RIGATONI
Large, ridged, hollow pasta.

PIPE RIGATE
Ridged, hollow pasta resembling
snail shells.

GNOCCHETTI DI ZITA LUNGHI RIGATI
Short, thick, ridged, hollow pasta.

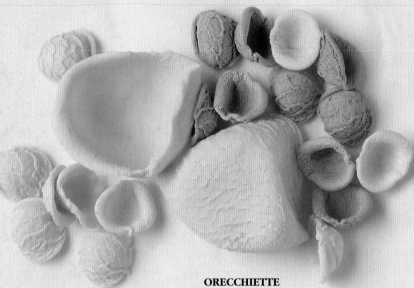

ORECCHIETTE
Small, ear-shaped pasta.
ORECCHIETTE MISTI
Small, ear-shaped pasta, a mix of green (spinach), red (chilli) and yellow (plain) pasta.
ORECCHIOTTE
Giant, ear-shaped pasta, suitable for stuffing and baking.

CONCHIGLIE RIGATE
Shell-shaped, hollow pasta.
CONCHIGLIONI RIGATI
Giant, shell-shaped, hollow pasta.

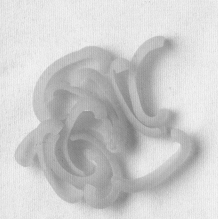

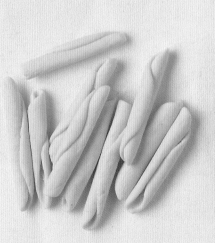

SPACCATELLA
Curved, hollow pasta, split open.

FRICELLI
Short lengths of hand-rolled pasta.

MILLERIGHE
Medium, finely
ridged, hollow pasta.

RISSONI
A rice-shaped pasta, similar to puntalette and orzo.

ACINI DI PEPE
Peppercorn-shaped pasta.

STELLINE
A star-shaped pasta. Also known as **stellette**.

ALFABETO
Tiny letters of the alphabet.

FILINI
Thin, short threads of pasta. Also known as **fedelini tagliati**.

PASTA MISTA
Mixed short pasta shapes.

DITALI
Short, hollow 'thimbles'. Also known as **tubetti**.

CONCHIGLIETTE PICCOLE
Tiny pasta shells.

CORALLINI
Tiny, bead-shaped, hollow pieces of pasta.

AGNOLOTTI

FAGOTTINI

TORTELLONI

MIXED TORTELLINI

RAVIOLI

FRESH PASTA AND GNOCCHI

Fresh egg pasta is made from white, unbleached flour or durum flour and fresh eggs, preferably free-range. Fresh pasta does not have the *al dente* quality of dried, but is meltingly tender. Use with sauces that are delicate in both flavour and texture. Unless you have easy access to a shop where the pasta is actually made and you can rely on the freshness, buying dried pasta is often a better option. Be wary of packages which claim to be 'fresh'.

Filled pasta is made of fresh pasta and comes in many shapes and sizes, and a huge variety of fillings. On offer could be anything from beef and black olives, Atlantic salmon and ginger, bacon and mushroom, to kangaroo and asparagus. Rightly or wrongly, **gnocchi** is included in the pasta world. It may be made of flour and water, potato and flour, spinach, ricotta and flour, or polenta. Gnocchi is mostly simmered in water and dressed with a sauce or placed in a *gratin* dish, topped with cheese or a sauce, and baked in the oven.

184

TRIANGOLI

PANZOTTI

GNOCCHI

SORRENTINO

185

DRIED SPINACH NOODLES
Spinach-flavoured wheat noodles.

DRIED WHEAT NOODLES (MIEN)
Light, quick-to-prepare noodles come packaged in tangled cakes.

BEAN THREAD NOODLES
Also known as **cellophane noodles** or **green bean vermicelli**. Bean thread noodles come in one-person servings, tied in small or large bundles. Good in stir-fries and salads.

CHINESE WHEAT NOODLES (HO FEN)
Flat sticks which take a sauce well.

WON TON WRAPPERS
These square, pastry-like wrappers range from small to large, and from thin to medium thickness. They can be filled and then fried, steamed or used in soups. Buy the thinnest ones available and keep frozen. They may be used instead of pasta dough in dishes, such as ravioli.

FRESH WHEAT NOODLES (YANG CHUE)　　　**FRESH YELLOW EGG NOODLES (HOKKIEN)**

THICK RICE STICK

**FRESH WHEATFLOUR
NOODLES**

RICE NOODLES
Made from rice flour and
water and available as rice
stick, threads or vermicelli.
Translucent appearance
remains when cooked.
Easily confused with
beancurd noodles, rice
noodles are good stir-fried,
and with rich, highly
flavoured sauces.

DRIED EGG NOODLES
Available in thin or medium thickness, these noodles are made from wheatflour,
egg and water. Popular and versatile, they are good for stir-frying, hold a
dressing well and are a good, starch side dish. Also good deep-fried.

THIN EGG NOODLES
A Chinese-style, dried noodle. Available by
themselves or as 2-minute noodles with
flavour sachets. Good in soups and casseroles.

RICE VERMICELLI

187

RAMEN
Made from wheatflour, egg and water, these fresh Japanese noodles are especially suitable for hot noodle soups. Boil for 2–3 minutes.

RICE PAPERS
Made from rice flour, water and salt, these paper-thin wafers are dried in the sun on mats, which gives them their checkered imprint. Available in dry form only, in round or triangular sheets, which are stiff and hard. Soften the papers for a few seconds, one by one, in warm water, before using to wrap spring rolls. When soaked in beer, the spring roll will become beautifully crisp and golden.

MEN KOBO ZARU SOBA

DRIED SOBA
Made with buckwheat and plain flour, these thin, but filling, Japanese noodles are either green or brown, which makes them an interesting addition to stir-fries and soups. Good eaten cold.

SHINSHU SOBA

HARADA CHA SOBA

FRESH SOBA
Highly nutritious Japanese
buckwheat and plain flour
noodles with a chewy quality.
Good in hot noodle soups or as
a cold dish.

SHOEI JEAU PASTRY
Used for making spring rolls.

MILK UDON
Made from wheatflour and water.

SOMEN
Very fine and
thin Japanese
wheatflour
noodles used
in stir-fries or
noodle soups.

**BOILED SOFT WHEATFLOUR
NOODLES (NAMA UDON)**

Fresh & preserved seafood

It is quite an adventure to go shopping for seafood, and on visiting the fish markets one could not be blamed for being overwhelmed by the glistening diversity on offer.

Fish is one of the healthiest foods in the modern diet. Packed with protein, low in fat, and containing essential vitamins, not surprisingly it has become a favourite choice for everyday eating as well as special occasions.

With the surge of interest in international cooking, dishes such as garlic prawns, Thai fish curry, bouillabaisse, and even simple country ideas such as moules marinière, are now as popular as fish and chips.

Good supermarkets and fishmongers stock a world-wide range of fresh fish and shellfish. Fresh fish should always be exactly that, and bought on the day it is intended to be eaten.

White fish fillets should have a pearly appearance and the flesh should be firm and moist. In whole fish, look for bright eyes, red gills and a glossy sheen to the skin. Shellfish such as mussels, clams and oysters must be tightly closed. Any that remains open after a sharp tap with the back of a knife should be discarded.

Crustacea ranges from crabs and lobsters to brown shrimps. Cooked lobsters and crabs should feel heavy in relation to size, with pert claws and feelers. All fish and shellfish must smell fresh, with an aroma of the sea.

Smoking is one of the best ways to preserve fish. There are two ways of doing this. Cold smoking simply flavours the fish over a heat not high enough to cook it. Hot smoking cooks the fish at the same time.

Canned fish is a great staple for the larder. Always keep a supply of canned tuna, sardines, salmon and anchovies for pastas, pizzas, sandwiches and snacks.

BRILL
Scophthalmus rhombus
Similar to the turbot, it is a disc-shaped, flat fish with delicate, firm flesh and a sweet flavour. It is used in classic fish dishes, often with a cream sauce. Available throughout the year and sold whole or in fillets.

DOVER SOLE
Solea solea
A much-sought-after, expensive, flat fish, native to the North Sea and so named because it used to be most easily sourced at the port of Dover. Renowned for its excellent flavour and meaty texture, it is the subject of many classic fish dishes. It should be skinned before cooking. The main bone is easy to remove once cooked. Available throughout the year, it is best grilled, fried or poached.

PLAICE
Pleuronectes platessa
An inexpensive flat fish with moist, white flesh and a mild flavour. Available throughout the year, either whole or in fillets, it is delicious crumbed, fried in batter or poached as fillets.

LEMON SOLE
Microstomus kitt
A flat fish with a plump body,
its flesh is firm and creamy with a
taste and texture similar to that of the
Dover sole, although it is not related.
Lemon sole is the less expensive of
the two, and is available throughout
the year, whole or in fillets. It is
best cooked simply.

*left
handed*

TURBOT
Scophthalmus maximus or
Psetta maxima
Known as the prince of flat fish
because of its firm, meaty, excellently
flavoured, moist flesh. Usually very
expensive, it is available all year
round as cutlets or whole. There is a
special pan called a *turbotière* for
cooking the whole fish.

193

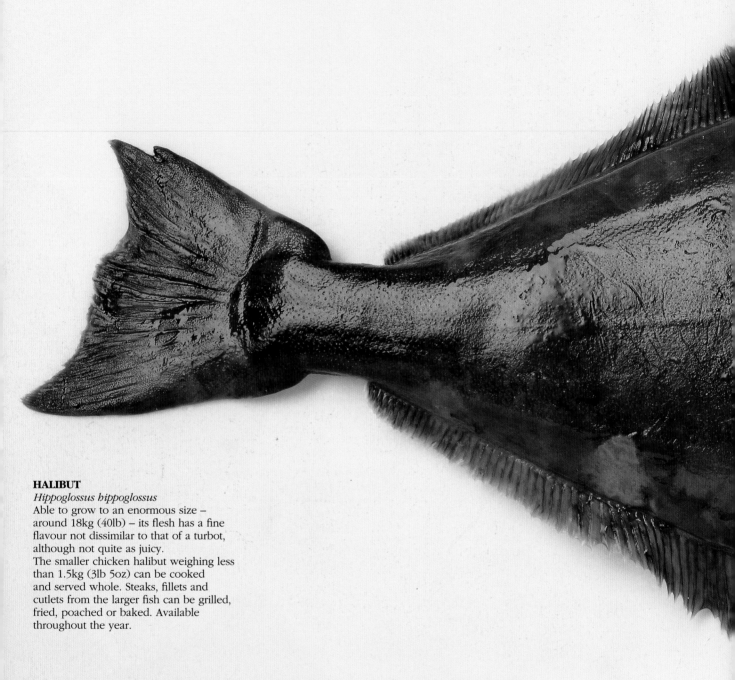

HALIBUT
Hippoglossus hippoglossus
Able to grow to an enormous size –
around 18kg (40lb) – its flesh has a fine
flavour not dissimilar to that of a turbot,
although not quite as juicy.
The smaller chicken halibut weighing less
than 1.5kg (3lb 5oz) can be cooked
and served whole. Steaks, fillets and
cutlets from the larger fish can be grilled,
fried, poached or baked. Available
throughout the year.

RED MULLET
Mullus barbatus
Pink/gold in colour, it is always
sold whole. The flesh is firm and full of
flavour. The liver is also a delicacy, but only
worth looking for in older fish. Excellent slashed
then grilled or barbecued; also a good ingredient
in fish soups – especially those with
Mediterranean flavourings. The bones are
sharp, but are thick and easy to remove.
Best fish available in summer.

SEA-BREAM
Pagellus centrodontus
Several varieties are available. From the home
waters, the most frequently seen is **black bream**
(*Spondyliosoma cantharus*), a round, white fish
with firm-textured flesh. Always sold whole, it is
good for grilling, barbecuing or steaming, and is
delicious with herbs and black pepper.

SNAPPER
Lutjanus campechanus
Found around the Gulf of Mexico, this flavoursome
fish has a delightful texture and is sold whole, or in steaks and
fillets. Available all year, it is best poached, grilled or baked whole.

GURNARD
Triglidea spp.
Also known as **gurnet** or **sea robin**. A plentiful, inexpensive fish with
a firm flesh and a sweet flavour. Usually sold whole,
it makes a good choice for fish stews and soups.
Sold all year, except July–September.

196

GREY MULLET
Mullus capito, Mugil cephalus, Crenimugil labrosus, Liza ramada
Many varieties are classed as grey mullet, although it is no relation to the red mullet. Its flesh is delicate and moist and resembles that of sea bass. Good grilled, or stuffed with lemon, garlic and breadcrumbs. Its salted roe is the correct one for making taramasalata, though smoked cod's roe is often used instead. Available throughout the year.

MACKEREL
Scomber scombrus
A beautiful, silver-blue, oily fish with moist, pinkish-brown flesh. It grills to perfection to give a crisp skin, and is delicious served simply with lemon. Usually sold whole, or as fillets with the skin on, it has large, easy-to-remove bones. Fresh mackerel are found in late spring and early summer. Smoked mackerel is also available.

HERRING
Clupea harengus
An inexpensive and underrated round, oily fish. Rich in vitamins, it has a soft, delicate flesh with a creamy texture. Usually sold whole, it is delicious grilled or fried. Cold, smoked herring is the kipper and pickled herring the rollmop. Available throughout the year, but best in summer.

GILTHEAD
Sparus aurata
Also called **daurade**, this is one of the best breams. Recognised by the gold band running between its eyes and on each cheek. With a delicious, moist flavour and texture, it is often used in Mediterranean dishes where it has an affinity with fennel. Available throughout the year.

197

COD
Gadus morhua
One of the Britain's most popular fish, it has firm, flaky,
white flesh and a good flavour. Since it grows to a large size, it
can be sold as fillets with the skin off, steaks and cutlets – or as a
small, whole fish with big, easy-to-spot bones. In Europe, it is
sometimes salted and dried to make **bacalao**, much loved by the
Spanish and Portuguese. The delicious roe is used for
taramasalata. Available throughout the year and can be used
in most methods of cooking.

HAKE
Merluccius vulgaris
A deep-water member of the cod family, which frequently features in Spanish and Portuguese recipes. The flesh is soft, pink and flaky with a creaminess of texture. It is excellent deep-fried, or pan-fried with garlic and tomatoes. It is sold whole or in fillets and steaks.

BASS
Labrax lupus
Usually from the warmer Mediterranean waters, the **silver sea bass** can be served whole in cutlets, or in fillets from a large fish. Often very expensive, it has delicate-flavoured, white flesh. Like most fish of excellence it is best cooked simply, and when served whole it has an easy-to-peel-out backbone and skeleton.

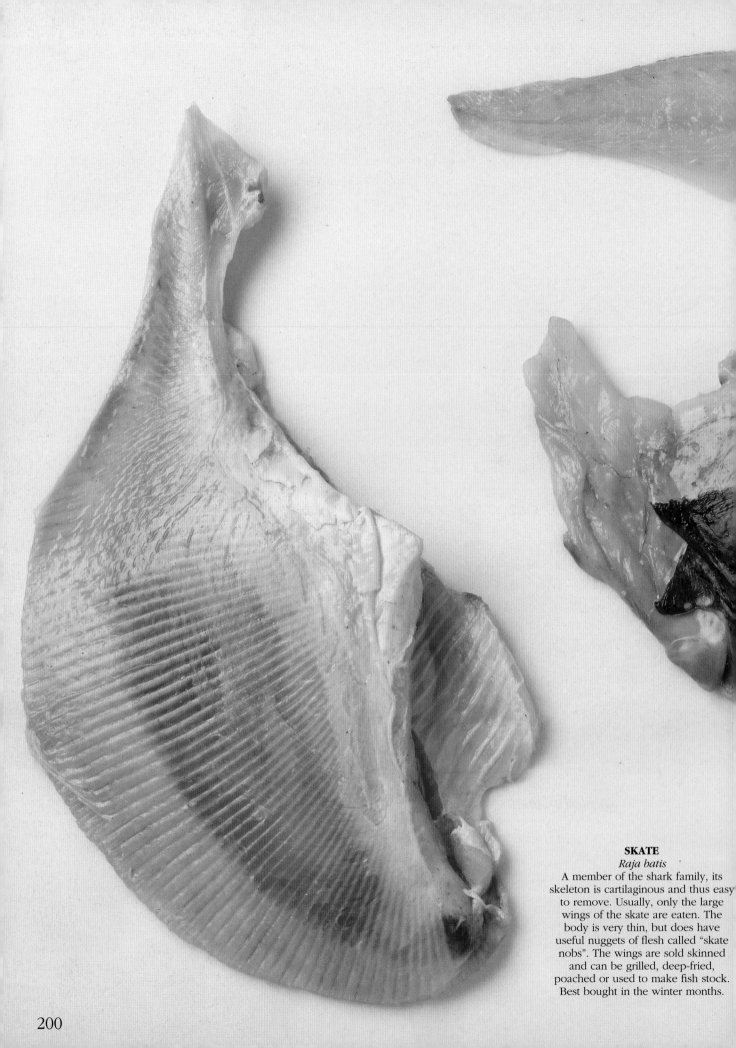

SKATE
Raja batis
A member of the shark family, its
skeleton is cartilaginous and thus easy
to remove. Usually, only the large
wings of the skate are eaten. The
body is very thin, but does have
useful nuggets of flesh called "skate
nobs". The wings are sold skinned
and can be grilled, deep-fried,
poached or used to make fish stock.
Best bought in the winter months.

200

HADDOCK
Melanogrammus aeglefinus
A similar fish to cod, haddock is popular
for its firm, light, flavoursome flesh.
Available in steaks or fillets, it is often
smoked. (See smoked haddock.)
Available throughout the year, it is
delicious deep-fried.

MONK FISH
Lophius piscatorius
Also known as **angler fish**, it is a
deep-sea fish with a huge, ugly head.
Because of its appearance, only the
slender meaty tail is usually sold. The
flesh is dense, succulent and juicy, and
has been likened to that of lobster. Poach,
grill or, when flesh is firm enough to stay
on a skewer, barbecue as kebabs. A
versatile fish that tastes good with many
flavours from curry spices to
Mediterranean tomatoes and peppers.
Available throughout the year.

201

SMOKED SPRAT
Small fish, often enjoyed in
Germany, eaten with rye
bread and butter.

**NATURAL SMOKED
HADDOCK**
Cold-smoked, prime
haddock fillet.

FINNAN HADDOCK
Also known as **finnan
haddie**. From the village of
Findon in Aberdeenshire,
Scotland. This is a cold-
smoked haddock which can
be poached or grilled. Serve
with a pat of butter as a
breakfast dish.

DYED SMOKED HADDOCK
Inexpensive smoked haddock
which is dyed to give it a
bright colour.

SMOKED HALIBUT
Usually sold in thin slices like smoked salmon. Serve with black pepper and lemon.

SMOKED TROUT FILLET
Moist and tender, hot-smoked fish fillets. Serve with horseradish sauce and bread and butter.

203

ZANDER
Stizostedion lucioperca
A round, perch-like, freshwater fish
which is sometimes available fresh or,
more likely, frozen. Delicious in fish
stews or baked, it can also be steamed,
poached or microwaved.

EEL
Anguillidae spp.
Young eels are known as
elver. Small and
transparent, they are best
soaked then fried. The
mature silver eel is rich
and meaty and is
delicious with mash. Best
bought live, eel is
available all year round.

205

PIKE
Esox lucius
A bony, freshwater fish with firm, white flesh. It can be baked or braised and, in France, it is used to make *quenelles* (light fish dumplings) served with white wine sauce.

WILD SALMON
A sought-after fish which is much more expensive and intensely flavoured than the farmed variety. It is firm textured because of its long journey from the sea back to the river to spawn.

SARDINES
Clupea pilchardus
From the herring family, these oily fish are excellent barbecued or grilled so that the skin becomes crisp and the flesh meltingly moist.

SMELT
Osemrus eparlanus
Small, semi-transparent member of the salmon family, it has an excellent flavour and is usually eaten whole and deep fried.

CAT FISH
Pimelodus catus
A freshwater fish usually sold in fillets. The flesh is white and sweet, and can be griddled, grilled or baked.

SEA TROUT
Salmo trutta
Also known as **salmon trout**. A large sea fish with pale, delicate flesh. Roast whole or poach and serve cold. Also available smoked.

207

HUSS
Scyliorhinus stellaris
From the shark family, also sometimes
known as **rock salmon** or **dog fish**. An
underrated fish which is brilliant fried in
batter or used in kebabs or curries,
because of its firm, tasty flesh.

WHITING
Merlangius merlangus
An inexpensive, round, white fish with sweet, flaky, delicate
flesh. Bake whole or fry in breadcrumbs.

TORBAY SOLE
Soleidae spp.
Sole which comes from
around the south-west
coast of England. Use
like Dover sole.

CONGER EEL
Conger conger
Growing up to 10ft (3m) long,
it has firm, well-flavoured
flesh. Cook as for cod.

DAB
Pleuronectes limanda
The smallest flat fish available. Usually sold
whole, it is inexpensive and underrated; the
flesh is sweet and tender. However, the
bones are small and difficult to remove.
Shallow fry or grill.

FLOUNDER
Platichthys flesus
An inexpensive, flat, marine fish
with moist, white flesh. Best fried.

208

POLLACK
Pollachius pollachius
An inexpensive, round, white fish from the cod family. Use for fish cakes and fish pies.

CARP
Cyprinus carpio
Native to Asia but available in fresh European waters. Usually farmed, it has bony but tasty flesh. Soak the cleaned, scaled fish in mildly salted water for 3 to 4 hours to ensure it doesn't have a muddy flavour. Oven bake whole.

GOLDEN TROUT
Salmo aguabonita
A farmed member of the trout family. Use like rainbow trout.

COLEY FILLET
Pollachius virens
Also known as **coalfish** and **saithe**, it is a round, white fish similar to cod but with darker flesh. Use for fish cakes and rissoles.

WHITEBAIT
From the herring family, these small fish are eaten whole, usually dipped in milk and flour, then deep fried.

209

BREAM
Acanthopagrus spp.
These fish have white, fine-textured, sweet flesh.
Available whole and in fillets. Smaller sizes may
be served whole for each person.
VARIETIES: black bream, pikey bream,
yellowfin bream and the freshwater species, bony
bream (*Nematalosa erebi*).

BREAM FILLET

BLUE-EYE COD
Hyperoglyphe antarctica
Available in fillets, steaks and cutlets, smaller cod are
sold whole. Scoring is essential for better heat
penetration of the thick, moist flesh.

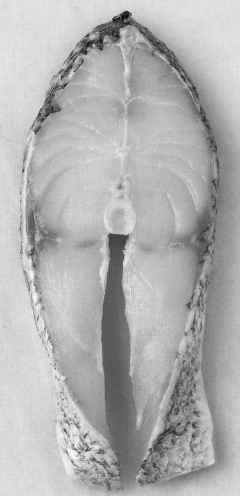

BLUE-EYE COD CUTLET

BLUE-EYE COD FILLET

TUNA
Thunnus spp.
With pink-red, coarse-grained flesh and rich flavour, this oily fish is found in warmer waters and is commonly sold as steaks; particularly suitable for sashimi.
VARIETIES: albacore, bigeye, longtail, mackerel, skipjack, southern bluefin, yellowfin.

TUNA STEAK

TUNA SASHIMI

SASHIMI
Sashimi is a Japanese dish which has become universally popular. It consists of a selection of thin slices of raw fish, arranged on a platter accompanied by a small bowl of soy sauce, mixed with wasabi. Tuna, salmon, Atlantic salmon and yellowtail kingfish are excellent served in this manner.

SALMON CUTLET

SALMON SASHIMI

SALMON
Salmo salar
Increasingly raised on fish farms, it has firm flesh with a rich flavour. Buy whole, in steaks, cutlets or fillets. Poaching is a classic treatment for the whole fish; pan-fry steak, cutlets, fillets.

TIGER FLATHEAD
Neoplatycephalus richardsoni
This is a member of the extended flathead family. Fine, white, firm flesh; a good fish to cook whole or filleted.
VARIETIES: bartail, bluespot, deepwater, dusky, northern sand, rock, sand and southern flathead.

FLATHEAD FILLET
The flesh of the flathead is very dry, so a moist cooking method, such as in a casserole or curry is suitable. When frying, coating the fillets keeps in the moisture. The best flesh of this fish is in the 'tail' part of the fillet.

REDFISH
Centroberyx affinis
Found in the Atlantic and Pacific oceans, these small fish are available whole, but are often sold as skinless fillets. Because of their tight-knit scales, cooking the whole fish is not recommended. Redfish fillets are suitable for pan-frying or deep-frying. The pale pink flesh has a delicate flavour and texture, so it is best to use a protective coating, such as a batter, breadcrumbs or flour before cooking.

REDFISH FILLET

WHITING, Pacific
Sillago spp.
This is a delicious fish — sweet flavour, tender, fine, white flesh with a fine bone structure. The whole fish may be grilled or fried as the skin keeps in the moisture. Poaching is a suitable method. Fillets need a protective coating with batter, crumbs or flour to retain moisture. Poaching fillets is also recommended.

SAND WHITING FILLET

GARFISH

There are many varieties of this slender, silvery fish. They are similar but can be distinguished by the length of their 'beaks' and their colour. They have a fine, sweet, delicately flavoured flesh. Usually sold whole; fillets are sometimes available. Pan-fry, deep-fry, bake, grill or poach.

GARFISH FILLET

RIVER GARFISH

NORTHERN GARFISH

GEMFISH FILLET

SILVER WAREHOU
Serioletta punctata
This warm-water fish has firm, creamy-pink, mild-flavoured flesh with a large flake. Usually available as fillets. The skin should be removed before cooking. Pan-fry, casserole, bake, poach or grill.

GEMFISH
Rexea solandri
This large, warm-water fish is rarely seen whole. Score thick fillets to allow even heat penetration. Poach, pan-fry, grill, bake or barbecue. Generally too thick for deep-frying.

SILVER WAREHOU FILLET

215

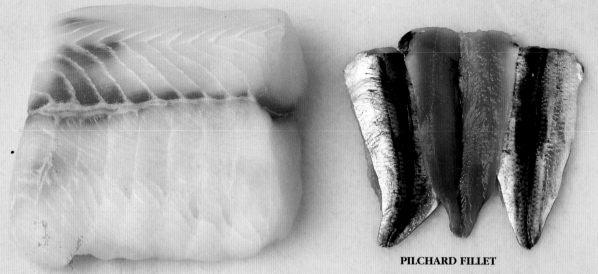

PILCHARD
Sardinops neopilchardus
A fast-moving, silvery fish, low in fat in winter, but very fatty in summer. Butterfly, after removing head and cleaning out stomach cavity. Deep- or pan-fry, barbecue.

PILCHARD FILLET

SHARK
Species var.
There are many varieties of shark, but universally flesh is firm and boneless, making it especially suitable for children. Usually sold in fillets, it is ideal for frying, grilling or barbecuing.

SNAPPER
Pagrus auratus
This warm-water fish develops a bump on the head when older. With firm, white flesh and a mild flavour, this is one of Australia's more popular fish. Bake, barbecue or poach. Fillets and cutlets are also available. Score thick fillets for even heat penetration. Pan-fry or bake.

SNAPPER FILLET

JOHN DORY
Zeus faber
Sometimes known as
St Peter's fish, it is one of the
best table fish, with fine, white,
sweet flesh, which is moist and
tender. The skin has no scales and
the fillets contain no bones.

JOHN DORY FILLET

SILVER DORY FILLET
Cyttus australia
Native to Australian waters, this fish has fine scales and
pink fins. The flesh is white with a fine-to-medium
texture. Poach or fry gently or apply a protective coating
before baking.

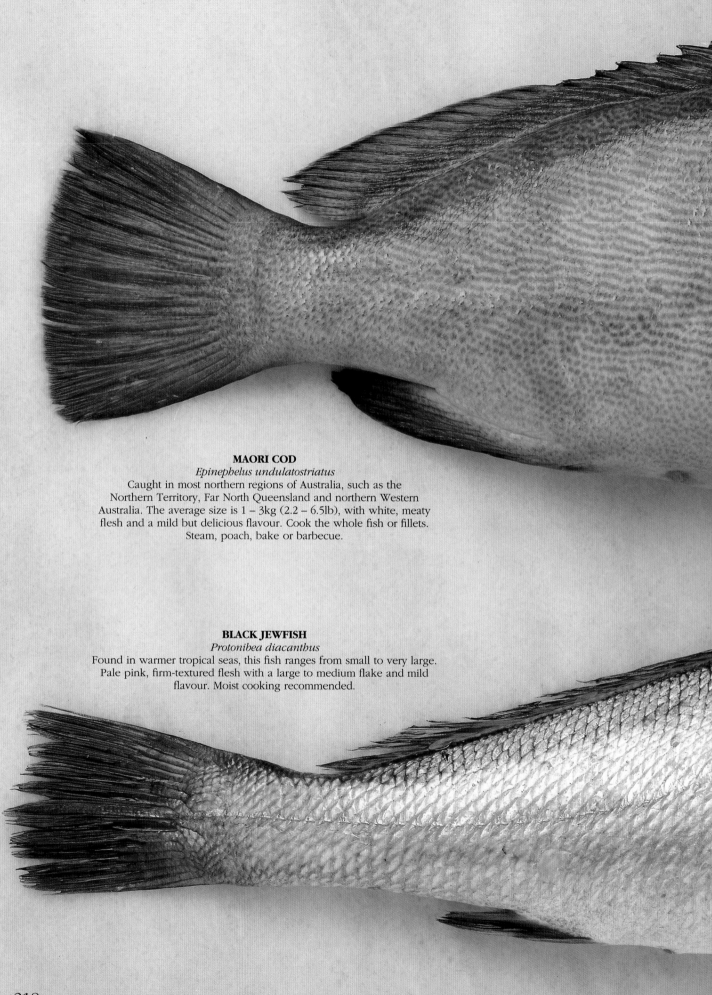

MAORI COD
Epinephelus undulatostriatus
Caught in most northern regions of Australia, such as the
Northern Territory, Far North Queensland and northern Western
Australia. The average size is 1 – 3kg (2.2 – 6.5lb), with white, meaty
flesh and a mild but delicious flavour. Cook the whole fish or fillets.
Steam, poach, bake or barbecue.

BLACK JEWFISH
Protonibea diacanthus
Found in warmer tropical seas, this fish ranges from small to very large.
Pale pink, firm-textured flesh with a large to medium flake and mild
flavour. Moist cooking recommended.

BARRAMUNDI
Lates calcarifer
This mildly flavoured fish is tender and firm
with a large flake. Found in northern
Australia, it grows to a huge size. Available
whole, in fillets and cutlets. Poach, bake,
barbecue, grill or pan-fry.

BABY BARRAMUNDI

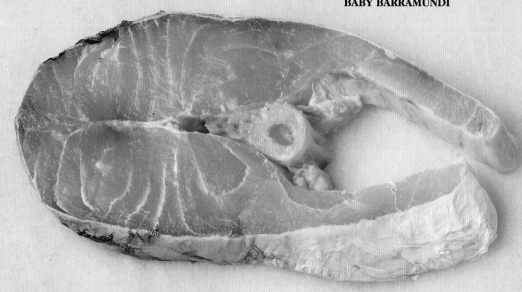

BARRAMUNDI CUTLET

RAINBOW TROUT
Salmo gairdnerll
This freshwater fish makes excellent eating. It has soft, moist,
white to pink flesh and can be identified by its dark spots and
a red stripe running lengthways along the sides of the male.
Poach, pan-fry, grill, barbecue or bake. Also available smoked.

OCEAN PERCH
Helicolenus spp.
Found in the Atlantic and Pacific
oceans, it is available whole and as steaks
and fillets. It has white, firm, moist
flesh with a mild flavour. Pan-fry, bake,
poach, steam, grill or barbecue.

SWORDFISH
Xiphias gladius
One of the best fish to eat, with flesh similar to tuna
and marlin, but more moist. This warm-water fish is
available in steaks. Barbecue, grill, poach, pan-fry.

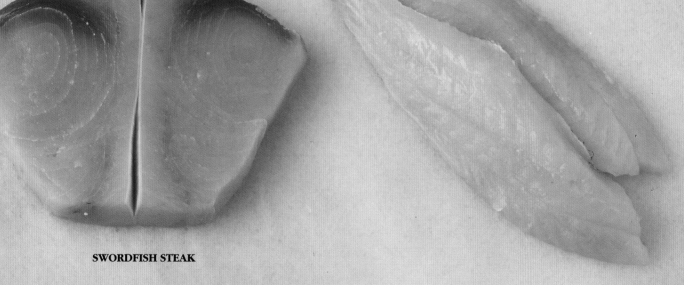

SWORDFISH STEAK

OCEAN PERCH FILLET

MULLET, Pacific
Mugilidae spp.
Available whole or as fillets.
Moist, oily, dark pink flesh
with a distinctive taste. Bake,
barbecue, pan-fry or grill.
Good smoked.

221

BROOK TROUT
Oncorhynchus mykiss
This small- to medium-sized, freshwater fish has soft, white to pink flesh with a moist texture and a mild flavour. Colour varies according to its species. Available whole. Bake, pan-fry, poach, grill, barbecue.

222

CORAL TROUT
Plectropomus maculatus
Found in warmer waters, these
fish live around coral reefs. White,
firm-textured, sweet flesh; sold
whole or as fillets. Score whole
fish and thick fillets before
cooking. Bake, pan-fry, poach,
grill or barbecue.

SEA TROUT
Salmo trutta
Also known as **salmon trout**, this is
the **rainbow trout** which has moved
downstream and out to sea, becoming a
saltwater fish. It has grown much larger,
and the most suitable cooking method
is poaching, but it may also be baked.
Available as fillets and cutlets.

223

VELVET LEATHERJACKET
Parika scaber
Found in tropical waters, this fish has white, soft flesh and a mild flavour. The skin is tough, hence the name. Bake, pan-fry, poach, grill or barbecue.

RAY
Rajidae spp.
A flat relative of the shark, also sold as **skate**. The flesh is soft, sweet and delicious. The tough skin should be removed before cooking; plunge into boiling water and peel off. The 'flaps' of large skates are available. Pan-fry.

BLUE MACKEREL
Scomber australasicus
Found in warmer waters, this fish has white, soft, dry flesh, with a mild flavour. Also available as fillets. Bake, pan-fry, grill or barbecue.

LUDERICK
Girella tricuspidata
An estuarine and rock fish from Australia. These fish are good for eating if they are bled as soon as they are caught. White, moist, soft flesh with a distinctive flavour. Also available as fillets. Bake, pan-fry, grill or barbecue.

PEARL PERCH
Glaucosoma spp.
A marine fish found in tropical trawling grounds near reefs, it has white, soft flesh, with a delicate, sweet flavour. Bake, pan-fry, poach, grill or barbecue.

GOLDEN PERCH
Macquaria ambigua
This freshwater fish is also available in fillets. Dry, white, firm flesh with a mild but distinctive flavour. Bake, pan-fry, poach, grill or barbecue.

GREAT TREVALLY
Caranx sexfasciatus
With firm, white flesh, this fish is very good to
eat when small, but becomes a little
flavourless when older. Bake, pan-fry, poach,
grill or barbecue.

PARROT FISH
Scaridae spp.
This brightly coloured reef fish has
white, moist, soft flesh with a delicate
flavour, which makes it excellent to
eat. Bake, pan-fry, poach,
grill or barbecue.

RED ROCK COD
Scorpaena cardinalis
Popular in southern Europe for making
bouillabaisse, it has firm, white flesh which makes
good eating. The Chinese also like its slightly fatty
flavour. An ideal fish for steaming.

GREENBACK FLOUNDER
Rhombosolea tapirina
This flat fish has a fine bone structure, white, soft, succulent flesh
with fine flake and a very sweet taste. It is one of the most
delicious fish. Coat the soft skin with flour before pan-frying. Also
available as fillets. Bake, pan-fry, poach, grill or barbecue.

BARBOUNIA
Mullidae spp.
These small fish, members of the mullet family, are good to eat, with a
rich, oily flavour. Barbecue, bake, pan-fry or grill.

RED EMPEROR
Lutjanus sebae
A reef fish from tropical waters, with a
salmon pink body and red fins. With firm,
white flesh, a sweet flavour and large
flake, this is a delectable fish. Also
available as fillets. Bake, pan-fry, poach,
grill or barbecue.

EMPEROR
Lethrinus spp.
A reef fish from warmer waters, it has firm, white
flesh, a sweet flavour and large flake, making it one
of the most delicious fish. Also available as fillets.
Bake, pan-fry, poach, grill or barbecue.

BLUE WAREHOU
Seriolella brama
Found in Australian waters, it has firm-textured and mild-flavoured flesh with a large flake and very few bones. Good for soups, casseroles and salads.

LING FILLET
Genypterus spp.
Ling is a member of the cod family and is mostly sold as fillets. Buy skinless fillets and score to ensure even cooking. Grill, poach, pan-fry, bake, steam or barbecue. Can also be salted, smoked or dried.

GOLDBAND SNAPPER
Pristipomoides spp.
This warm-water snapper has moist flesh with a mild flavour. May be cooked whole or cut into cutlets. Bake, grill, steam, pan-fry or barbecue.

RED SNAPPER
Centroberyx spp.
Usually sold as skinless fillets. Has
pale pink flesh with fine-to-medium
flake and delicate flavour. Pan-fry or
deep-fry in batter. Cooking this fish
whole is not recommended.

BONITO
Sarda spp.
Also known as **Pacific bonito**, this fish is not
good to eat when fresh, but is excellent when
dried. Adds a 'fishy' flavour to otherwise
bland dishes.

ALBACORE
Thunnus alalunga
A member of the tuna family, this fish grows to
about 1.5m (5ft). The flesh is pink-red in colour. Buy
in cutlets or cut off the bone. Cook lightly. Pan-fry,
grill, barbecue or casserole. Large pieces may be
wrapped in foil and baked.

ABALONE
Haliotis spp.
A gastropod mollusc (single shell and single muscle), the edible part is the muscle by which it clings to rocks. Slice thinly and tenderize before cooking. Cook very quickly or simmer for a long time; anything in between will result in tough flesh.

CONCH
Melo amphora
This gastropod mollusc (single shell and single muscle) is caught in southern waters. The orange, brittle shell is broken to remove the meat, which is then cleaned. Sought-after for Asian and Caribbean dishes.

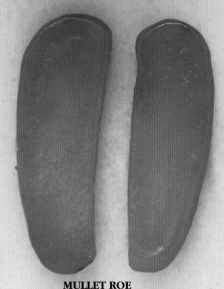

MULLET ROE
Mugil cephalus
This is the salted, dried roe of the grey mullet, and always comes in pairs. Has a not-too-salty, mildly fishy flavour and grainy texture. Remove skin before slicing thinly. Serve on bread or crackers or use to make *taramasalata,* the Greek *hors d'oeuvre.*

SEA URCHIN ROE
Heliocidaris spp.
Sea urchin is sometimes available in the shell, but the roe is more commonly sold in boxes. May be briefly cooked or served raw, sprinkled with a little lemon juice on bread or crackers.

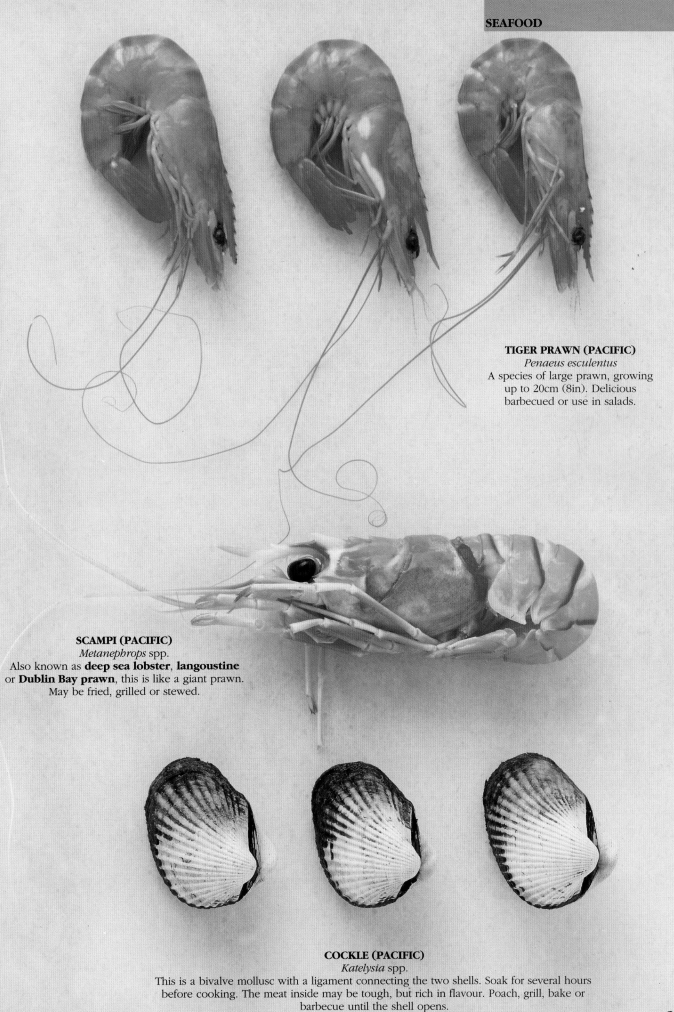

TIGER PRAWN (PACIFIC)
Penaeus esculentus
A species of large prawn, growing
up to 20cm (8in). Delicious
barbecued or use in salads.

SCAMPI (PACIFIC)
Metanephrops spp.
Also known as **deep sea lobster**, **langoustine**
or **Dublin Bay prawn**, this is like a giant prawn.
May be fried, grilled or stewed.

COCKLE (PACIFIC)
Katelysia spp.
This is a bivalve mollusc with a ligament connecting the two shells. Soak for several hours
before cooking. The meat inside may be tough, but rich in flavour. Poach, grill, bake or
barbecue until the shell opens.

233

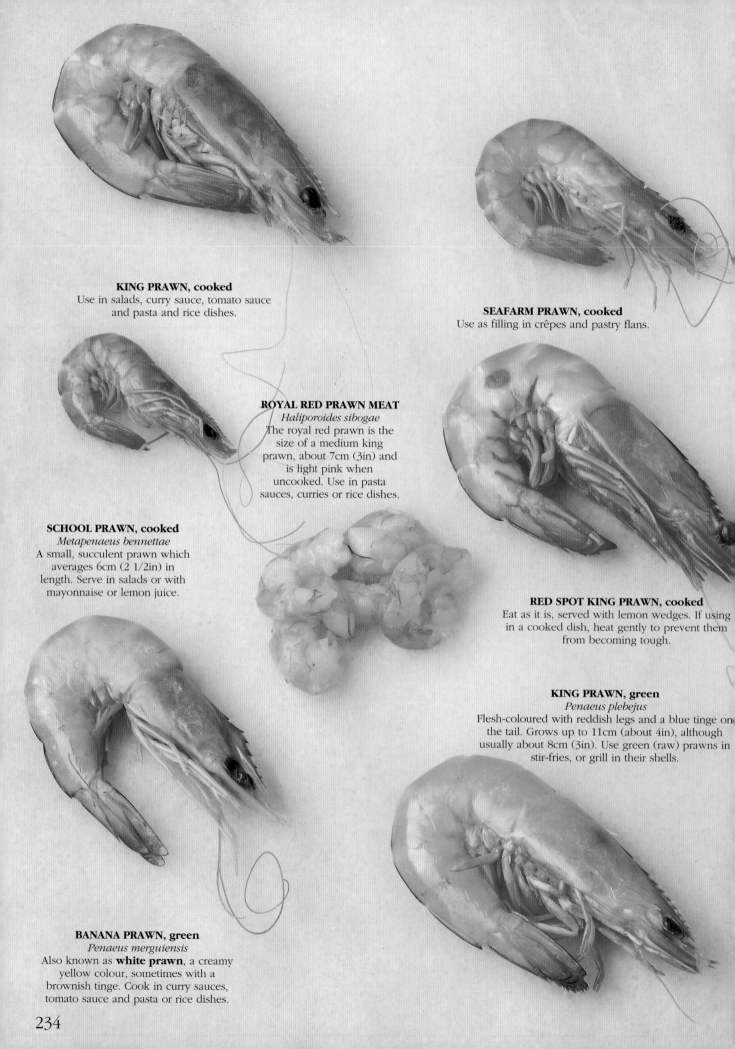

KING PRAWN, cooked
Use in salads, curry sauce, tomato sauce
and pasta and rice dishes.

SEAFARM PRAWN, cooked
Use as filling in crêpes and pastry flans.

ROYAL RED PRAWN MEAT
Haliporoides sibogae
The royal red prawn is the
size of a medium king
prawn, about 7cm (3in) and
is light pink when
uncooked. Use in pasta
sauces, curries or rice dishes.

SCHOOL PRAWN, cooked
Metapenaeus bennettae
A small, succulent prawn which
averages 6cm (2 1/2in) in
length. Serve in salads or with
mayonnaise or lemon juice.

RED SPOT KING PRAWN, cooked
Eat as it is, served with lemon wedges. If using
in a cooked dish, heat gently to prevent them
from becoming tough.

KING PRAWN, green
Penaeus plebejus
Flesh-coloured with reddish legs and a blue tinge on
the tail. Grows up to 11cm (about 4in), although
usually about 8cm (3in). Use green (raw) prawns in
stir-fries, or grill in their shells.

BANANA PRAWN, green
Penaeus merguiensis
Also known as **white prawn**, a creamy
yellow colour, sometimes with a
brownish tinge. Cook in curry sauces,
tomato sauce and pasta or rice dishes.

PERIWINKLE (PACIFIC)
Littorinia unifasciata
A variety of the small snail found on the coast, clinging to rocks between high and low tides. Usually boiled for 10 minutes, picked from the shell with a pin, and fried or used in omelettes, pasta sauces or in dips.

TASMANIAN SCALLOP
Pecten fumatus
The white meat is surrounded by the coral (roe). Usually available with or without the coral. Cook in pasta sauces, pan-fry or grill.

BABY CLAM (PACIFIC)
Meretrix spp.
Also known as **vongola**, this small, hard-shell, bivalve mollusc has delectable meat, although it is frequently very gritty. Available in the shell, clams should be cooked until they open. Use in pasta sauces or chowders.

BLUE MUSSEL
Mytilus edulis
Also known as **Tasmanian mussel**. Delectable in flavour and texture, this mussel may be cooked by itself or in a sauce. Always buy mussels that are closed, or will close when tapped. Discard any which stay closed after cooking.

PIPI (PACIFIC)
Plebidonax deltoides
Sold in the shell, but avoid those which have opened. Cook only until the shell opens. Use with rice and in pasta sauces.

GREEN-LIP MUSSEL
Perna canaliculus
Imported from New Zealand, this large mussel is not as tender as the Tasmanian mussel. When cooked in dishes or sauces, it may have to be cut up to be more manageable.

235

LOBSTER
Homarus vulgaris
Largest of the crustaceans, the prime examples come from the cold waters around Scotland, Ireland, Brittany and Maine. Best bought when they're alive and blue in colour. Bright red, cooked lobsters are also available. Serve simply with a sauce or butter, or in a salad.

CREVETTE GRIS
Crangon crangon
Tiny brown shrimps. Only available cooked, these make delicious appetisers or can be used to make potted shrimp, peeled and mixed with spicy cayenne butter.

NATIVE OYSTER
Ostrea edulis
These are wild oysters which thrive in cold waters. Recognised by their roundish, slightly rough shells and creamy meat, they are best served *au naturel*, straight from the shell or with a squeeze of lemon or a dash of Tabasco sauce.

CLAM
Various, including
Mya arenaria, Venus mercenaria, Pinna dolobiatia
A delicious bivalve mollusc. There are dozens of edible varieties found around the world. American "clam bake" favourite *Mya arenaria*, has now colonised British waters.

WHELK
Buccinum undatum
Sold cooked and ready to eat, usually with vinegar and brown bread and butter, they are similar to winkles but larger and less difficult to uncoil from the shells. They can also be used in seafood soups and stews.

LANGOUSTINE
Nephrops norvegicus
Also known as **Norwegian lobster**, because they were plentiful around the coast of Norway, and **Dublin Bay Prawns**, since this is where the trawlers unloaded the catch. They are available live, cooked, fresh or frozen, and their delicate flavour is not unlike lobster. Excellent barbecued, grilled, or lightly boiled and used in salads.

236

COCKLE
Cerastoderma edulis
A tiny bivalve with a grooved shell, it can be eaten raw or cooked and brined. Best in summer for use in shellfish salads.

WINKLE
Littorina spp.
Usually sold cooked, and in the UK they are often served with a cork with pins stuck into it. The pins are used to uncoil the little fellows out of their shells before eating only the first part of the body. Fresh winkles should be boiled in their shells in salted water for 10 minutes.

MUSSEL
Mytilus edulis
Can be purchased live, cooked or frozen. Fresh mussels should be thoroughly cleaned, and the beards removed. Always buy mussels that are closed, and discard any with damaged shells, and those that stay closed after cooking.

COMMON EUROPEAN CRAB
Cancer pagurus
These delicious crustaceans are at their best during summer. Sold cooked, or live, the hen crab (*below*) usually has smaller front claws than the cock crab (*above*) and a broader tail flapped against its underside. The hen carries a delicious roe and more abundant meat in the tail than the male. The male crab, however, is often more expensive due to its front claws which are full of white meat. Body meat of both hen and cock crabs is creamy, and delicious eaten cold with mayonnaise.

237

YABBY
Cherax destructor
Also known as **freshwater crayfish**, found in creeks, dams, rivers and lakes. Usually brown. Eat the fresh-tasting, moist meat in the tail and claws.

BALMAIN BUG
Ibacus peronii
Also known as the **shovelnose lobster**, **flying saucer** or **southern bay lobster**, this is a species of sand lobster, similar to a Moreton Bay bug. White flesh with good, briny flavour, makes excellent eating.

PACIFIC OYSTER
Crassotrea gigas
Also known as the **Coffin Bay oyster** or **Japanese oyster**, much larger than the Sydney rock oyster. Greyish-white in colour, briny flavour.

SOUTHERN ROCK LOBSTER
Jasus edwardsii
This is a crayfish. Also known as the **cray**, **spiny lobster** or **rock lobster**, this is smaller than the Eastern rock lobster. The colour may range from creamy yellow and orange to purple. Excellent eating.

SYDNEY ROCK OYSTER
Saccostrea commercialis
The most commonly farmed oyster in Australia. Creamy flesh with full-bodied flavour.

EASTERN ROCK LOBSTER
Jasus verreauxii
This is a crayfish. Also known as **rock lobster**, this species is primarily found along the New South Wales coast. Uncooked, the lobster is green, turning to bright orange when cooked. Excellent eating with good meat in the legs.

NAMBUCCA ROCK OYSTER
Saccostrea commercialis
A variety of the Sydney rock oyster.

WALLIS LAKE OYSTER
Saccostrea commercialis
A variety of the Sydney rock oyster.

TASMANIAN PACIFIC OYSTER
Crassotrea gigas
A variety of the Pacific oyster.

239

BLUE CRAB
Portunus pelagicus
Found on the east coast of America, Australia and the eastern Mediterranean, this crab turns orange-red when cooked. Excellent, fine-textured, sweet meat is present in the legs and claws.

QUEENSLAND SAND CRAB (COOKED)
Portunus pelagicus
When alive, the skin is mottled with blue. With good meat in the body, the best is in the legs and claws.

SPANNER CRAB (COOKED)
Ranina ranina
Also known as **frog crab**,
it is found along Australia's north-eastern
coast. It can grow to more than 20cm
(8in) in length. Fine, sweet, white meat,
sometimes a bit 'shelly'.

MUD CRAB (GREEN)
Scylla serrata
Also known as a **black**, **brown** or
green crab, this crab lives in
mangroves and muddy waters and
grows up to 2kg (4.5lb) in weight.
Usually sold uncooked or alive, it
turns a bright orange when cooked.
The best flesh is in the claws, with
the body meat a little coarser.

241

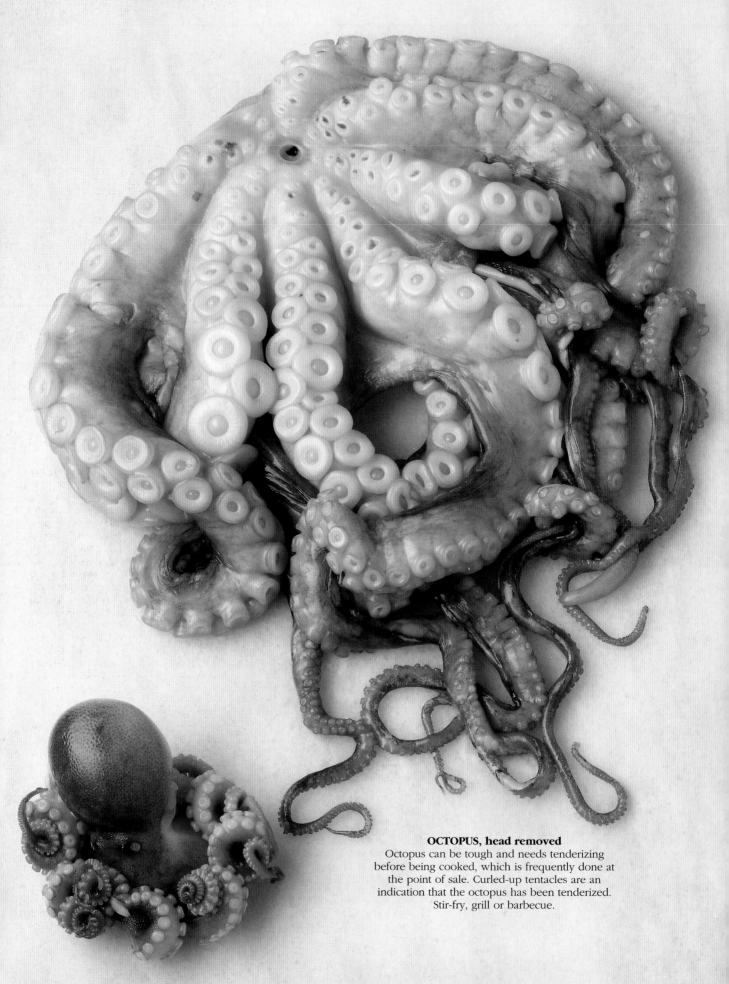

OCTOPUS, head removed
Octopus can be tough and needs tenderizing before being cooked, which is frequently done at the point of sale. Curled-up tentacles are an indication that the octopus has been tenderized. Stir-fry, grill or barbecue.

BABY OCTOPUS

SQUID TUBE
The body or mantle of the squid, skin removed.
Frequently stuffed and baked or casseroled, or
cut into rings.

BOTTLE SQUID
Loligo etheridgi
This small squid is found in estuarine and inshore
waters. Very tender to eat, but also used as bait. Best
when cooked quickly or it can be tough.

**SOUTHERN
SQUID**
*Sepioteuthis
australis*
Found in
temperate waters,
and also known as
calamari, it has a
cylindrical body,
or mantle, with
fins towards the
tail, a head with
eyes and 10
tentacles encircling
a beak. Inside,
there is a delicate
backbone or 'quill'.
All of the body,
except for the
head, may be
eaten. Best very
quickly cooked,
1–2 minutes only.

SQUID RINGS
The skin is removed from the body, or mantle, of
the squid, which is then cut into rings. Pan-fry or
deep-fry. It is frequently crumbed or battered.

CUTTLEFISH
Sepia spp.
Found in temperate waters, it is generally smaller
than squid, with a thicker body and a hard bone
(cuttlebone) inside. Two of its 10 tentacles are
significantly longer than the others. The body,
tentacles and ink sac may be used in cooking. Best
cooked very quickly (2–3 minutes) or
the meat will be tough.

243

GRAVAD LAX, GRAVLAX, GRAVALAX
Scandinavian pickled salmon. The fillets are sprinkled with salt, sugar and chopped fresh dill, pressed flesh sides together, wrapped in foil, refrigerated, and turned over every day. Serve, in thin slices cut obliquely towards the skin, with mustard sauce. Also available pre-packed from delicatessens.

SALT COD
Also known as **bacalao**, this is cod which has been salted and sometimes dried. It makes up many classic dishes from Spain, Portugal and Provence. However, the cod usually comes from Norway, and is bought in chunks, the thickest being the best. It will keep in the fridge for up to 2 months but, before use, needs to be soaked for at least a day in several changes of water.

BISMARK HERRING
Baltic herring, filleted and soaked in white wine vinegar. The white flesh is delicious served with onion rings, sour cream or new potatoes.

SWEET CURED ORKNEY HERRING
Filleted herrings which have been brined and then marinated in a secret sweet cure. Use as *hors d'œuvres*, or in main dishes with boiled potatoes.

FILLET OF SMOKED HERRING
A smoked herring or kipper, which has been filleted and, usually, bottled or canned in oil with seasoning.

ARBROATH SMOKIES
Small haddocks which are beheaded and gutted, then tied together in pairs and hot smoked. They are usually eaten warm, after being brushed with butter and placed in the oven. NB: Hot smoking means the fish can be eaten as it comes. Cold smoking is carried out at a lower temperature, so the fish is not actually cooked, just flavoured, and needs further cooking before being eaten – with the exception of salmon, which is cold smoked and eaten raw.

245

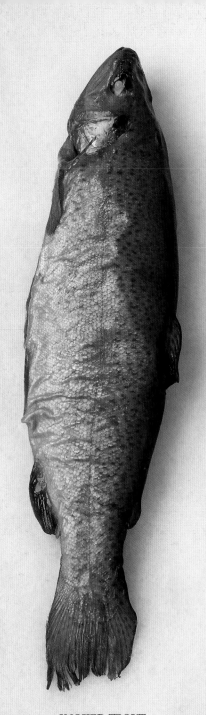

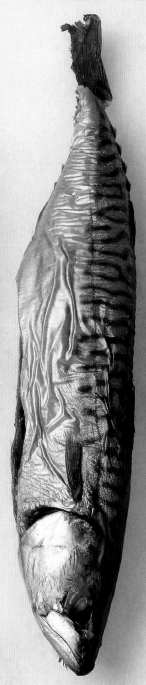

SMOKED MACKEREL
Oily flesh has a smoky, strong, salty flavour. The skin is easily removed. Store in the fridge for up to one week. Serve as *hors d'œuvre* on buttered toast or in salads. Lemon juice is a good addition.

SMOKED TROUT
A smoky, yet delicate flavour. The skin comes easily off the pink flesh. Store in the fridge for up to one week. Serve as *hors d'œuvre* on buttered toast or in salads.

SMOKED SALMON
Mildly smoky, delicate flavour, soft flesh and slightly moist surface. Available sliced. Store in the fridge for up to one week. Serve as *hors d'œuvre* on buttered toast or in salads. Lemon juice is a good addition.

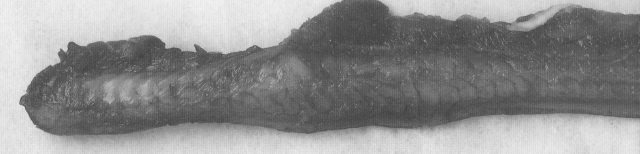

SMOKED HADDOCK
The skin, which can range from orange to yellow, hides white flesh with a mildly smoky flavour. Store in the fridge for up to one week. Fry, bake, barbecue, steam or poach gently.

**SMOKED NEW ZEALAND
BLUE COD**
A cold-smoked fish with a high salt
content. Use for fish pies and
kedgeree, the classic English breakfast
dish of fish and rice.

KIPPER
Herring, which is split and cured
by salting, drying and cold-smoking.
Popular English breakfast fare when
grilled. Refrigerate for up to
one week.

SMOKED EEL
Very fatty, salty flavour; it has many
dedicated followers. Remove the skin and
serve as *hors d'œuvre* with horseradish.
Refrigerate for up to one week.

SMOKED OYSTER
Also available unsmoked and in a variety
of sauces, these salty molluscs may be
stored for up to 12 months, but refrigerate
and eat within 24 hours once opened.
Serve on crackers.

SMOKED MUSSEL
Also available unsmoked and in a variety of sauces.
Refrigerate and eat within 24 hours once can is opened.
Serve as *hors d'œuvre* on crackers.

247

KIPPER FILLET
This is herring, which is split and cured. Refrigerate for up to one week.

CANNED CRAB
Flaky, salty, sweet meat with white to pink tones. Store for up to 12 months, but refrigerate and consume within 24 hours once opened. Serve as *hors d'œuvre*, in salads, pasta sauces or dips.

CANNED RED SALMON
Pink salmon is also available. The soft, salt flesh contains edible bones. May be stored f longer than 12 months, but refrigerate and consume within 24 hours once opened. Serv as *hors d'œuvre*, in salads, sauces or dips.

SMOKED TUNA SLICES
Smoky flavoured, these canned tuna slices are perfect for sandwiches and salads. Store for up to 12 months, but refrigerate and consume within 24 hours once opened.

CANNED TUNA
Available in different varieties: salt-free, packed in oil or brine. Has a full-bodied fish flavour. May be stored for up to 12 months, but refrigerate and consume within 24 hours once opened. Use in sandwiches, sauces, *gratins*, *hors d'œuvre* or salads.

ANCHOVY FILLET
Available rolled or 'flat'. Strongly flavoured; use in salads, meat, fish and vegetable dishes, pasta and on pizza.

CANNED SARDINES
Canned in oil or tomato sauce, sardines may be eaten, whole or mashed, on toast, in sandwiches or as *hors d'œuvre*. Lemon juice is a good addition.

CANNED MACKEREL
With a strong, salty flavour, these are canned in oil or various sauces. May be stored for up to 12 months, but refrigerate and eat within 24 hours once opened. Use for *hors d'œuvre* or in salads.

KAMABOKO
A Japanese speciality, these are processed fish cakes with a delicate flavour and fairly rubbery texture. Slice thinly and add to a dish at the end of cooking. Store in the fridge.

CANNED SAITHE
Saithe is the Scottish name for 'coalfish', a close relative of cod. Perfect for sandwiches and salads. Store for up to 12 months, but refrigerate and consume within 24 hours once opened.

ROLLMOP
Made from unskinned, boned fillets of herring. Usually wrapped around gherkins, fastened with toothpicks and pickled in spiced vinegar. Keep refrigerated once opened.

CONPOY
Dried Chinese sea scallops cut into discs, with a full-bodied briny flavour. Reconstitute by lengthy soaking, then use to enhance flavours of steamed or stewed dishes. Store indefinitely in an airtight jar in a cool, dark place.

RED LUMPFISH ROE
The dyed eggs of the lumpfish, not deserving of the name 'caviar'. Fishy, salty flavour, sometimes used when the 'real thing' is too expensive. Refrigerate once opened, and consume within eight weeks. Use as *hors d'œuvre*.

BLACK LUMPFISH ROE
The dyed eggs of the lumpfish, not deserving of the name 'caviar'. Fishy, salty flavour, sometimes used when the 'real thing' is too expensive. Store in the fridge once opened, and consume within eight weeks. Use as *hors d'œuvre*, in salads and with other fish.

SALTED SALMON ROE
The eggs are considerably larger than those of the lumpfish and are bright orange with a fresh, briny flavour. Store in fridge once opened and consume within two weeks. Use as *hors d'oeuvre*, with sour cream, or in pasta sauces.

CHINESE FISH BALLS
With a chewy texture and well seasoned, these cooked balls are a version of fish cakes; usually sliced and added to a dish at the last moment. Store in the fridge and eat within one week of opening.

CANNED SHRIMP
Small prawns, peeled and canned whole in brine. Store indefinitely, but consume within 24 hours once opened. Use in pasta sauces, mornay, shrimp cocktail or as *hors d'œuvre*.

CANNED CLAM
Salty, usually canned in oil. Store in a cool place for up to 12 months, but refrigerate and consume within 24 hours once can is open. Use as *hors d'œuvre* or in pasta sauce.

DRIED CUTTLEFISH
With a strong flavour and aroma, these flattened, sun-dried molluscs are a popular ingredient in most South-East Asian countries. May be used in cooking or eaten as a snack. Store in a cool, dark, dry place.

DRIED SQUID
These flattened, sun-dried molluscs are used to give full-bodied flavour to soups, stews and braised dishes. To reconstitute, soak in warm water for several hours, then simmer in clean water. Store in a cool, dark, dry place.

BOMBAY DUCK
A small, dried, strongly flavoured variety of fish, caught off the west coast of India. Usually sold in strips. Cut into pieces and serve deep-fried with rice and curry. Store in an airtight container in a cool, dark place.

DRIED SARDINE
With an intense, fishy flavour and crisp texture, these tiny sardines are eaten as a snack or incorporated with other foods, especially rice dishes. Store in a dark, cool, dry place.

DRIED BONITO FLAKES
Shaved pieces of filleted and dried bonito, a close relative of the mackerel family. Essential ingredient in Japanese soup stock (*dashi*), bonito flakes give full-bodied flavour to otherwise bland dishes. Store in a cool place.

DRIED SEA CUCUMBER
Sea cucumbers may be reconstituted by soaking in water for several hours. Steamed or braised, the flavour is bland, but receptive to taking on other flavours, such as garlic, ginger and chillies.

DRIED CONGER PIKE MAW

A spongy membrane, removed from the stomach of the conger pike, dried and deep-fried to a honeycomb crispness. Soak in warm water to soften, then cook in acidulated water for a few minutes. Squeeze out remaining water before adding to other ingredients. Bland itself, it readily takes on other flavours. Store in a cool, dry place.

DRIED POLLACK

A member of the cod family, with a strongly concentrated flavour and aroma. Soak in warm water for 30 minutes, then remove any bones. Chop to cook with other food. Store in a cool, dry place.

SHARK'S FIN

The longer the strands, the higher the quality and the more expensive. The fins need many days of soaking and further preparation; shark's fin soup is a Chinese delicacy, with only the slightest hint of fishiness.

SALTED JELLYFISH

With a pungent sea smell, it is heavily salted and needs to be soaked for several hours in cold water, changing the water frequently. Before cooking, shred finely and soak for 20 minutes in a mixture of hand-warm water, rice wine, spring onions and sliced ginger. Lends a crunchy texture to dishes.

251

LAVER
Porphyra vulgaris
A purplish-red seaweed used by the
Welsh to make laverbread. Known as
nori in Japan, it is pressed into sheets,
dried and used to
make sushi.

MARSH SAMPHIRE
Salicornia europaea
Also known as **glasswort**,
this is a wild plant found
growing in estuaries and salt
marshes. In season mid-
summer, it is best stir-fried in
a wok or lightly blanched in
boiling water to maintain its
crisp texture. Its salty,
peppery flavour complements
fish dishes.

WAKAME
Undaria pinnatifidia
A dark green, Japanese seaweed.
Also known as **salad seaweed**, it is rich in minerals and is
used for salads, soups and as a garnish. It should only be
lightly cooked.

SEA LETTUCE
Ulva lactuca
Delicate, green, gos-
samer-thin leaves
which can be used to
wrap meats and fish
before cooking, like
blanched spinach.
Usually sold salted, so
needs a thorough
washing in plenty of
cold water.

DULSE
Rhodymenia palmata
A red seaweed with
ribbon-like fronds and a
fishy, salty flavour. It needs
thorough washing if sold
salted, and can be used in
salads and egg dishes. A
squeeze of lemon juice helps
to keep its colour.

SEAKALE
Crambe maritima
A member of the mustard
family, it grows wild in sandy
English coastal regions. The
delicate, white stems with
frilled leaves can be eaten raw
like celery, or boiled or
steamed and served
with butter.

HARICOT DE MER
Himanthalia elongata
Seaweed which resembles
haricot beans, at least in
texture if not taste. Use to add
character to risottos, or as a
bed for baked fish. Blanched
and deep fried, it makes
an interesting crisp addition
to salads.

Fresh & processed meats

With a new emphasis on healthy eating, and the changes brought by our varied multicultural society, the role of meat has changed. The good news is that, instead of the emphasis being on quantity, it is now on an unprecedented range of quality produce, and there has probably never been a time when the quality has been more reliable. Over the past decade, the concern over the welfare of livestock has led to changes in the meat industry. Strict regulations are laid down to control the living conditions, diet and rearing of animals, resulting in excellent meat from butchers and supermarkets. This is especially true of the beef industry.

Meat is no longer at the centre of the plate; portions are smaller and are generously supplemented with vegetables, pulses and grains, Many cuts these days are tailored for cooks with busy lifestyles, where quick preparation and cooking are as important as the flavour. The vast choice of ready-prepared meat is staggering.

On the health issue, there's been a move towards breeding animals with less fatty meat, although some supporters of 'old-fashioned' taste have their reservations about the overall benefit. A little marbling in beef actually delivers the flavour. There are few, however, who would disagree that it's a good idea to trim off excess fat when cooking meat.

Offal has its fans and foes: people either love it or loathe it. When photographing the many and varied items for this book, there was no shortage of takers afterwards when distributing meats, fish, pasta, cheeses, etc. When it came to offal, though, it was an entirely different matter. However, it is one of the cheapest and most nutritious forms of meat, and is frequently used in fashionable dishes cooked with a difference.

What used to be a midweek staple — the sausage — has also taken on 'designer' status. The humble banger has been elevated into the realms of a gourmet dish. The choice is phenomenal with scores of tastes and blends.

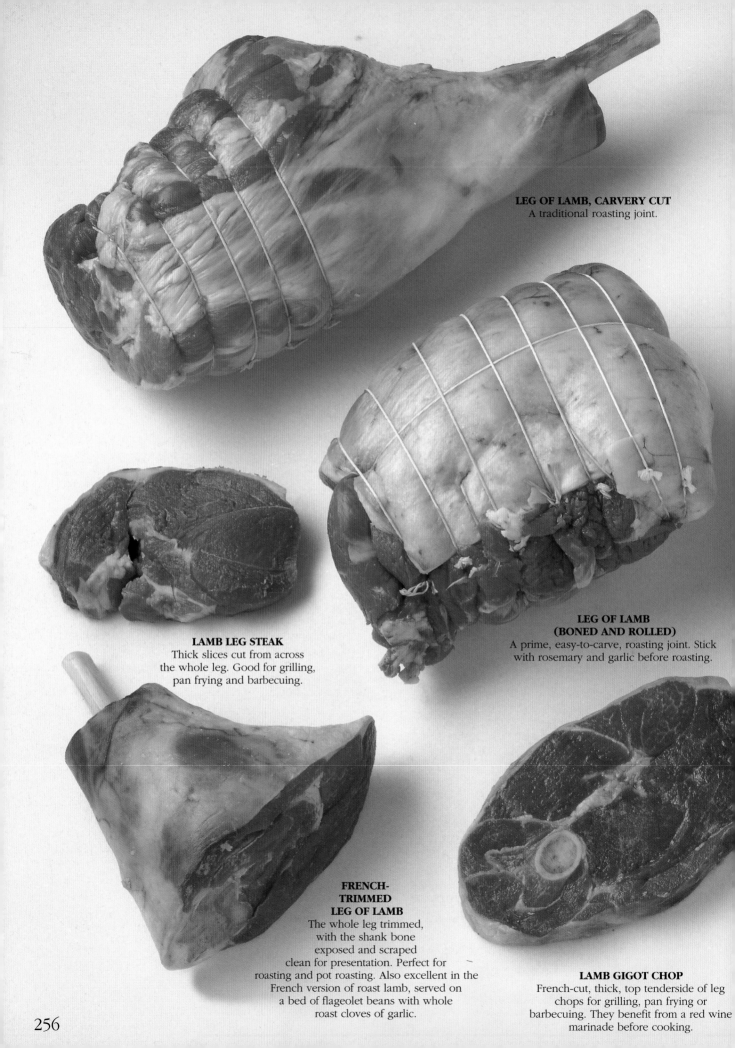

LEG OF LAMB, CARVERY CUT
A traditional roasting joint.

**LEG OF LAMB
(BONED AND ROLLED)**
A prime, easy-to-carve, roasting joint. Stick
with rosemary and garlic before roasting.

LAMB LEG STEAK
Thick slices cut from across
the whole leg. Good for grilling,
pan frying and barbecuing.

**FRENCH-
TRIMMED
LEG OF LAMB**
The whole leg trimmed,
with the shank bone
exposed and scraped
clean for presentation. Perfect for
roasting and pot roasting. Also excellent in the
French version of roast lamb, served on
a bed of flageolet beans with whole
roast cloves of garlic.

LAMB GIGOT CHOP
French-cut, thick, top tenderside of leg
chops for grilling, pan frying or
barbecuing. They benefit from a red wine
marinade before cooking.

DRESSED SADDLE OF LAMB
Prepared with all the bones and
internal fat removed, and dressed to
include the kidneys. It is a prime roasting
joint for a large dinner party.

**SHORT CUT SADDLE OF LAMB
(BONED AND ROLLED)**
A prime roasting joint with all
bones removed.

257

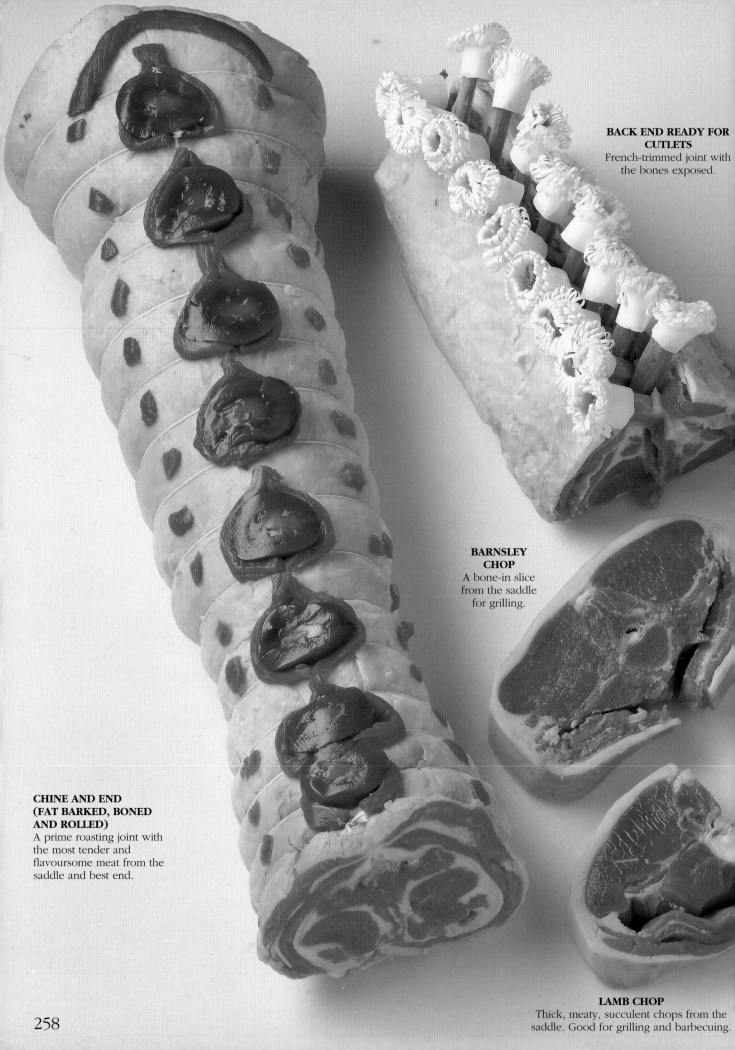

BACK END READY FOR CUTLETS
French-trimmed joint with the bones exposed.

BARNSLEY CHOP
A bone-in slice from the saddle for grilling.

CHINE AND END (FAT BARKED, BONED AND ROLLED)
A prime roasting joint with the most tender and flavoursome meat from the saddle and best end.

LAMB CHOP
Thick, meaty, succulent chops from the saddle. Good for grilling and barbecuing.

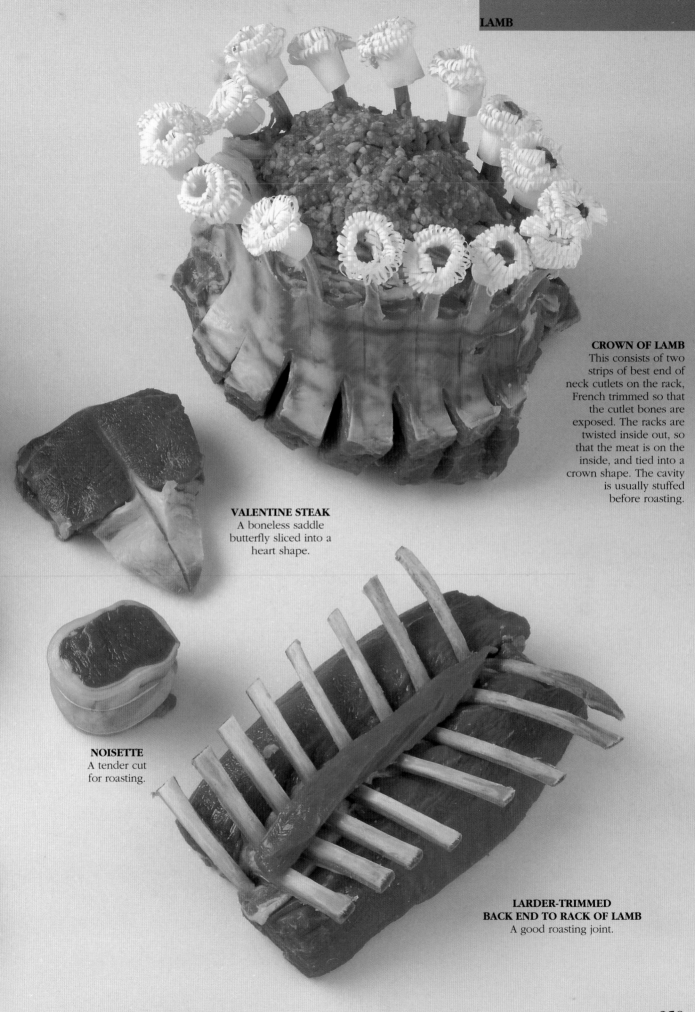

CROWN OF LAMB
This consists of two strips of best end of neck cutlets on the rack, French trimmed so that the cutlet bones are exposed. The racks are twisted inside out, so that the meat is on the inside, and tied into a crown shape. The cavity is usually stuffed before roasting.

VALENTINE STEAK
A boneless saddle butterfly sliced into a heart shape.

NOISETTE
A tender cut for roasting.

LARDER-TRIMMED BACK END TO RACK OF LAMB
A good roasting joint.

SHOULDER OF LAMB
A forequarter joint, best slow roasted for deliciously tender meat and crisp skin. Also available as half shoulders – either the blade end or the knuckle end – which are enough for two.

CHUMP CHOP
Thick, meaty chops cut from the chump end of the lamb.

SHOULDER STEAK
A braising cut traditionally used in the Greek dish, *kleftiko*, with herbs and garlic.

CHUMP OF LAMB CUT INTO RUMP OF LAMB
A good, small, roasting joint for one portion.

**LAMB SHOULDER
(BONED AND ROLLED)**
An easy-to-carve roasting
joint which is especially
good stuffed.

MIDDLE NECK FILLET
Taken from the middle neck, this is an
inexpensive, boneless, tender cut best cooked
slowly for curries, stews, casseroles and pies.

MIDDLE NECK
A good stewing or
braising cut.

**MIDDLE NECK CUT
TO CUTLET**
A meaty stewing or
braising cut.

DICED LAMB
Tender lamb cut
nto cubes, suitable for
casseroles and stews.

LAMB MINCE
Excellent for meatballs,
burgers, shish kebabs,
moussaka and
shepherd's pie.

LEG

CHUMP

LOIN

BREAST (BONED AND ROLLED)
Good for stuffing and slow roasting.

MIDDLE NECK (FILLETS REMOVED)
Ideal for a lamb stockpot.

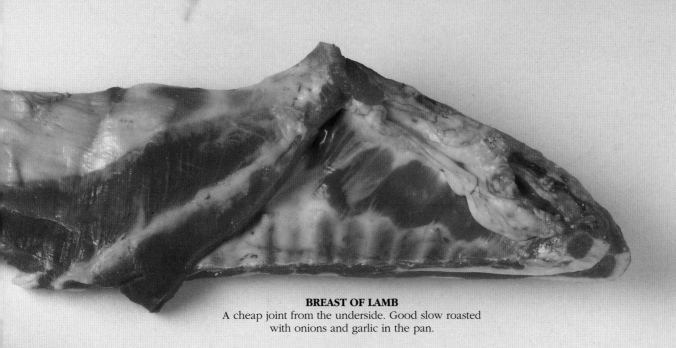

BREAST OF LAMB
A cheap joint from the underside. Good slow roasted
with onions and garlic in the pan.

BREAST

BEST END

SHOULDER

ROLLED SIDE OF LAMB (BONELESS)
Prepared from the side which is folded,
rolled and strung once all bone, cartilage, thick
gristle and internal fat has been removed.
Rarely used whole, except for large banquets,
it can be divided into smaller roasting
joints as shown.

263

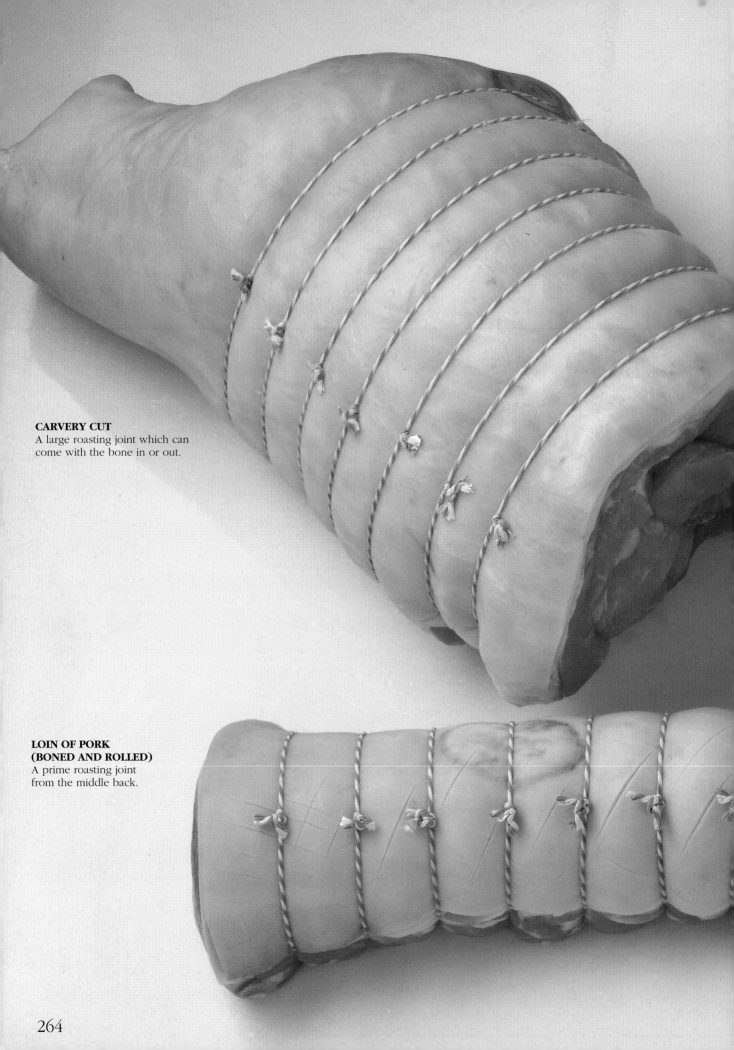

CARVERY CUT
A large roasting joint which can come with the bone in or out.

**LOIN OF PORK
(BONED AND ROLLED)**
A prime roasting joint from the middle back.

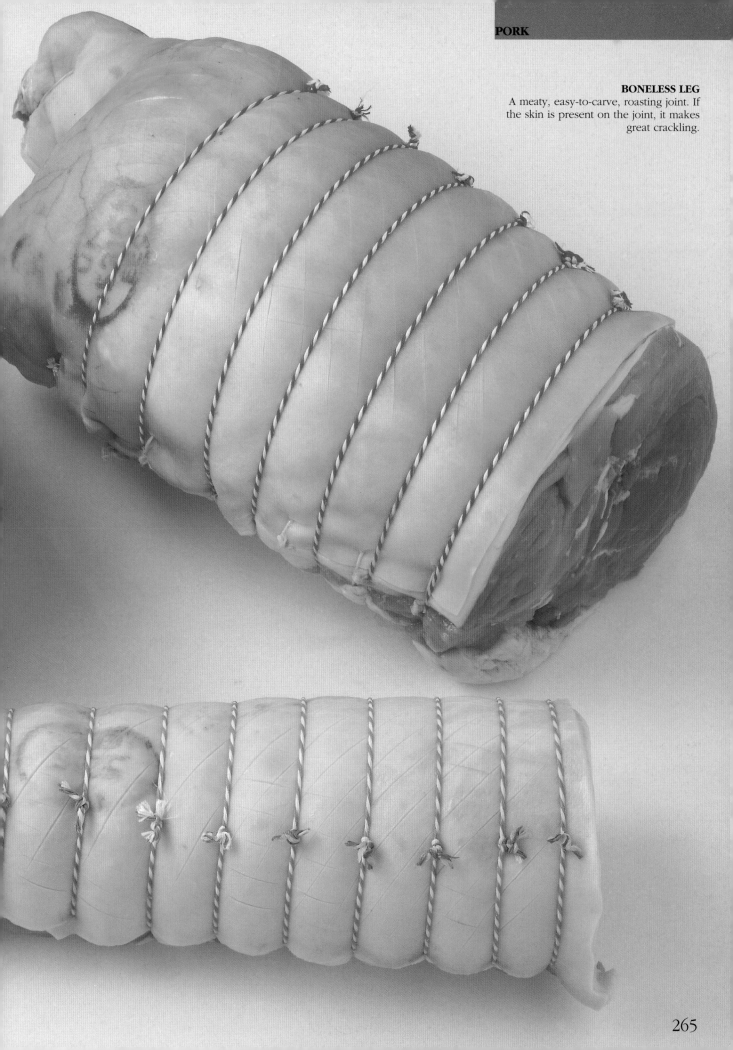

BONELESS LEG
A meaty, easy-to-carve, roasting joint. If the skin is present on the joint, it makes great crackling.

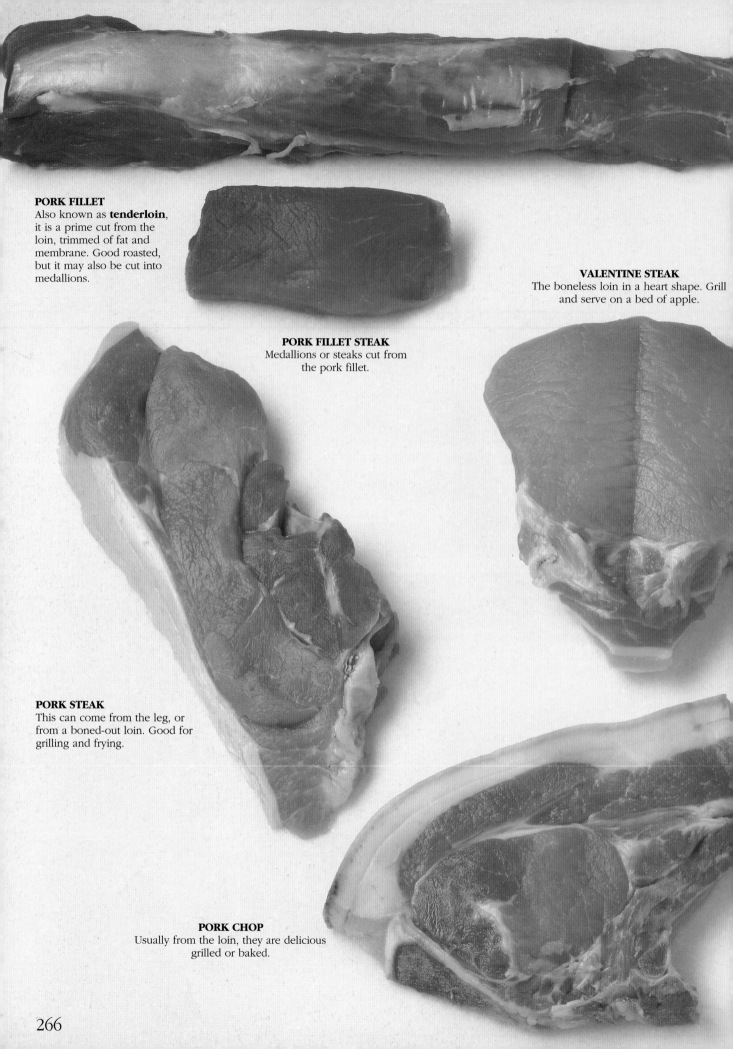

PORK FILLET
Also known as **tenderloin**,
it is a prime cut from the
loin, trimmed of fat and
membrane. Good roasted,
but it may also be cut into
medallions.

VALENTINE STEAK
The boneless loin in a heart shape. Grill
and serve on a bed of apple.

PORK FILLET STEAK
Medallions or steaks cut from
the pork fillet.

PORK STEAK
This can come from the leg, or
from a boned-out loin. Good for
grilling and frying.

PORK CHOP
Usually from the loin, they are delicious
grilled or baked.

NECK END (BONED AND ROLLED)
An inexpensive roasting joint.

NECK END CHOP
Also known as a
spare rib chop, and
not to be confused
with spare ribs, it is
meaty, succulent, and is
best slow roasted,
grilled or fried.

267

PORK BELLY
An inexpensive, thin, flat joint on the bone with loads of crackling. Slow roasting is best, as the fat melts off, leaving a fragrant and tender meat.

PORK BELLY (SLICE)
Best for grilling or oven roasting. It can also be minced, with the skin and bones removed, for sausages and pork pies.

PORK SPARE RIBS
From the underside of the belly, these are good cooked Chinese style with five-spice and chilli, marinated and barbecued, or cooked in a spicy barbecue sauce.

PORK MINCE
Good for meatballs, burgers and wonton stuffings.

DICED PORK
Convenient for stews, casseroles or pork pies.

269

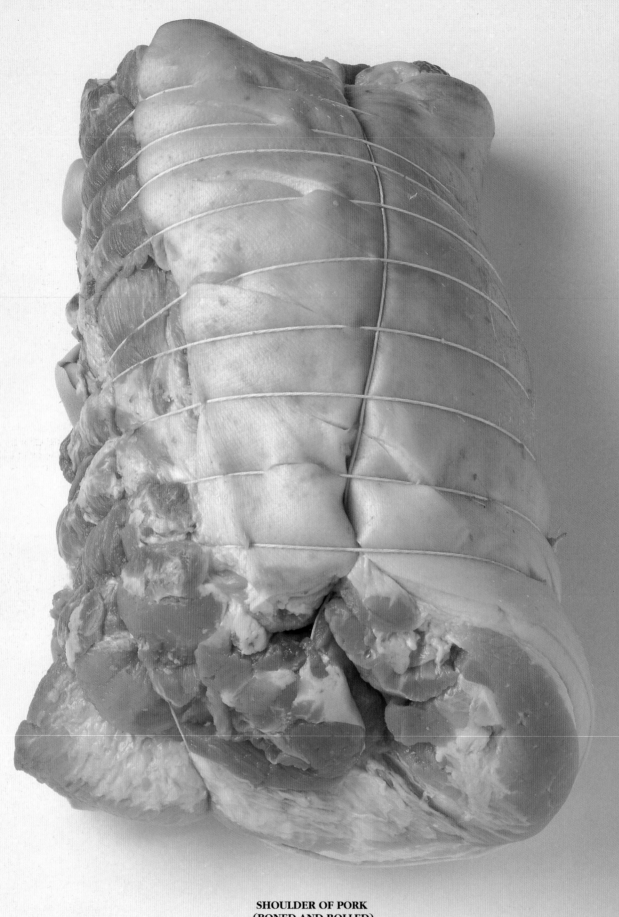

**SHOULDER OF PORK
(BONED AND ROLLED)**
Tender, sweet meat from the forequarter.
Good for slow roasting.

LARGE PORK SAUSAGEs
Jumbo sausages for hot dogs and main courses.

PORK ESCALOPE
A thinly sliced, low-fat cut for pan
frying and stir-fries.

PORK SAUSAGE
Thick pork sausages for dishes
such as Toad in the Hole or
Sausage and Mash.

THIN PORK SAUSAGE

COCKTAIL SAUSAGES
Tiny chipolatas for mini sausage rolls, or
for serving on cocktail sticks with drinks.
Also a typical accompaniment to the
turkey roast at Christmas.

PORK SAUSAGE MEAT
Finely minced sausage meat combined
with spices. Use for homemade sausages
or stuffings.

271

TOPSIDE
The top muscle of the meaty leg, which is tender, full of flavour and suitable for roasting or pot roasts.

**SIRLOIN
(BONED AND
ROLLED)**
A prime
roasting joint.

272

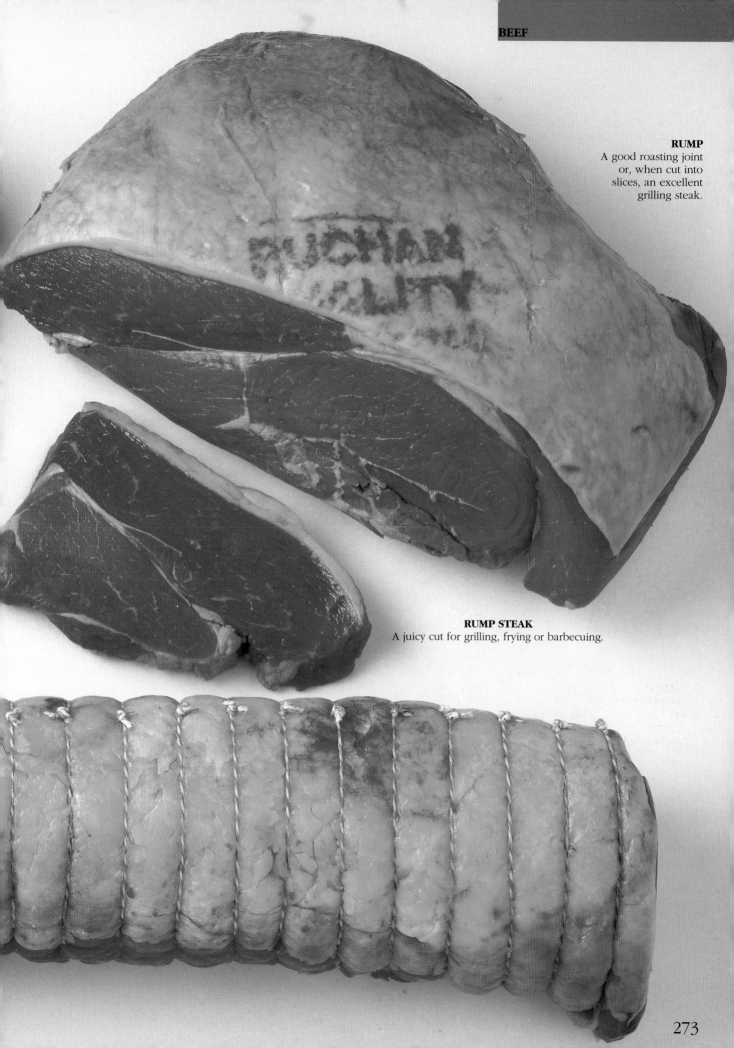

RUMP
A good roasting joint
or, when cut into
slices, an excellent
grilling steak.

RUMP STEAK
A juicy cut for grilling, frying or barbecuing.

273

SIRLOIN, BONELESS
A delicious cut for roasting or for
cutting into steaks.

SIRLOIN STEAK
A prime-quality grilling steak.

274

WHOLE FILLET
The most expensive and most tender
cut of beef, it makes a delicious roast
on its own or wrapped in pastry and
topped with duxelles for
beef Wellington.

**FORERIB
(BONED AND ROLLED)**
A good roasting joint.

FILLET STEAK
Thick slices of fillet for grilling or
pan frying.

275

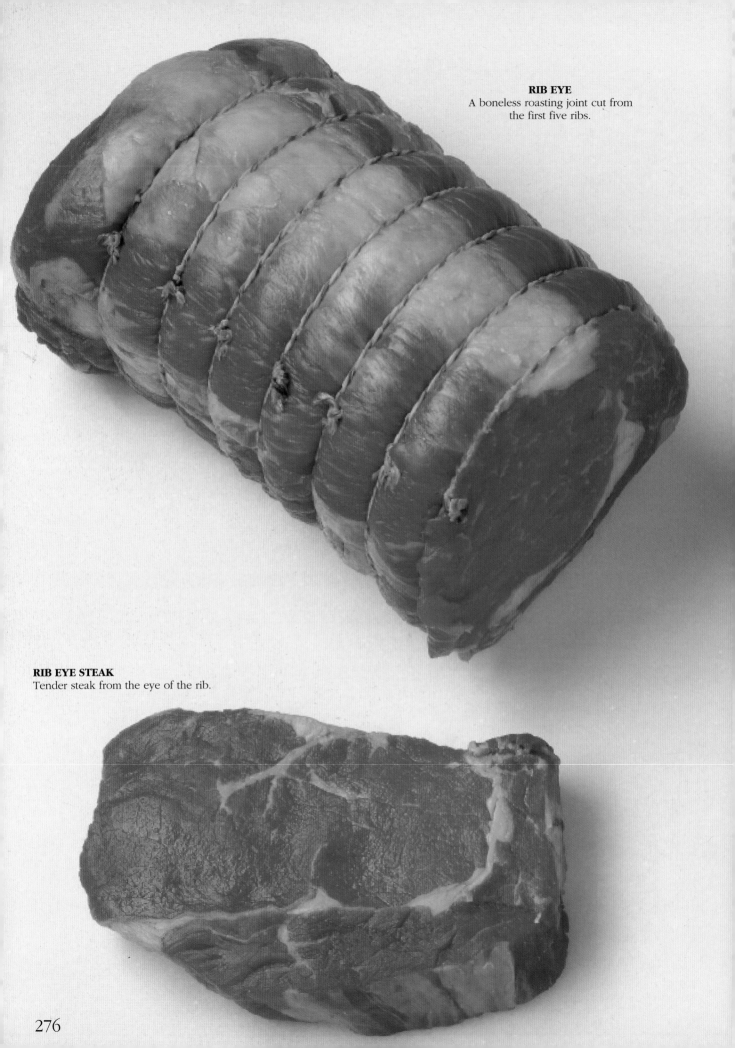

RIB EYE
A boneless roasting joint cut from
the first five ribs.

RIB EYE STEAK
Tender steak from the eye of the rib.

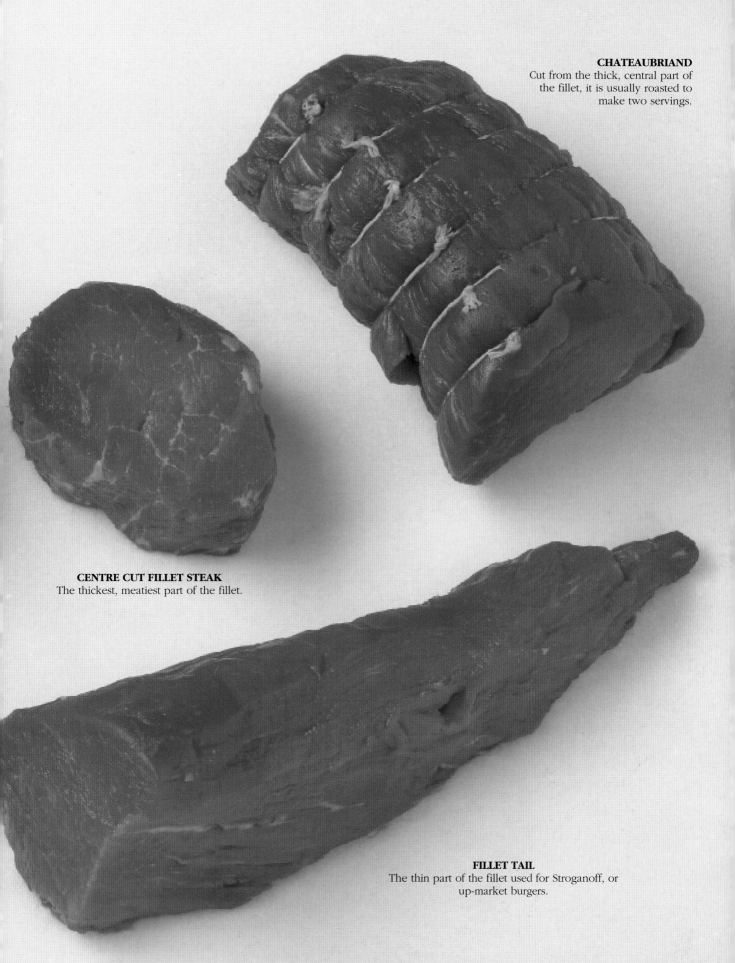

CHATEAUBRIAND
Cut from the thick, central part of
the fillet, it is usually roasted to
make two servings.

CENTRE CUT FILLET STEAK
The thickest, meatiest part of the fillet.

FILLET TAIL
The thin part of the fillet used for Stroganoff, or
up-market burgers.

BEEF PATTY
Used for burgers.

BEEF MINCE
Look for mince which is deep red,
as pale mince has fat through it.
Use for shepherd's pie, bolognese
and burgers.

CHUCK ROLL
A braising joint. It is often
thickly sliced for braising
and stewing, and has an
excellent flavour. It is also
available diced.

SILVERSIDE
From the hindquarter, this cut
can be roasted, but is best
known as the joint for boiled
beef or salt beef.

278

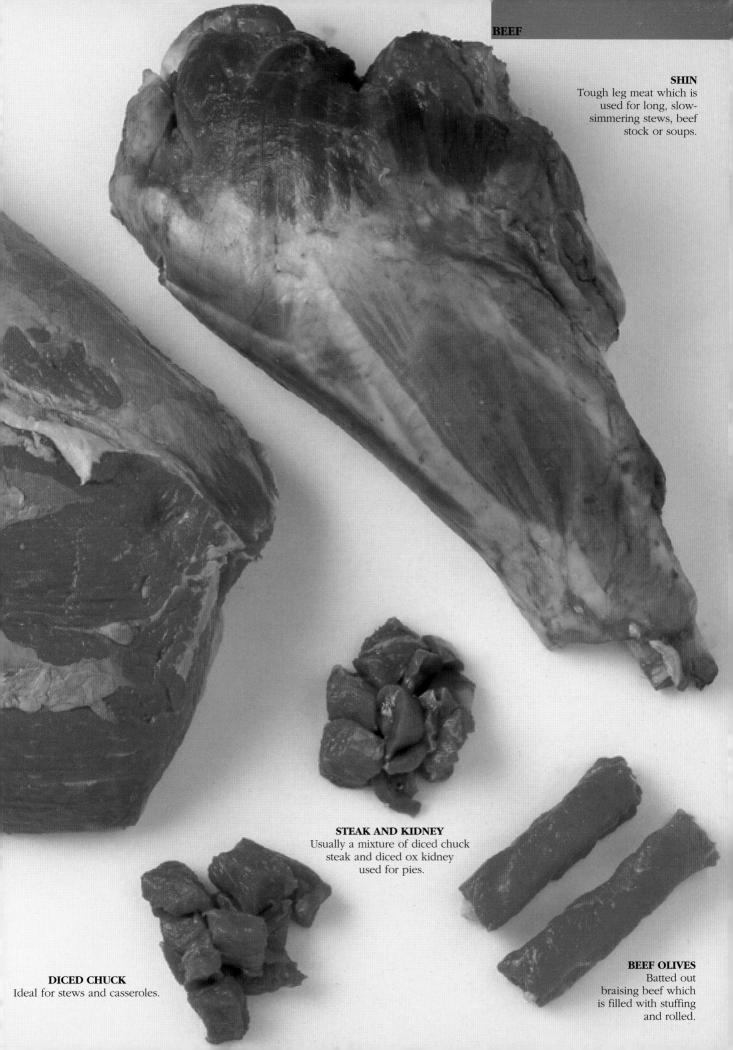

SHIN
Tough leg meat which is used for long, slow-simmering stews, beef stock or soups.

STEAK AND KIDNEY
Usually a mixture of diced chuck steak and diced ox kidney used for pies.

BEEF OLIVES
Batted out braising beef which is filled with stuffing and rolled.

DICED CHUCK
Ideal for stews and casseroles.

ESCALOPE
Thinly sliced prime cut of veal.
Often coated with breadcrumbs
and fried.

DICED
Trimmings cut from the
shoulder and breast; use for
pies and stews.

T-BONE STEAK
A large steak, with the bone in,
taken from the fillet end of the
sirloin. Grill or fry.

ENTRECÔTE STEAK
A tender, thick steak from the
sirloin. Grill or pan fry.

280

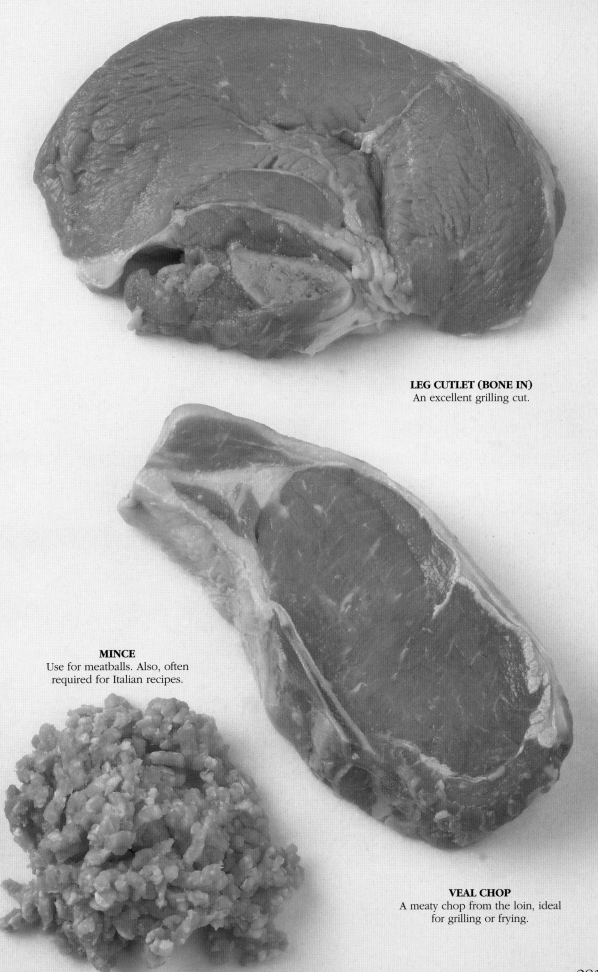

LEG CUTLET (BONE IN)
An excellent grilling cut.

MINCE
Use for meatballs. Also, often
required for Italian recipes.

VEAL CHOP
A meaty chop from the loin, ideal
for grilling or frying.

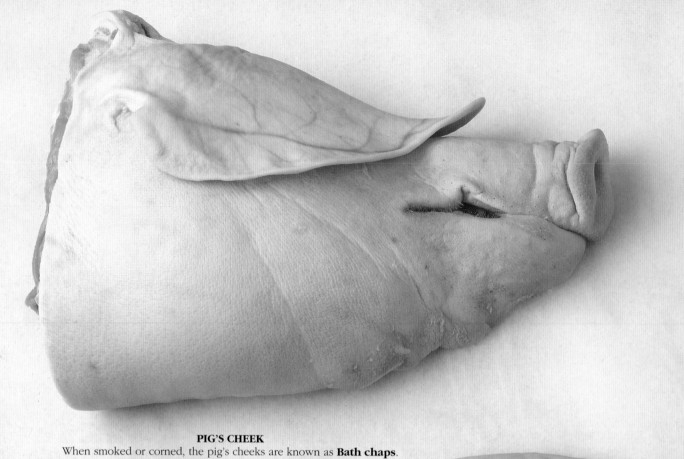

PIG'S CHEEK
When smoked or corned, the pig's cheeks are known as **Bath chaps**.
These may be simmered and eaten cold like ham.

PIG'S EAR

EARS
Pig's and calf's ears consist
mainly of cartilage and are a
popular food in China, where
they are usually fried, grilled or
stuffed. Usually cooked with
spices. Singe the hair before
cooking the calf's ear.

CALF'S EAR

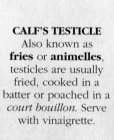

CALF'S TESTICLE
Also known as
fries or **animelles**,
testicles are usually
fried, cooked in a
batter or poached in a
court bouillon. Serve
with vinaigrette.

SHEEP'S EYEBALL
These are considered a delicacy in
the Middle East. Usually the
eyeballs are removed after the
whole head is cooked, and are
eaten immediately, either by
themselves or with sauce.

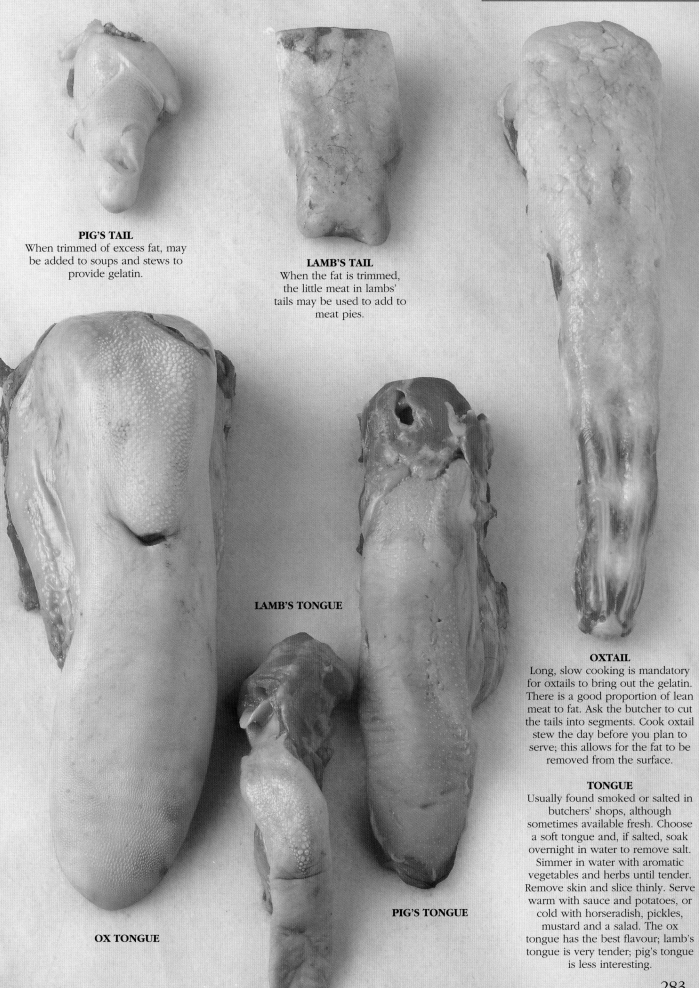

PIG'S TAIL
When trimmed of excess fat, may be added to soups and stews to provide gelatin.

LAMB'S TAIL
When the fat is trimmed, the little meat in lambs' tails may be used to add to meat pies.

LAMB'S TONGUE

OXTAIL
Long, slow cooking is mandatory for oxtails to bring out the gelatin. There is a good proportion of lean meat to fat. Ask the butcher to cut the tails into segments. Cook oxtail stew the day before you plan to serve; this allows for the fat to be removed from the surface.

TONGUE
Usually found smoked or salted in butchers' shops, although sometimes available fresh. Choose a soft tongue and, if salted, soak overnight in water to remove salt. Simmer in water with aromatic vegetables and herbs until tender. Remove skin and slice thinly. Serve warm with sauce and potatoes, or cold with horseradish, pickles, mustard and a salad. The ox tongue has the best flavour; lamb's tongue is very tender; pig's tongue is less interesting.

PIG'S TONGUE

OX TONGUE

283

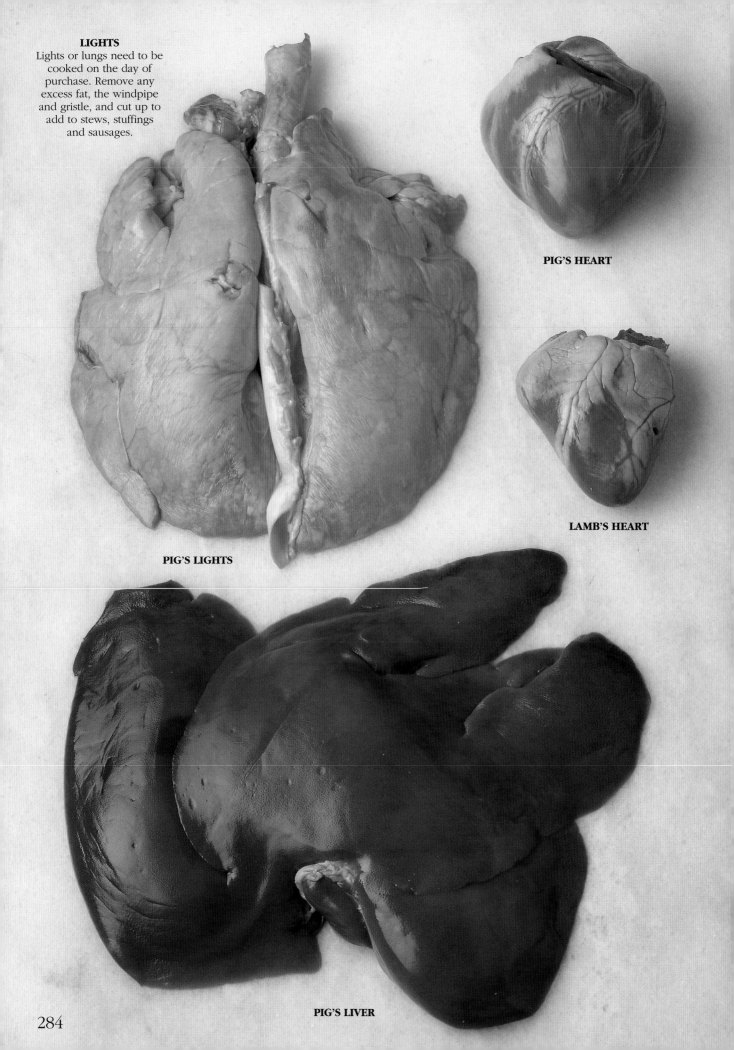

LIGHTS
Lights or lungs need to be cooked on the day of purchase. Remove any excess fat, the windpipe and gristle, and cut up to add to stews, stuffings and sausages.

PIG'S HEART

LAMB'S HEART

PIG'S LIGHTS

PIG'S LIVER

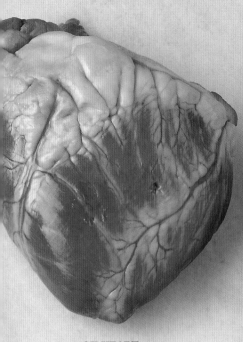

OX HEART

HEART
After removing any excess fat and flaps, soak in cold water with vinegar added for 1–3 hours. Rinse and dry. May be grilled or roasted, cut into bite-size pieces and added to stews, or left whole and stuffed and roasted. Don't overcook or the meat will be tough.

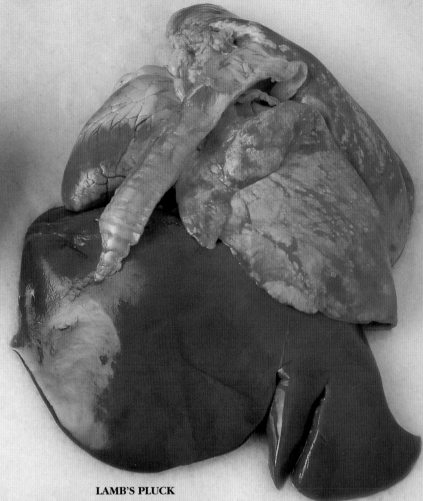

LAMB'S PLUCK

LAMB'S LIVER

PLUCK
A combination of heart, lungs and liver of lamb, goat or pig.

LIVER
After rinsing, remove the silvery membrane. For pig's and ox liver, slice and soak in milk for one hour to reduce the strong flavour. Roast or braise pig's liver; braise or stew ox liver; grill, fry or roast lamb's or calf's liver. Sliced livers may be used in pâtés and terrines.

CALF'S LIVER

285

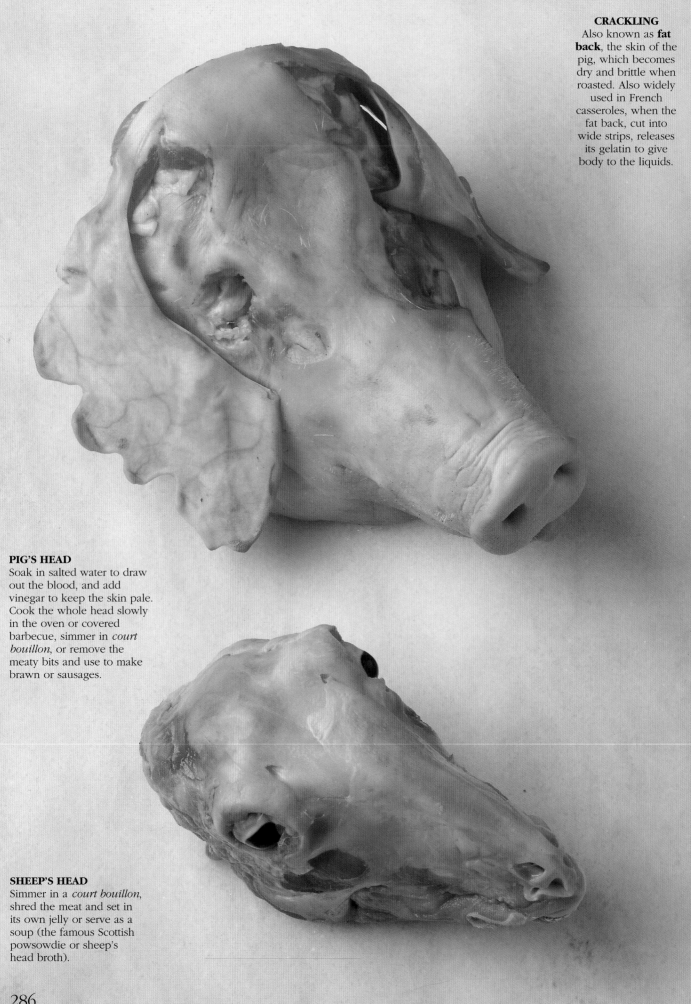

CRACKLING
Also known as **fat back**, the skin of the pig, which becomes dry and brittle when roasted. Also widely used in French casseroles, when the fat back, cut into wide strips, releases its gelatin to give body to the liquids.

PIG'S HEAD
Soak in salted water to draw out the blood, and add vinegar to keep the skin pale. Cook the whole head slowly in the oven or covered barbecue, simmer in *court bouillon*, or remove the meaty bits and use to make brawn or sausages.

SHEEP'S HEAD
Simmer in a *court bouillon*, shred the meat and set in its own jelly or serve as a soup (the famous Scottish powsowdie or sheep's head broth).

286

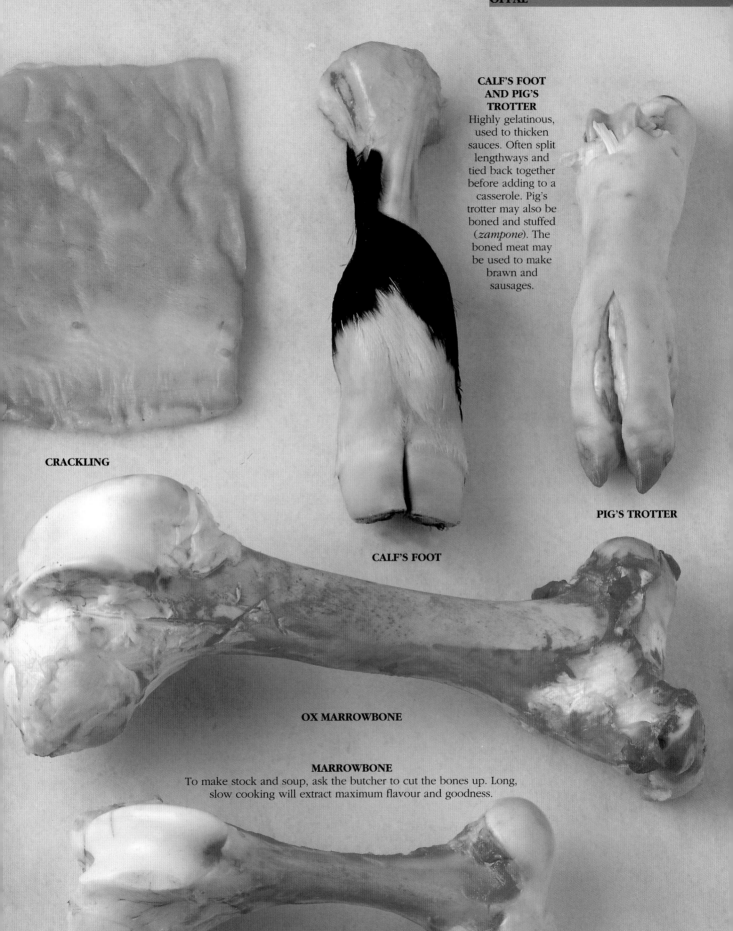

CRACKLING

CALF'S FOOT AND PIG'S TROTTER
Highly gelatinous, used to thicken sauces. Often split lengthways and tied back together before adding to a casserole. Pig's trotter may also be boned and stuffed (*zampone*). The boned meat may be used to make brawn and sausages.

CALF'S FOOT

PIG'S TROTTER

OX MARROWBONE

MARROWBONE
To make stock and soup, ask the butcher to cut the bones up. Long, slow cooking will extract maximum flavour and goodness.

CALF'S MARROWBONE

287

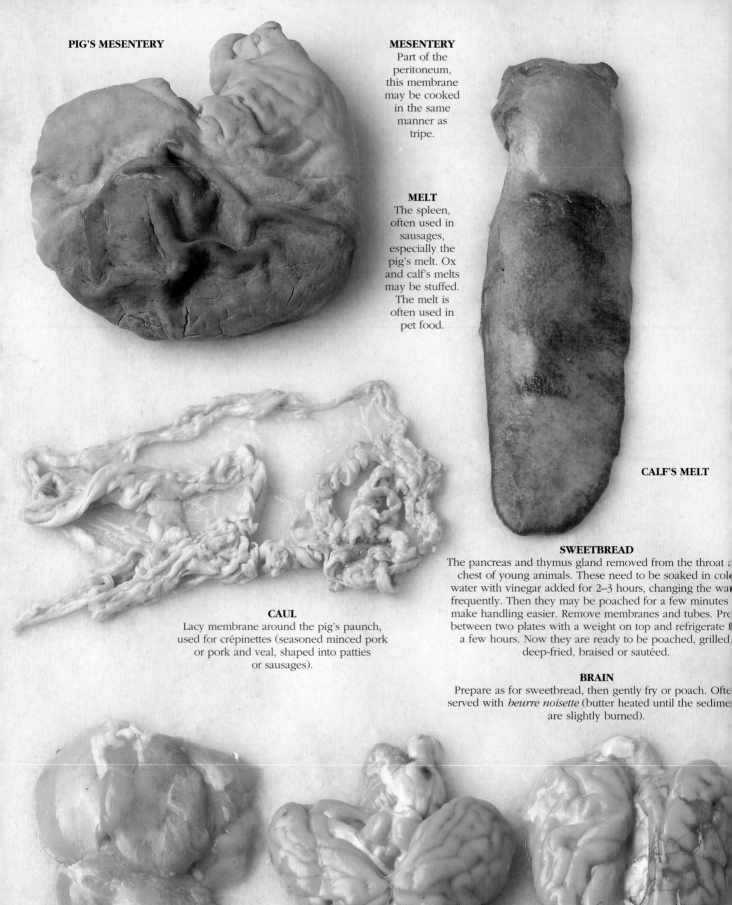

PIG'S MESENTERY

MESENTERY
Part of the peritoneum, this membrane may be cooked in the same manner as tripe.

MELT
The spleen, often used in sausages, especially the pig's melt. Ox and calf's melts may be stuffed. The melt is often used in pet food.

CALF'S MELT

CAUL
Lacy membrane around the pig's paunch, used for crépinettes (seasoned minced pork or pork and veal, shaped into patties or sausages).

SWEETBREAD
The pancreas and thymus gland removed from the throat a chest of young animals. These need to be soaked in col water with vinegar added for 2–3 hours, changing the wa frequently. Then they may be poached for a few minutes make handling easier. Remove membranes and tubes. Pre between two plates with a weight on top and refrigerate f a few hours. Now they are ready to be poached, grilled deep-fried, braised or sautéed.

BRAIN
Prepare as for sweetbread, then gently fry or poach. Ofte served with *beurre noisette* (butter heated until the sedime are slightly burned).

LAMB'S SWEETBREAD

LAMB'S BRAIN

PIG'S BRAIN

TRIPE

The lining of the first and second stomachs, usually from ox or calf. Choose tripe which has a fresh white to creamy yellow colour. Honeycomb (right) is considered the superior. Most butchers pre-cook tripe to shorten cooking time at home. Blanket tripe (left) stands up to long cooking times without disintegrating. Boil, grill, sauté, deep-fry or casserole.

PIG'S KIDNEY

KIDNEY
Look for firm, sweet-smelling specimens. Remove the membrane, halve and remove gristle. For a tender result, either grill or sauté quickly or simmer long and slowly.

LAMB'S KIDNEY

CALF'S KIDNEY

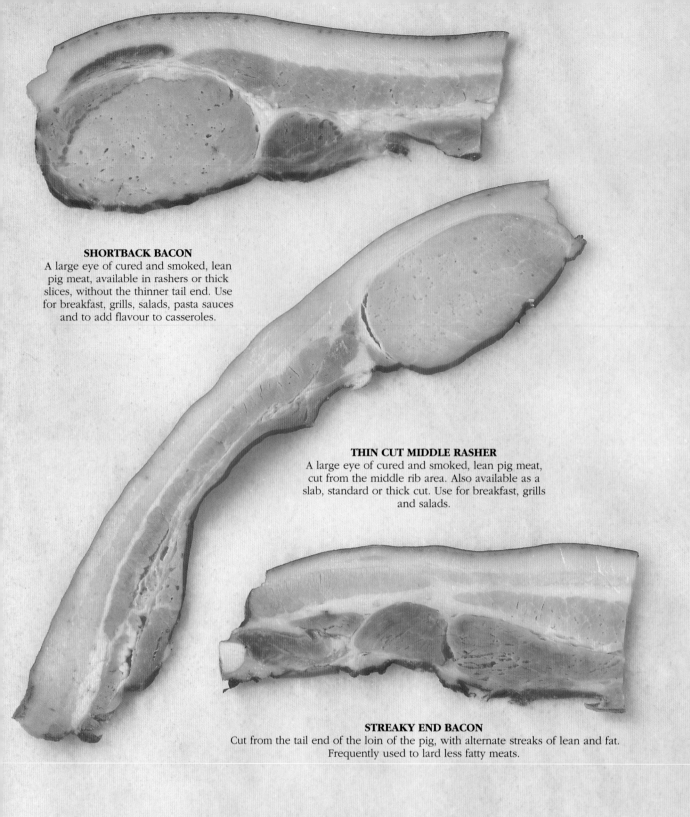

SHORTBACK BACON
A large eye of cured and smoked, lean pig meat, available in rashers or thick slices, without the thinner tail end. Use for breakfast, grills, salads, pasta sauces and to add flavour to casseroles.

THIN CUT MIDDLE RASHER
A large eye of cured and smoked, lean pig meat, cut from the middle rib area. Also available as a slab, standard or thick cut. Use for breakfast, grills and salads.

STREAKY END BACON
Cut from the tail end of the loin of the pig, with alternate streaks of lean and fat. Frequently used to lard less fatty meats.

STREAKY BACON (THINLY SLICED)
Very finely cut streaky bacon which crisps easily, and is perfect for cooking in the microwave.

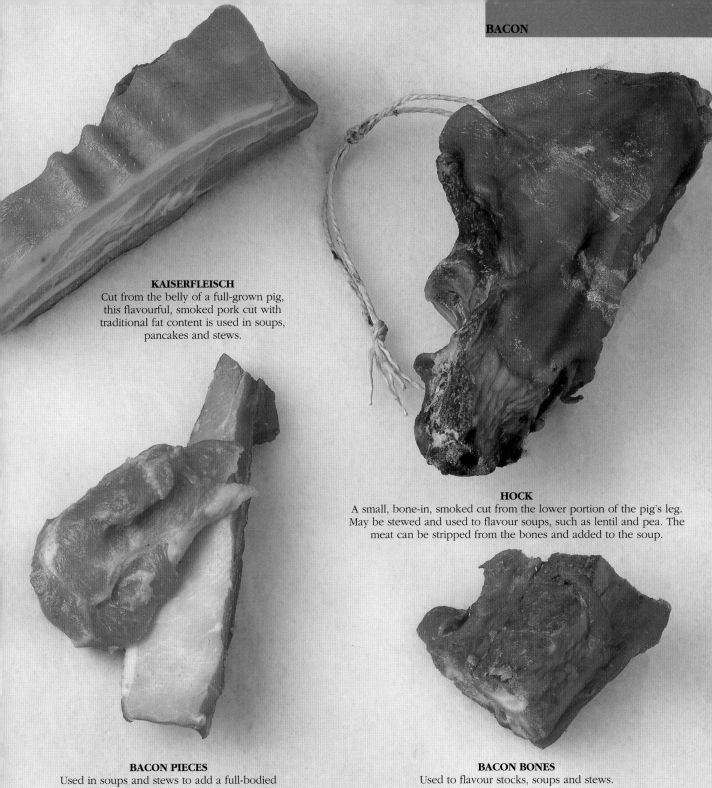

KAISERFLEISCH
Cut from the belly of a full-grown pig,
this flavourful, smoked pork cut with
traditional fat content is used in soups,
pancakes and stews.

HOCK
A small, bone-in, smoked cut from the lower portion of the pig's leg.
May be stewed and used to flavour soups, such as lentil and pea. The
meat can be stripped from the bones and added to the soup.

BACON PIECES
Used in soups and stews to add a full-bodied
flavour. The meat may be removed after cooking
or cut up and added to the dish.

BACON BONES
Used to flavour stocks, soups and stews.

CHINESE-STYLE DRIED PORK BELLY
Also known as **Chinese bacon**, this full-flavoured pork is sliced or diced and used in stews and
steamed dishes, soups and stuffings.

CHAMPAGNE HAM
Smoked, boneless, leg ham. Ever popular for
sandwiches and salads.

LEG HAM
Carved off the bone. This
premium product is good for
sandwiches and salads.

PRAGUE HAM
Traditional European-style. A lightly smoked sweet ham.

HAM STEAK
Quick and easy to prepare, perfect for
barbecue and grill.

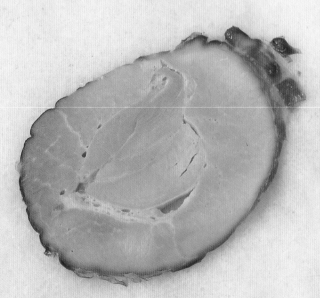

HONEY HAM
A sweet, moist, honey-cured ham
with delicate flavour.

SANDWICH HAM
Especially shaped to fit sandwiches for school
lunches; convenient and inexpensive.

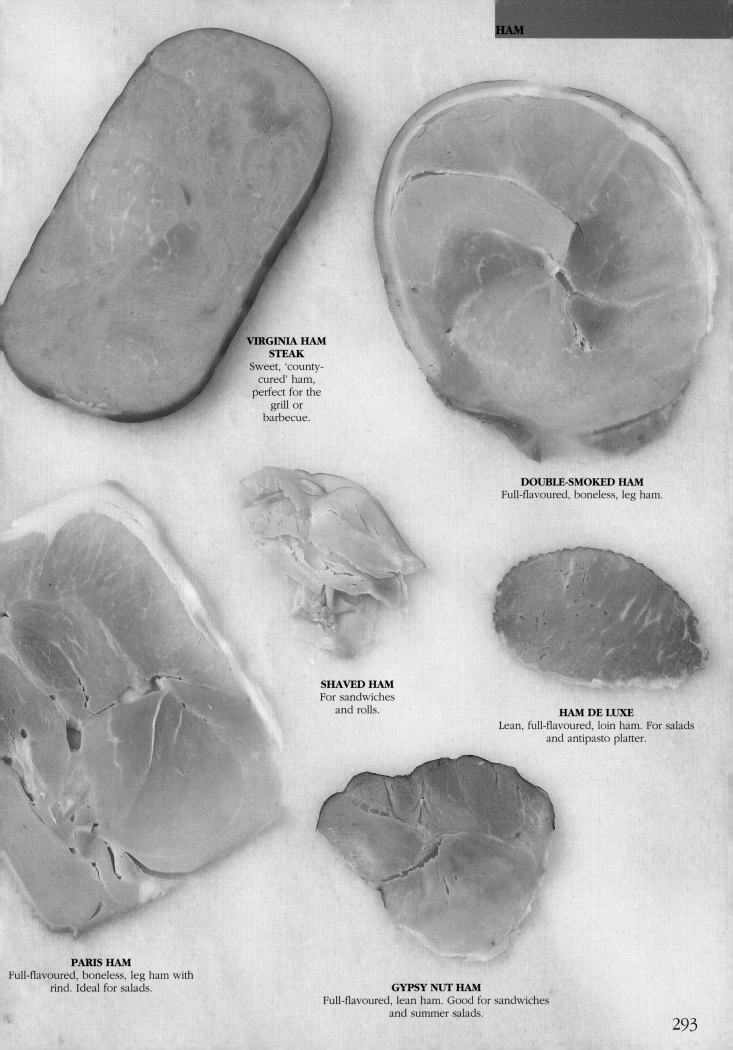

VIRGINIA HAM STEAK
Sweet, 'county-cured' ham, perfect for the grill or barbecue.

DOUBLE-SMOKED HAM
Full-flavoured, boneless, leg ham.

SHAVED HAM
For sandwiches and rolls.

HAM DE LUXE
Lean, full-flavoured, loin ham. For salads and antipasto platter.

PARIS HAM
Full-flavoured, boneless, leg ham with rind. Ideal for salads.

GYPSY NUT HAM
Full-flavoured, lean ham. Good for sandwiches and summer salads.

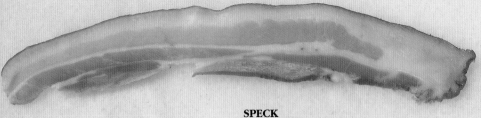

SPECK
Cut from the top side of the leg of an adult pig and smoked. May be substituted for bacon or pancetta in recipes, such as robust soups, stews or pasta sauces.

BLACK FOREST HAM
Double-smoked, with full-bodied flavour, made to a traditional European recipe.

KASSELER
From the boned loin of the pig, this traditional German speciality is cured and smoked.

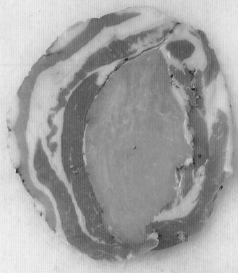

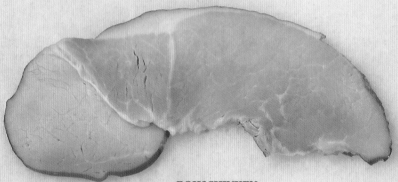

ROHSCHINKEN
A German speciality (lit. 'raw ham'), this is similar to prosciutto.

HOT PANCETTA
From the belly of the pig, rolled and cured with cayenne or chilli pepper. Serve thinly sliced.

LACHSSCHINKEN
Very tender (*Lachs* is German for salmon), this lightly brined ham is indeed like smoked salmon in taste and texture.

BASTOURMA
Similar to pastrami, this is highly spiced, air-dried beef with a spicy coating. Slice very thinly and ea as is or fry lightly.

PARMA HAM
Also known as **prosciutto**, or ***prosciutto crudo*** (*crudo* is Italian for raw). This is cut from the hind thigh of the pig, and salted, hung and dried for 12–18 months.

CLOBASSI
A spicy European-style smoked sausage made from pork and/or beef with herbs and spices. Eat as is or grill.

STRASSBURG
A fairly bland, European-style sausage made from beef and/or pork, with a light seasoning of coriander, pepper and nutmeg.

SLIM FRANKFURT
Usually made of pork or pork and beef and/or veal, seasoned with various spices and lightly smoked.

COCKTAIL FRANKFURT
Usually made of pork or pork and beef and/or veal, seasoned with various spices and lightly smoked.

CONTINENTAL FRANKFURT
Usually made of pork or pork and beef and/or veal, seasoned with spices and lightly smoked. Finely textured.

SMALL CHORIZO
A small variety of the
classic pork sausage
from Spain.

SALSICCES
Italian sausages made
with minced pork and
pancetta. There are
many versions, some
highly spiced, others
seasoned with herbs
and garlic.

CERVELAT SALAMI
From Germany,
a minced beef and
pork sausage which is
lightly smoked and
gently seasoned.

NAPOLI
A thin sausage made from pork
and beef, and spiced with red and
black pepper.

BOCKWURST
Made from finely ground beef and pork and lightly smoked. Slightly larger than frankfurters, these can be used in the same way.

HOT CHORIZO
Classic sausage from Spain; made with pork, and highly spiced with pimento.

WHITE PUDDING
Made with white meat, usually finely ground pork, chicken or veal.

LUCANICA
An Italian, thin, pure pork sausage, usually seasoned with herbs.

LANCASHIRE BLACK PUDDING
The best black pudding is said to come from the north of England — Bury in particular. This is made from pig's blood, fat, oatmeal and seasoning. Traditionally fried in bacon fat for breakfast, now used in modern salads, fried crisp into cubes.

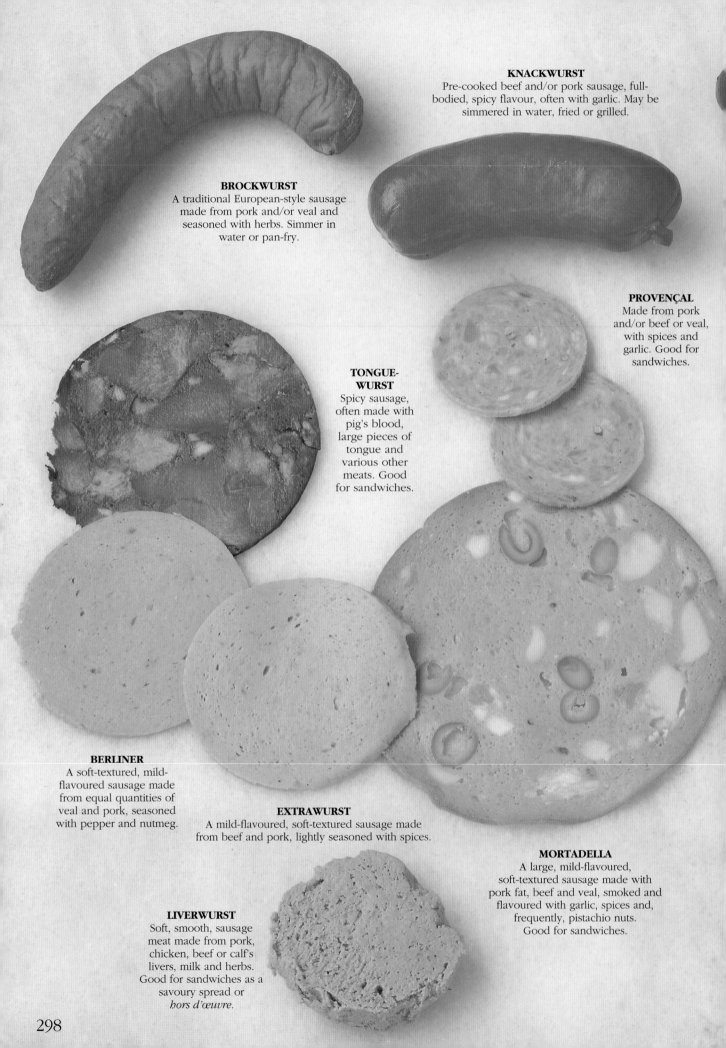

KNACKWURST
Pre-cooked beef and/or pork sausage, full-bodied, spicy flavour, often with garlic. May be simmered in water, fried or grilled.

BROCKWURST
A traditional European-style sausage made from pork and/or veal and seasoned with herbs. Simmer in water or pan-fry.

PROVENÇAL
Made from pork and/or beef or veal, with spices and garlic. Good for sandwiches.

TONGUE-WURST
Spicy sausage, often made with pig's blood, large pieces of tongue and various other meats. Good for sandwiches.

BERLINER
A soft-textured, mild-flavoured sausage made from equal quantities of veal and pork, seasoned with pepper and nutmeg.

EXTRAWURST
A mild-flavoured, soft-textured sausage made from beef and pork, lightly seasoned with spices.

MORTADELLA
A large, mild-flavoured, soft-textured sausage made with pork fat, beef and veal, smoked and flavoured with garlic, spices and, frequently, pistachio nuts. Good for sandwiches.

LIVERWURST
Soft, smooth, sausage meat made from pork, chicken, beef or calf's livers, milk and herbs. Good for sandwiches as a savoury spread or *hors d'œuvre*.

KRANSKY
A fairly coarse-textured sausage made from pork
and/or beef, smoked and strongly seasoned. Eat as
is, or simmer in water for a few minutes.

DEBRICINER
A traditional European-style sausage made from pork
and/or beef. Full-bodied flavour.

SCHAUESSEN
A traditional European-style sausage made from pork
and/or beef. Full-bodied flavour.

ALSACE
A traditional European-style sausage made from pork
and/or beef. Full-bodied flavour.

WESTPHALIAN
A traditional European-style sausage made from pork
and/or beef. Full-bodied flavour.

WEISSWURST
A delicate sausage (lit. 'white sausage') made with veal,
cream and eggs. Simmer in water.

BLACK PUDDING
A robust sausage made with pig's
blood, oatmeal and seasonings. May be
heated in simmering water or fried.

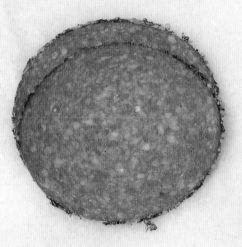

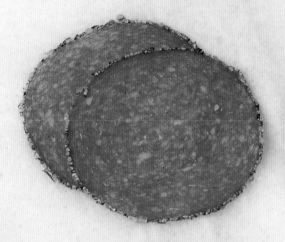

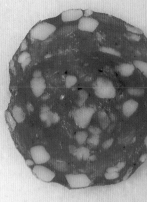

RED WINE, HERB AND GARLIC SALAMI
Spicy, but not hot, salami made from pork and/or beef, flavoured with red wine, herbs and garlic.

BLACK PEPPER AND BRANDY SALAMI
Spicy, hot salami made with pork and/or beef, flavoured with black pepper and brandy.

SICILIANO
A hot, salty salami with chewy texture made from pork and/or beef.

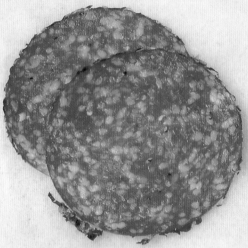

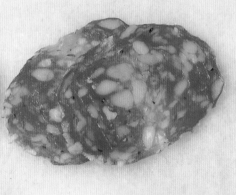

CHILLI SALAMI
Very hot salami made from pork and/or beef with spices and chillies.

CALABRESE
Moderately hot, spicy salami made with pork and/or beef, with chillies, spices, red wine and pieces of white fat.

FELINETTI
A luscious, mild salami made with pork and/or beef, white wine, peppercorns and garlic.

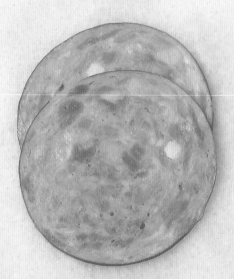

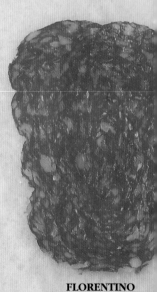

POLISH SALAMI
A non-spicy salami made with pork and/or beef, usually not too thinly sliced.

SPANISH SALAMI
A fine-textured, spicy, moderately hot salami made with pork and/or beef.

FLORENTINO
Moderately spicy salami made from pork and/or beef.

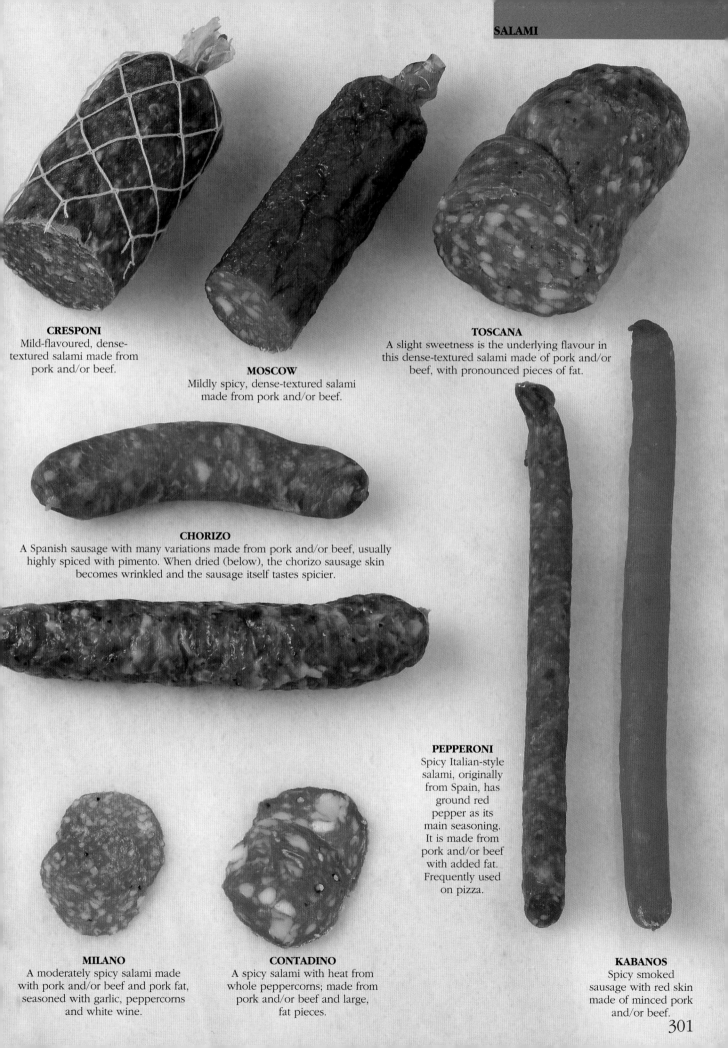

CRESPONI
Mild-flavoured, dense-textured salami made from pork and/or beef.

MOSCOW
Mildly spicy, dense-textured salami made from pork and/or beef.

TOSCANA
A slight sweetness is the underlying flavour in this dense-textured salami made of pork and/or beef, with pronounced pieces of fat.

CHORIZO
A Spanish sausage with many variations made from pork and/or beef, usually highly spiced with pimento. When dried (below), the chorizo sausage skin becomes wrinkled and the sausage itself tastes spicier.

PEPPERONI
Spicy Italian-style salami, originally from Spain, has ground red pepper as its main seasoning. It is made from pork and/or beef with added fat. Frequently used on pizza.

MILANO
A moderately spicy salami made with pork and/or beef and pork fat, seasoned with garlic, peppercorns and white wine.

CONTADINO
A spicy salami with heat from whole peppercorns; made from pork and/or beef and large, fat pieces.

KABANOS
Spicy smoked sausage with red skin made of minced pork and/or beef.

301

CASALINGA
This small salami may be either hot or mild. Usually made from pork and/or beef, with garlic and spices.

ITALIAN SALAMI
A non-spicy salami made from pork and/or beef, with little pieces of red pepper.

CAYENNE SALAMI
Very hot salami made from pork and/or beef, with cayenne pepper.

BELGIAN SALAMI
A hot, spicy salami made from pork and/or beef.

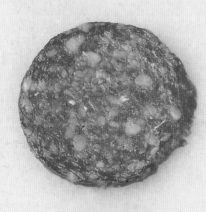

METTWURST
A soft-textured, German-type salami made with fresh pork; with and without garlic.

WHITE HUNGARIAN SALAMI
Takes its name from its white skin. Made from pork and/or beef and spices. Mildly flavoured.

GYULAI
A mildly spicy salami, originally from Hungary, made from pork and/or beef, smoked, with red pepper.

DANISH SALAMI
Coarse-textured, bright red colour, seasoned with garlic and pepper; made from pork and/or beef.

HOT HUNGARIAN SALAMI
A spicy, hot salami made from pork and/or beef and spices. As with all salamis, the flavour intensifies with age.

CACCIATORE
May be either hot or
mild; made from pork
and/or beef with garlic
and spices. Traditionally
small, so that a hunter
(*cacciatore*) could carry
a few in his pocket.

TWIGGY
Thin, spicy sausage
made from pork and/or
beef. Ideal for school
lunch boxes and
cocktail snacks.

PIZZA SALAMI
Especially for pizzas, a full
spicy flavour made from pork
and/or beef.

CSABAI
This Hungarian-type sausage
may be either mild or hot. It
is made from pork and/or
beef, seasoned with paprika
and peppercorns.

303

NEW YORK-STYLE PASTRAMI
Cured and spiced cold meat from the
eye of silverside. Dry-cooked, rubbed with chilli and
black peppercorns. Very lean, spicy meat. Slice
thinly for sandwiches.

AMERICAN-STYLE PASTRAMI
Cured and spiced cold meat, from the eye of
silverside. Dry-cooked, rubbed with chilli
and black peppercorns, this pastrami is
milder in flavour than New York-style
pastrami. Slice thinly for sandwiches.

BILTONG
Also known as
jerky. Dried strips
of very lean beef or
game, originally
from South Africa.
Can be grated or
sliced, but eat in
moderation, as
biltong swells in
the stomach and
can cause a
bloated feeling.

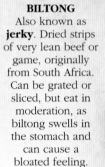

SMOKED BEEF
Silverside of beef which is cured and cold smoked.
This Dutch speciality is lean, with a subtle, salty,
smoky flavour, and should be cut very thinly for
sandwiches or cold meat platters.

SILVERSIDE

Cured, rolled brisket of beef; should have a clear,
rosy colour and a moist texture. Use for salads
or sandwiches.

SALT BEEF
Cured brisket of beef; should have a clear, rosy colour and a dry texture. Usually has a layer
of fat on one side, which may be removed. Use for salads or sandwiches.

PÂTÉ DE TÊTE
Originally only the head of the pig was used, but now other meats are included. A form of brawn set in gelatin. Use on sandwiches or as a light summer lunch with salad.

HURE DE PORC
Hure (head) is made of meat from the head of the pig, including the tongue. A form of brawn set in gelatin. Use on sandwiches or as a light lunch with a salad.

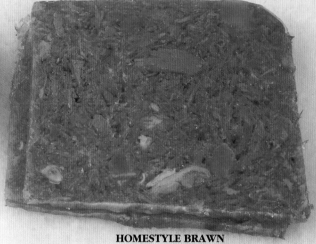

FANCY BRAWN
Originally made entirely from the head of the pig, but now other meats are used as well. Small pieces of red and green pepper are added, as well as gherkin. Set in gelatin. Use on sandwiches or as a light lunch with a salad.

HOMESTYLE BRAWN
Originally made entirely from the head of the pig, but now other meats are used as well. Set in gelatin. This mild-flavoured, cold meat is used on sandwiches or as a light lunch with a salad.

TERRINE
A mixture of meat, it may contain pork and pork products (such as bacon, speck or pancetta), beef, veal, lamb, poultry, and liver. It is usually highly seasoned and bound with egg. Originally cooked in a vessel called a 'terrine'. Serve sliced as a light lunch with a salad and cornichons.

PÂTÉ
The most famous — *pâté de foie gras* — is made with the liver of fattened goose. Pâté usually is a smooth mixture of puréed liver with other flavours, such as Grand Marnier, but the lines between pâté and terrine are sometimes blurred, so we may see a pâté with coarse pieces or a terrine which is smooth.

Poultry & game

There's nothing more welcoming than walking into a house where there's chicken roasting in the oven — delicious aromas wafting, all golden crisp skin on the outside and tender flesh within.

About 400 years ago, Henry IV of France (1589–1610) thought so highly of chicken that he pronounced, "I want there to be no peasant in my kingdom so poor that he cannot have a chicken in his pot every Sunday."

Today, chickens are more readily available and affordable, than even 40 years ago, due to improved conditions in farming. We have the choice of cornfed, free-range, organic and farmhouse, all available as whole birds or in joints and cuts to suit modern cooking.

Even turkey, once reserved as the celebration bird for Christmas, is now available all year round, again whole or as joints and cuts.

Duck, guinea fowl, poussin, quail and pigeon can also often be found in butcher's shops and food halls. However, the very special treats such as pheasant, partridge, grouse, wild duck and woodcock are only available in the game season, and can be bought by true devotees, still in feather.

Furred game also has its seasonal restrictions. However, venison, for instance, is farmed as well, making it readily available as a healthy alternative to other red meat. But real game enthusiasts will still opt for the wild variety because of its firmer texture and full gamy flavour.

Rabbit is also farmed and found jointed and ready to cook in many supermarkets. It is tender and flavoursome but, again, a true game fan will still opt for wild rabbits and hares bought from game butchers and poulterers. Wild rabbit and hare need longer and slower cooking, and they will benefit from robust marination.

**CHICKEN,
TIED AND DRESSED**
Ready-to-cook chicken,
trussed for the oven.

POULET NOIR
A black-legged chicken
from France, revered for its
superior flavour.

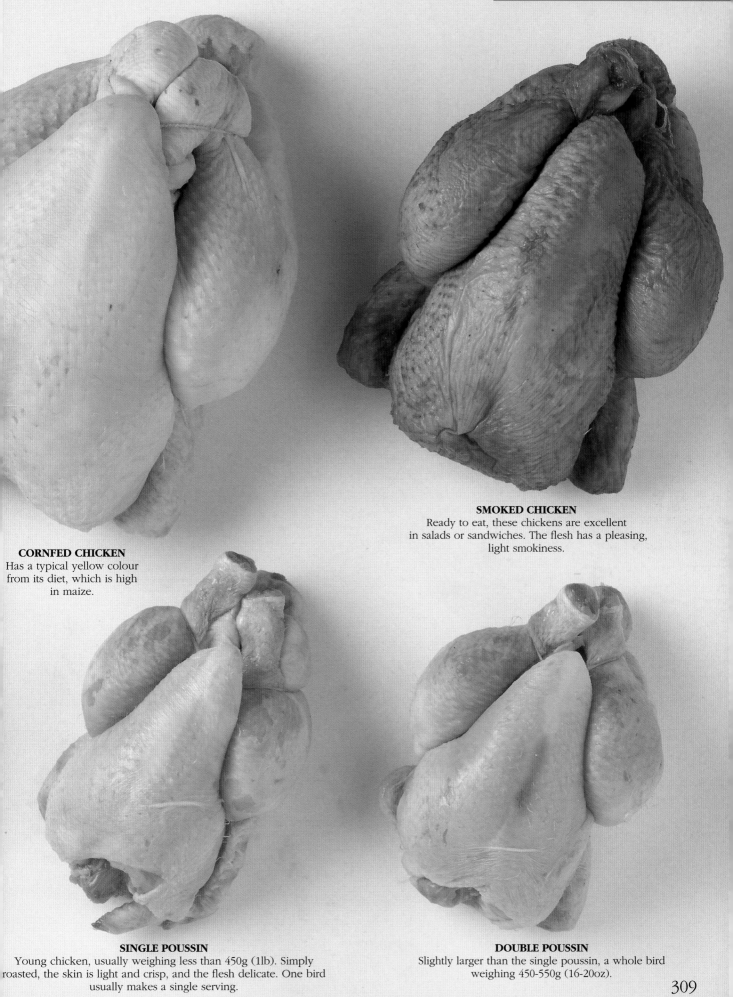

SMOKED CHICKEN
Ready to eat, these chickens are excellent
in salads or sandwiches. The flesh has a pleasing,
light smokiness.

CORNFED CHICKEN
Has a typical yellow colour
from its diet, which is high
in maize.

SINGLE POUSSIN
Young chicken, usually weighing less than 450g (1lb). Simply
roasted, the skin is light and crisp, and the flesh delicate. One bird
usually makes a single serving.

DOUBLE POUSSIN
Slightly larger than the single poussin, a whole bird
weighing 450-550g (16-20oz).

309

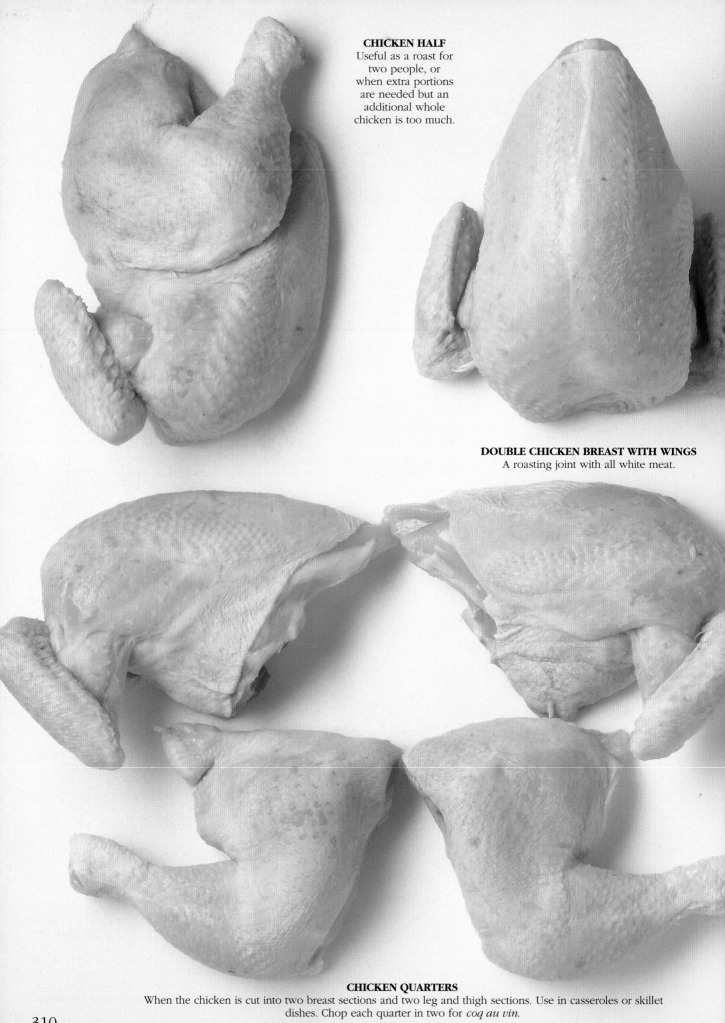

CHICKEN HALF
Useful as a roast for
two people, or
when extra portions
are needed but an
additional whole
chicken is too much.

DOUBLE CHICKEN BREAST WITH WINGS
A roasting joint with all white meat.

CHICKEN QUARTERS
When the chicken is cut into two breast sections and two leg and thigh sections. Use in casseroles or skillet
dishes. Chop each quarter in two for *coq au vin*.

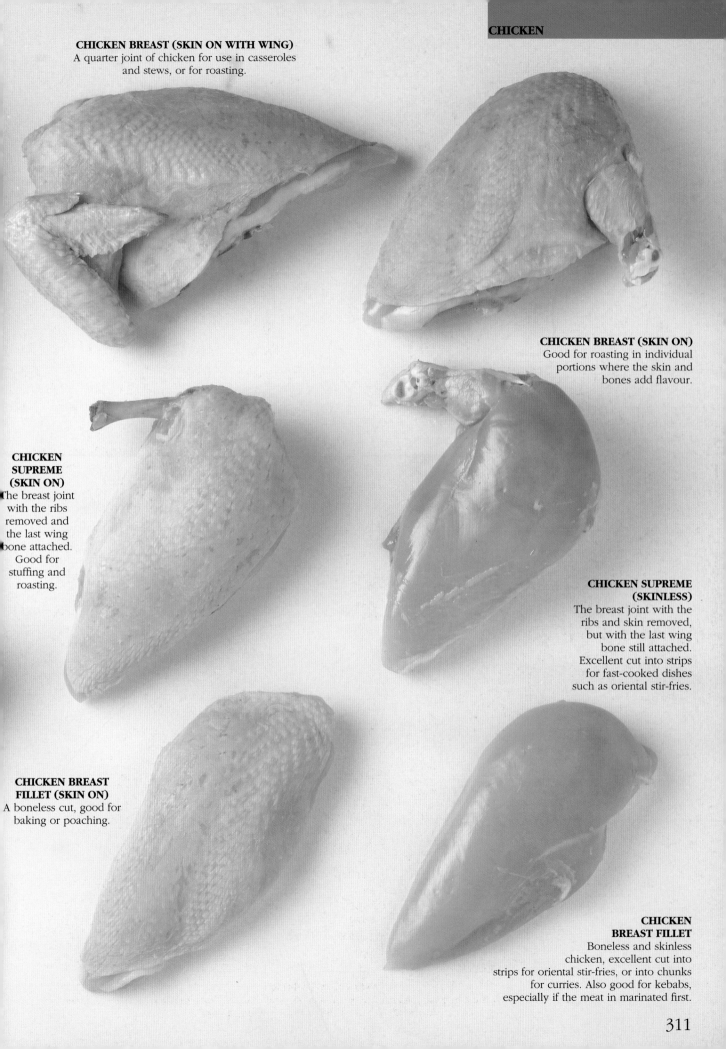

CHICKEN BREAST (SKIN ON WITH WING)
A quarter joint of chicken for use in casseroles and stews, or for roasting.

CHICKEN BREAST (SKIN ON)
Good for roasting in individual portions where the skin and bones add flavour.

CHICKEN SUPREME (SKIN ON)
The breast joint with the ribs removed and the last wing bone attached. Good for stuffing and roasting.

CHICKEN SUPREME (SKINLESS)
The breast joint with the ribs and skin removed, but with the last wing bone still attached. Excellent cut into strips for fast-cooked dishes such as oriental stir-fries.

CHICKEN BREAST FILLET (SKIN ON)
A boneless cut, good for baking or poaching.

CHICKEN BREAST FILLET
Boneless and skinless chicken, excellent cut into strips for oriental stir-fries, or into chunks for curries. Also good for kebabs, especially if the meat in marinated first.

311

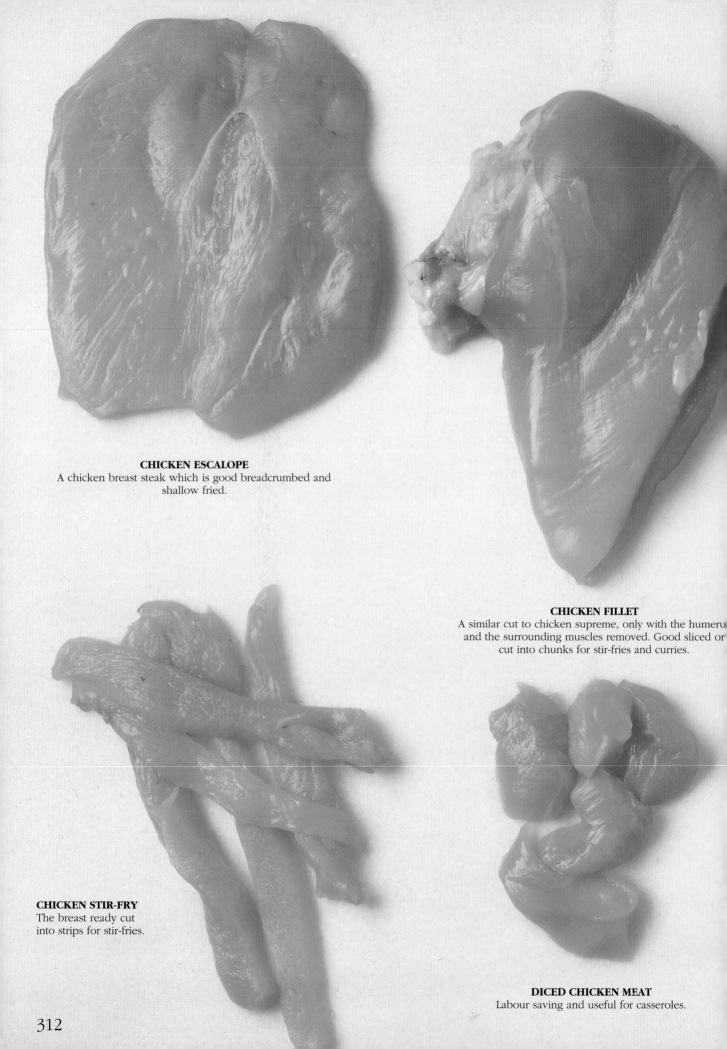

CHICKEN ESCALOPE
A chicken breast steak which is good breadcrumbed and
shallow fried.

CHICKEN FILLET
A similar cut to chicken supreme, only with the humeru
and the surrounding muscles removed. Good sliced or
cut into chunks for stir-fries and curries.

CHICKEN STIR-FRY
The breast ready cut
into strips for stir-fries.

DICED CHICKEN MEAT
Labour saving and useful for casseroles.

CHICKEN WING
They used to be confined to the stockpot, but these days they are marinated in soy, or painted with a mix of balsamic vinegar and runny honey, then roasted to make crisp, flavourful snacks.

CHICKEN WING TIP
Usually cut off the wings before roasting, these can be added to the stockpot.

CHICKEN WING, CENTRE CUT WITH WING TIP
Best baked, brushed with honey and soy, and used as finger food.

MINCED CHICKEN
erfect for low-fat burgers, also as a beef substitute for cottage pie, lasagnes and meatballs.

CHICKEN LIVER
One of the most underrated parts of the chicken, livers are inexpensive but deliciously tender and delicately flavoured. Use for smooth pâtés flavoured with brandy, or skillet dishes tossed with balsamic vinegar. Also chop and mix with ham for lasagne fillings or spaghetti topping.

CHICKEN CARCASS
The basis for chicken stock. Chop it roughly and place in a pan full of water with chopped onion, carrot and celery. Boil, covered, for an hour, topping up when necessary. Strain and discard bones and skin stock. Reduce before seasoning.

313

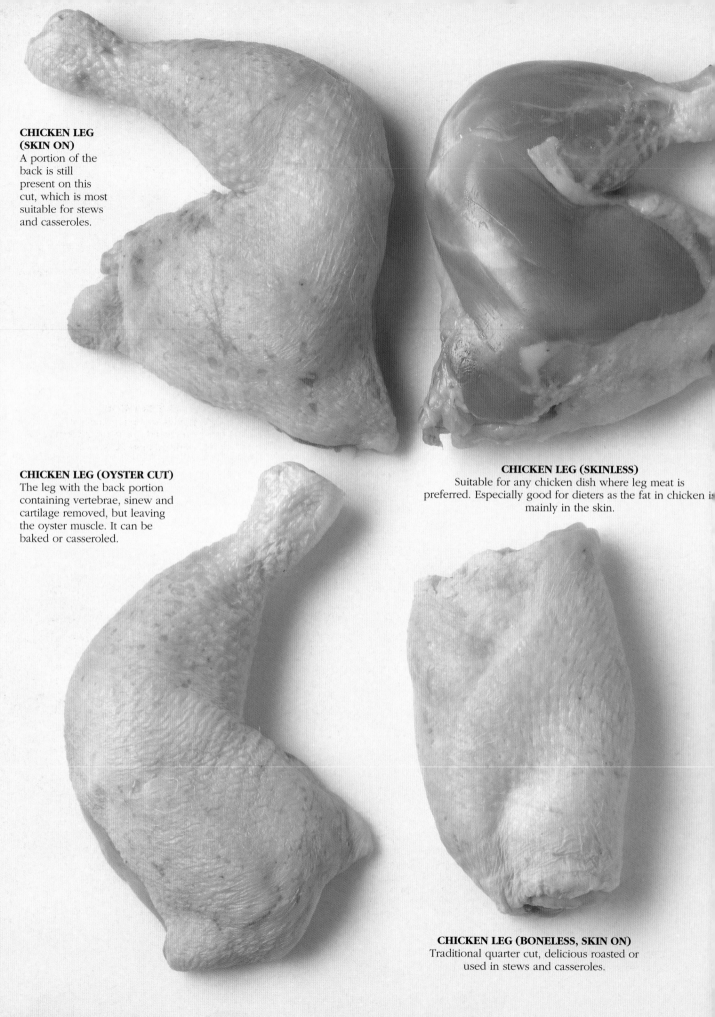

CHICKEN LEG (SKIN ON)
A portion of the back is still present on this cut, which is most suitable for stews and casseroles.

CHICKEN LEG (OYSTER CUT)
The leg with the back portion containing vertebrae, sinew and cartilage removed, but leaving the oyster muscle. It can be baked or casseroled.

CHICKEN LEG (SKINLESS)
Suitable for any chicken dish where leg meat is preferred. Especially good for dieters as the fat in chicken is mainly in the skin.

CHICKEN LEG (BONELESS, SKIN ON)
Traditional quarter cut, delicious roasted or used in stews and casseroles.

314

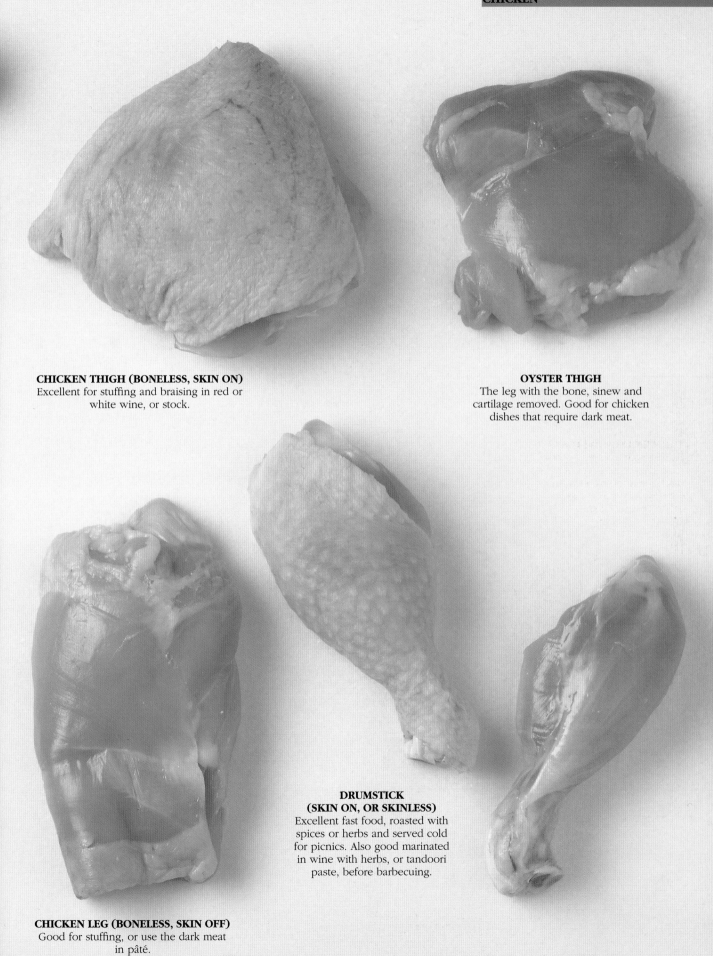

CHICKEN THIGH (BONELESS, SKIN ON)
Excellent for stuffing and braising in red or
white wine, or stock.

OYSTER THIGH
The leg with the bone, sinew and
cartilage removed. Good for chicken
dishes that require dark meat.

**DRUMSTICK
(SKIN ON, OR SKINLESS)**
Excellent fast food, roasted with
spices or herbs and served cold
for picnics. Also good marinated
in wine with herbs, or tandoori
paste, before barbecuing.

CHICKEN LEG (BONELESS, SKIN OFF)
Good for stuffing, or use the dark meat
in pâté.

315

HEN TURKEY
Generally, hen birds are used for oven-ready turkeys, as they are smaller than the males and have sweeter flesh.

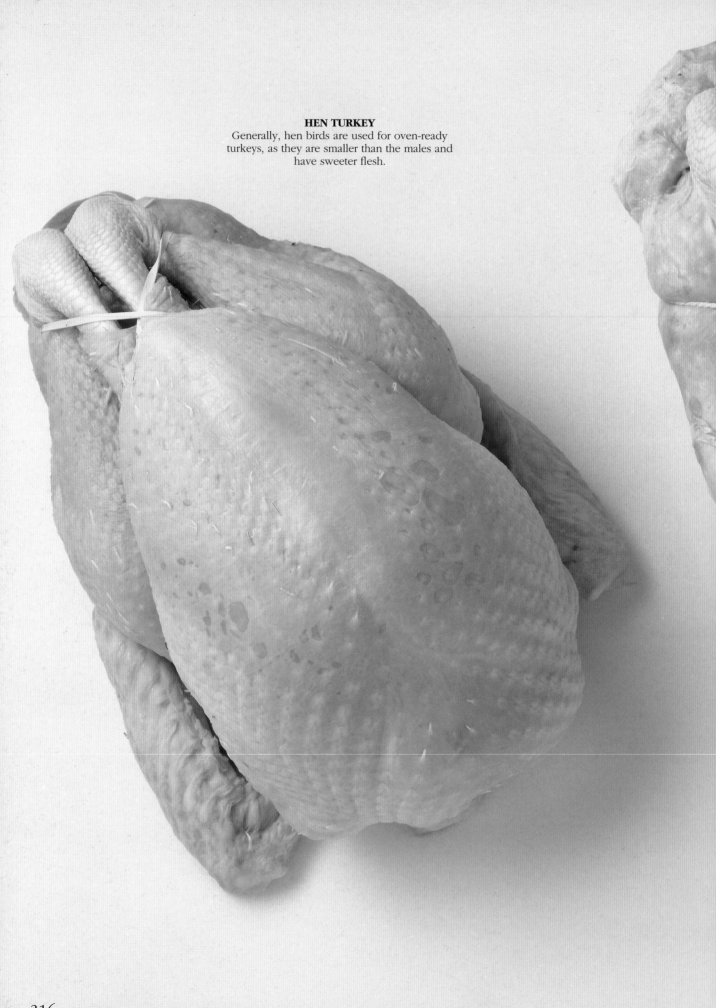

STAG TURKEY
The male birds are about 40 per cent larger than the hens, have a plumper breast, and are usually sold as turkey portions. Specialist farmers sell both hens and stags for roasting. The flesh of the stag is usually firmer.

317

TURKEY CROWN
An easy-to-carve roasting joint of
breast on the bone with the wing
bones attached.

TURKEY THIGH
The meaty part of the leg. Use chopped
for stews, or as mince.

TURKEY SUPREME (SKIN
Turkey breast on the bone w
the wing bone still attached. C
for roasting.

TURKEY BUTTERFLY
Crown roast with the bone in.

TURKEY, DOUBLE BREAST
The whole breast portion of the
bird, still on the bone. A tender
roasting joint.

**TURKEY SUPREME
(SKINLESS)**
A low-fat roasting
joint for two.

TURKEY ESCALOPE
The skinless turkey breast sliced
into thin steaks. Grill, pan fry or cut
into strips for stir-fries.

TURKEY LEG
The whole leg makes
an inexpensive roasting
joint for two, or it can
be used for stews.

**TURKEY LEG
(BONELESS, SKIN ON)**
A good, small, roasting
joint, or use for pot roasts.

**TURKEY LEG
(BONELESS, SKINLESS)**
Good in pot roasts.

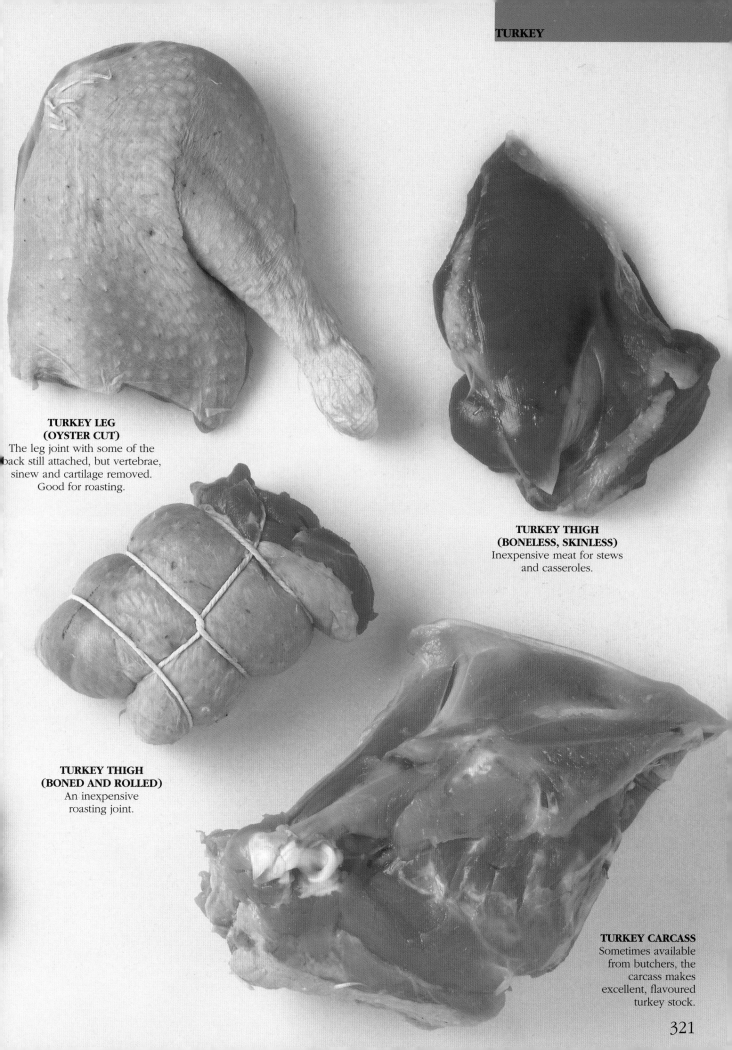

**TURKEY LEG
(OYSTER CUT)**
The leg joint with some of the
back still attached, but vertebrae,
sinew and cartilage removed.
Good for roasting.

**TURKEY THIGH
(BONELESS, SKINLESS)**
Inexpensive meat for stews
and casseroles.

**TURKEY THIGH
(BONED AND ROLLED)**
An inexpensive
roasting joint.

TURKEY CARCASS
Sometimes available
from butchers, the
carcass makes
excellent, flavoured
turkey stock.

DEBEN DUCK
From Suffolk, the style is a cross between a Peking and a Gressingham duck, both renowned for their excellent flavour and succulent flesh.

WATERMEADOW DUCK
A duck similar in character to those used by the Chinese for the dish, Peking Duck. Consequently, it is good for oriental dishes.

GOOSE
The original traditional Christmas roast bird, and still the main choice in parts of Europe. Excellently flavoured, its carcass is large in proportion to its limbs. Nevertheless, there is still dark meat to be had. During cooking, it produces copious amounts of fat which should be poured away from the roasting tin, but which can be used separately for roasting potatoes. Red cabbage is the traditional accompaniment.

BARBARY DUCK
Also known as
Muscovy duck. It is a
breed that has less fat
than others, and
produces the firm,
musky-flavoured meat
favoured by the French.
Excellent roasted.

GRESSINGHAM DUCK
A famous English duck,
somewhere between a
Peking and mallard in style.
The flesh is sturdy.

323

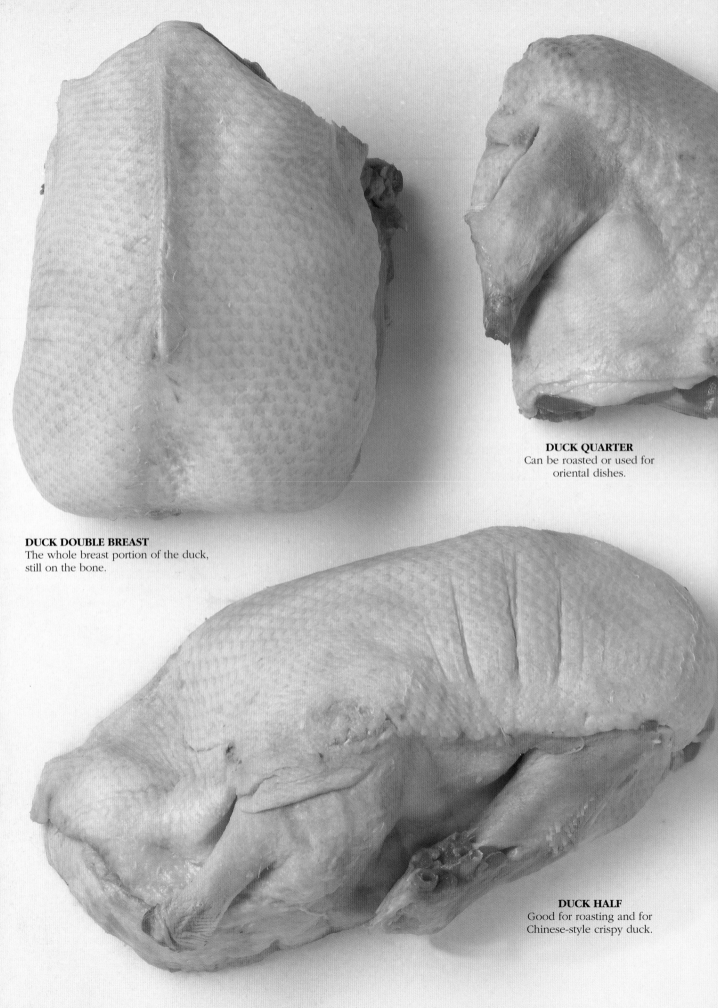

DUCK QUARTER
Can be roasted or used for
oriental dishes.

DUCK DOUBLE BREAST
The whole breast portion of the duck,
still on the bone.

DUCK HALF
Good for roasting and for
Chinese-style crispy duck.

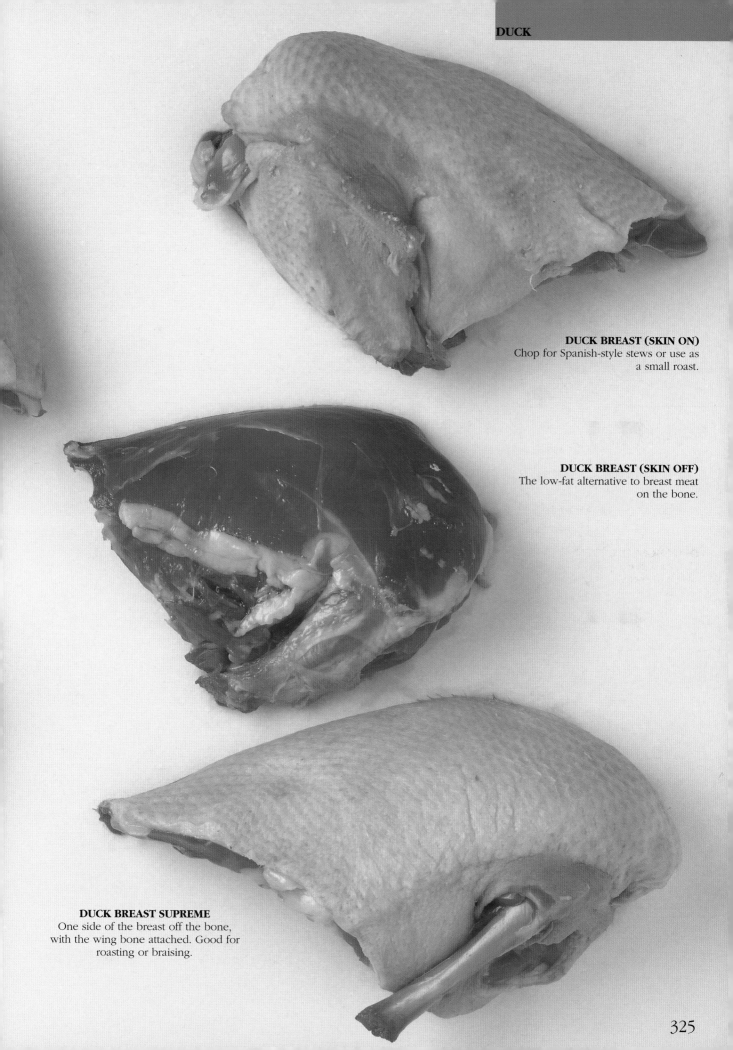

DUCK BREAST (SKIN ON)
Chop for Spanish-style stews or use as
a small roast.

DUCK BREAST (SKIN OFF)
The low-fat alternative to breast meat
on the bone.

DUCK BREAST SUPREME
One side of the breast off the bone,
with the wing bone attached. Good for
roasting or braising.

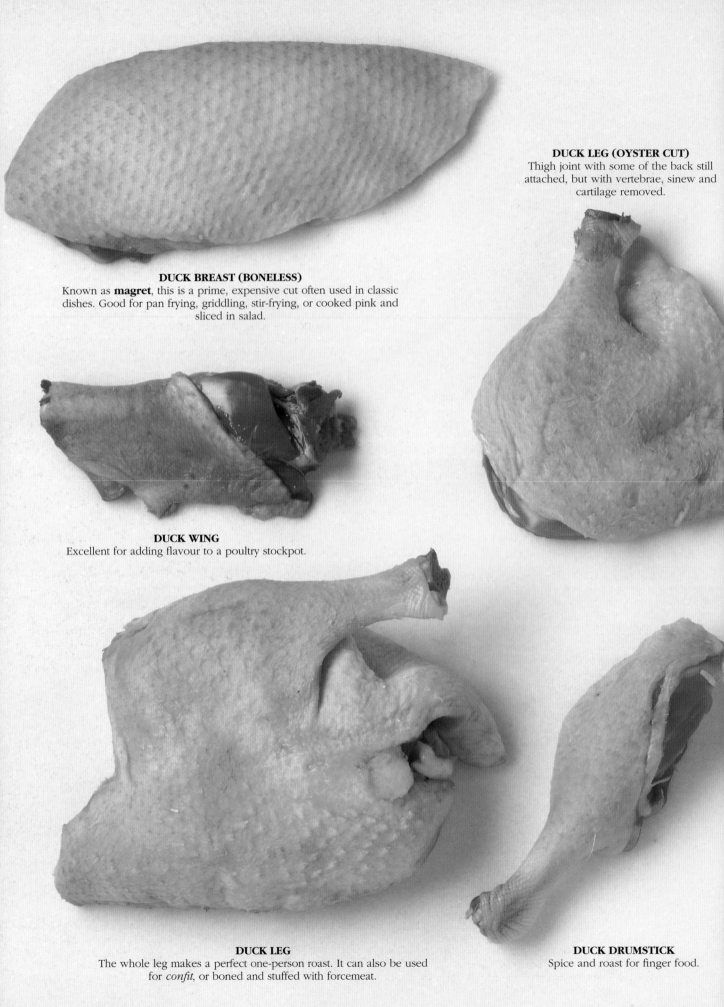

DUCK LEG (OYSTER CUT)
Thigh joint with some of the back still attached, but with vertebrae, sinew and cartilage removed.

DUCK BREAST (BONELESS)
Known as **magret**, this is a prime, expensive cut often used in classic dishes. Good for pan frying, griddling, stir-frying, or cooked pink and sliced in salad.

DUCK WING
Excellent for adding flavour to a poultry stockpot.

DUCK LEG
The whole leg makes a perfect one-person roast. It can also be used for *confit*, or boned and stuffed with forcemeat.

DUCK DRUMSTICK
Spice and roast for finger food.

DUCK THIGH (BONELESS, SKINLESS)
The meaty part of the leg, used for stews.

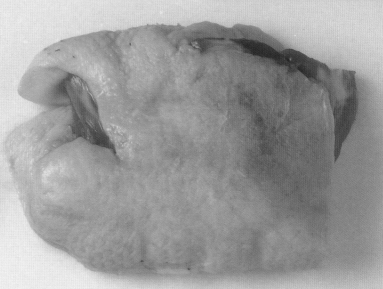

DUCK THIGH (BONE IN, SKIN ON)
A good casserole cut since the bones enrich the gravy. Very tasty cooked with chickpeas and tomatoes.

MINCED DUCK
Breast and leg meat minced. It is often used to make a coarsely textured country pâté, mixed with chopped streaky bacon, orange and Cointreau or brandy.

DUCK LIVER
Top quality liver which makes excellent, smooth pâté on its own, or mixed with pig's liver. A skillet meat, it also makes a wonderful breakfast dish served fried and on toast with lots of black pepper.

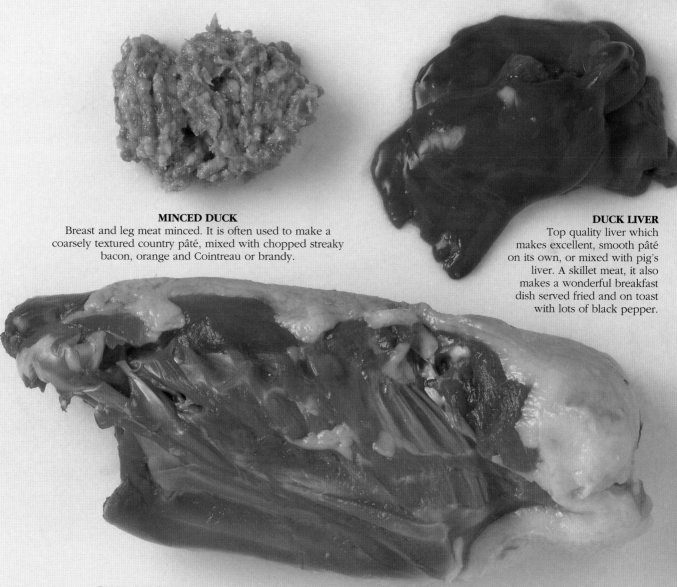

DUCK CARCASS
For the stockpot, carcasses are available from some butchers and game merchants. Simmer in water with carrots, onion, leeks and herbs.

WOODCOCK
A wading bird with a long bill,
one bird per person is required for
eating. When roasted, these birds are
not drawn or decapitated, although
the gizzard is removed before
cooking. The bill can be used to truss
the bird. English season is October 1
to January 31, Scottish season is
September 1 to January 31.

PHEASANT

Native to China, these birds are now found all over Europe. Hen birds are smaller, considered more tender and have sweeter flesh. Cocks may benefit from a marinade to soften the flesh for roasting, depending on the age. In general, older birds are more suitable for slow cooking in a pot roast or casserole. A cock and a hen bird together are called a brace. Season is October 1 to February 1.

WOOD PIGEON

One bird is required per person. There is very little meat on the legs, and often the tender plump breast is removed from the bone, pan-fried and sliced for warm salads. It is also good for game terrines, and pot roasts. Available all year round.

RED-LEGGED PARTRIDGE
Also known as the **French partridge**,
it was brought from France to Britain,
where it now thrives, by Charles II. Young
partridges have the texture of chicken but
a stronger taste, and are excellent for
roasting, while older birds need slow
cooking. The season is from
September 1 to February 1.

GREY-LEGGED PARTRIDGE
Native to Britain, it is reputedly a
better table bird than the red-legged
partridge because it is sweeter and
more succulent. Excellent roasted, it is
in season from September 1 to
February 1.

MALE MALLARD
A flavoursome, succulent bird
when roasted young with a little
fat. Older birds – and most are –
need long, slow casseroling,
preferably with a spell in a red
wine marinade first. Season
September 1 to January 31.

FEMALE MALLARD
Smaller birds than the male, and
usually more tender.
Season September 1 to January 31.

SQUAB
Columba palumbus
Plucked young wood pigeon which is ready for roasting. The breast meat is best. Available all year round.

PARTRIDGE
Perdix spp.
Flesh has the texture and flavour, only stronger, of chicken. Season is September 1 to February 1.

PHEASANT
Phasianidae spp.
With a full flavour, the cock bird provides two ample portions when roasted. Season is October 1 to February 1.

MALLARD
Anas platyrhynchos
One of Britain's best known and most delicious wild ducks, it has rich, gamy, dark meat. It is one of the best game birds for eating. Season is September 1 to January 31.

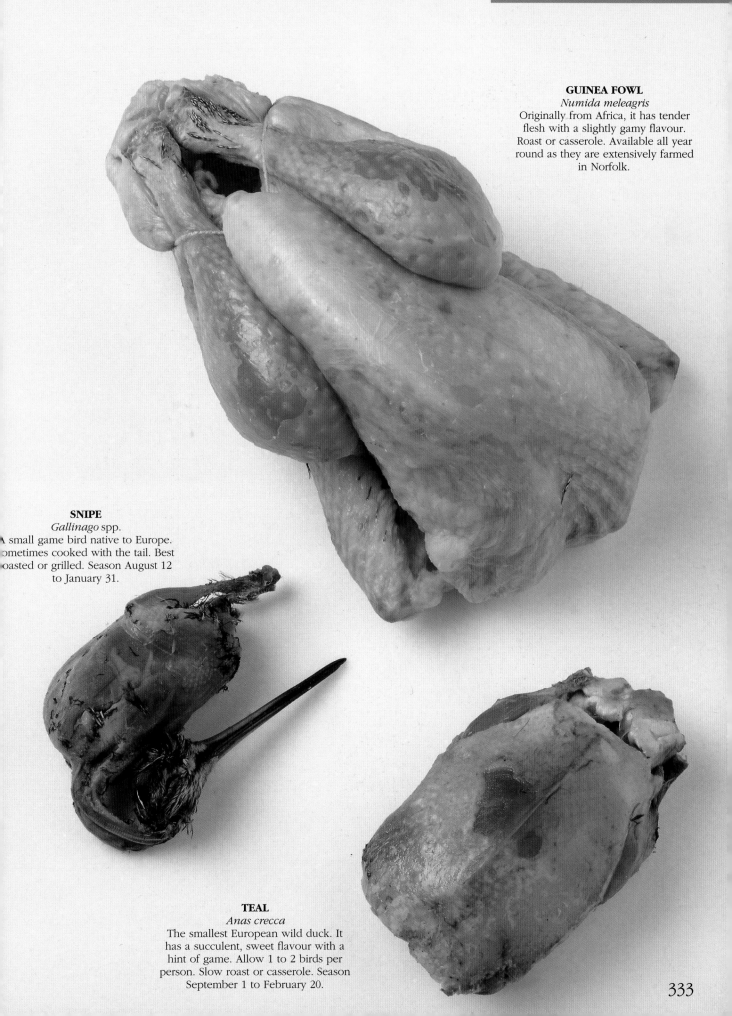

GUINEA FOWL
Numida meleagris
Originally from Africa, it has tender
flesh with a slightly gamy flavour.
Roast or casserole. Available all year
round as they are extensively farmed
in Norfolk.

SNIPE
Gallinago spp.
A small game bird native to Europe.
Sometimes cooked with the tail. Best
roasted or grilled. Season August 12
to January 31.

TEAL
Anas crecca
The smallest European wild duck. It
has a succulent, sweet flavour with a
hint of game. Allow 1 to 2 birds per
person. Slow roast or casserole. Season
September 1 to February 20.

333

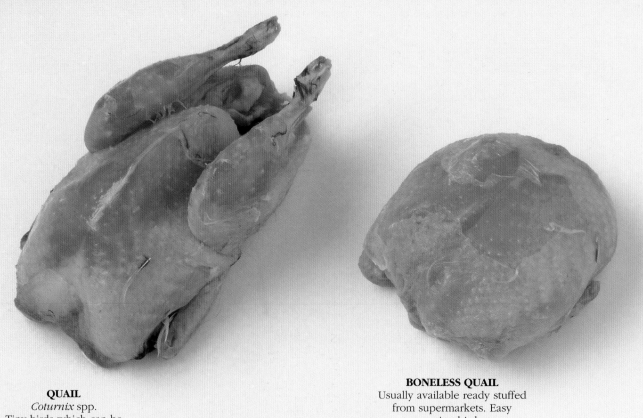

QUAIL
Coturnix spp.
Tiny birds which can be
roasted, sautéed,
barbecued or grilled.
Allow at least 1 bird per
person. Available all year
now they are farmed.

BONELESS QUAIL
Usually available ready stuffed
from supermarkets. Easy
carving birds.

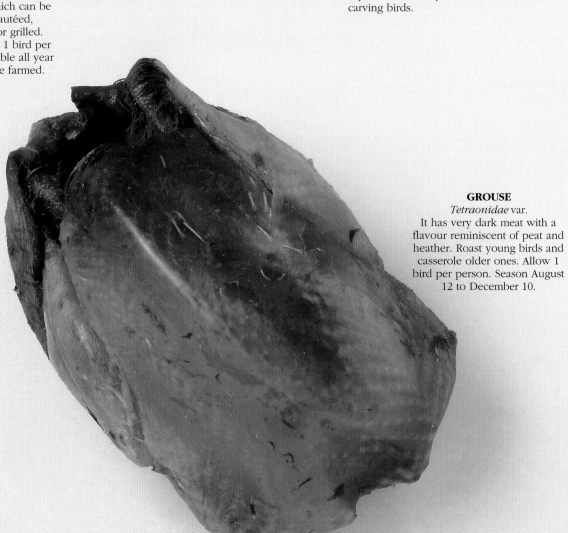

GROUSE
Tetraonidae var.
It has very dark meat with a
flavour reminiscent of peat and
heather. Roast young birds and
casserole older ones. Allow 1
bird per person. Season August
12 to December 10.

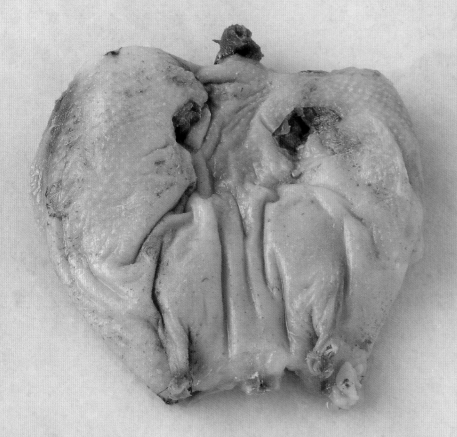

MUTTON-BIRD
Puffinus tenuirostris
Having been fed by their parents on small fish, these birds are exceedingly oily and salty. Bring to the boil in water three times, changing the water each time, before roasting or grilling. Also available smoked or pickled in brine.

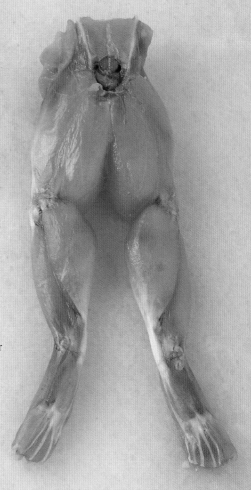

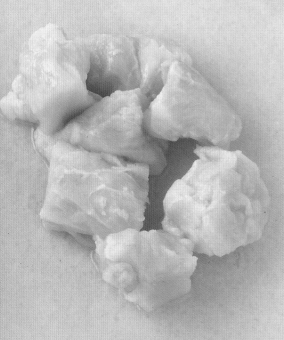

FROG'S LEGS
Rana esculenta
With delicate texture and flavour reminiscent of chicken, these are the hind legs of the frog, which are its only edible part. Look for pairs of legs that are plump and pink. Cook briefly, as over-cooking will toughen them. Pan-fry.

CROCODILE
Crocodylidae spp.
This white meat's taste is reminiscent of pork and chicken, and the flesh is fairly watery, not tough, but fibrous. Marinating improves the flavour. Cook briefly, as over-cooking will toughen the meat. May be chopped and shaped into patties. Pan-fry.

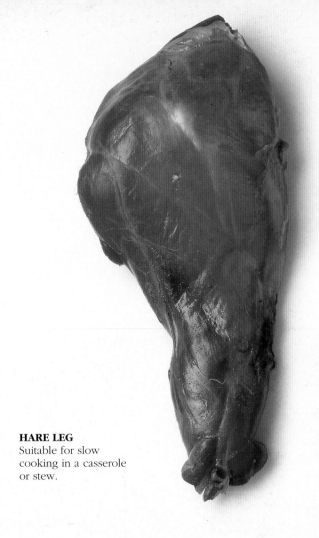

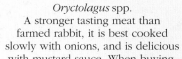

WILD RABBIT
Oryctolagus spp.
A stronger tasting meat than farmed rabbit, it is best cooked slowly with onions, and is delicious with mustard sauce. When buying, choose one that is well rounded rather than long and lanky. Half a small rabbit is usually sufficient per person.

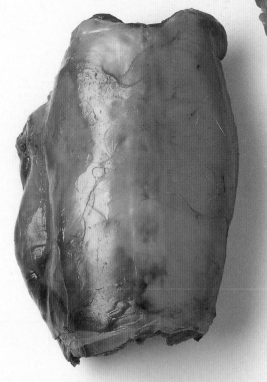

HARE LEG
Suitable for slow cooking in a casserole or stew.

HARE
Lepus spp.
Large and meaty, hares can weigh up to 5.5kg (12lb). The flesh is rich and gamy. Marinating in red wine enhances the flavour and tenderises the fibres. The most famous dish for this game is jugged hare, a slow-cooked casserole, traditionally thickened with the blood of the animal.

HARE SADDLE
A prime cut from the back of the hare. It includes the most tender meat, and is the best cut for roasting.

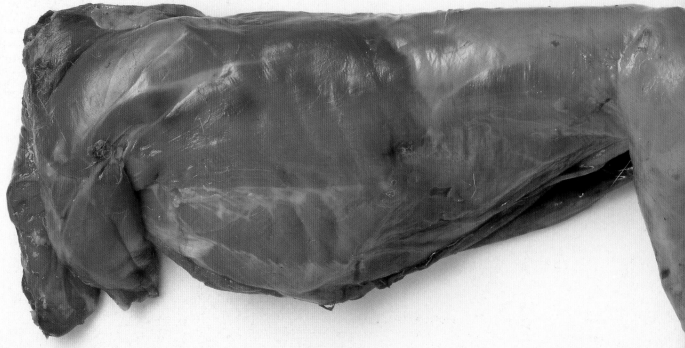

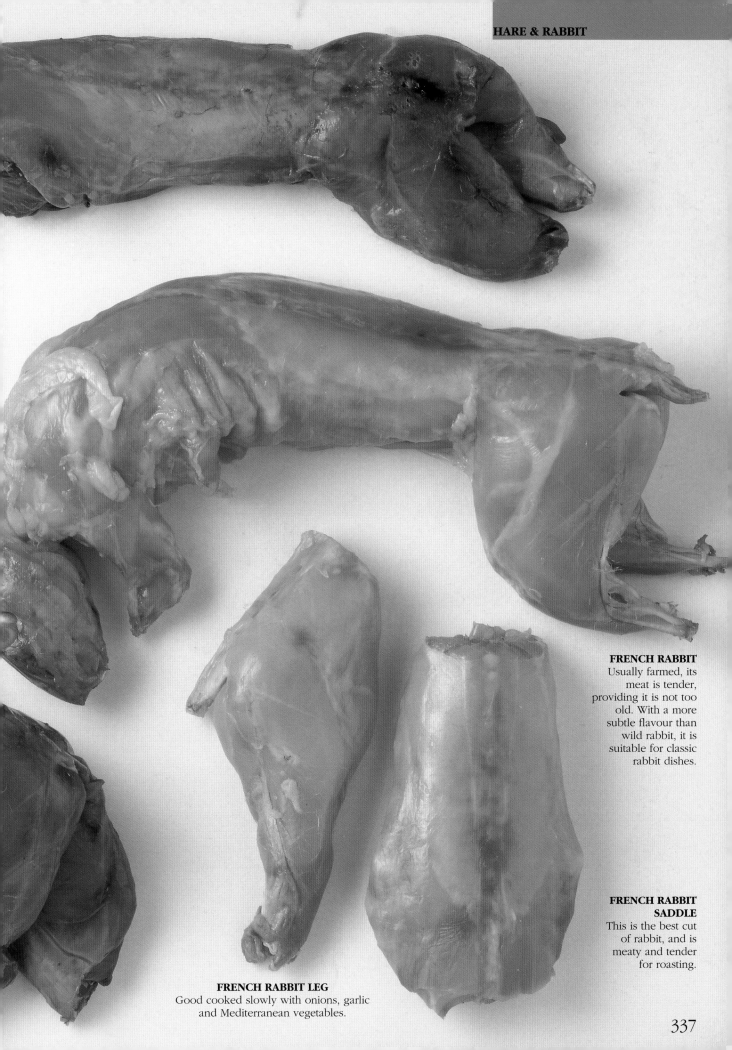

FRENCH RABBIT
Usually farmed, its meat is tender, providing it is not too old. With a more subtle flavour than wild rabbit, it is suitable for classic rabbit dishes.

FRENCH RABBIT SADDLE
This is the best cut of rabbit, and is meaty and tender for roasting.

FRENCH RABBIT LEG
Good cooked slowly with onions, garlic and Mediterranean vegetables.

337

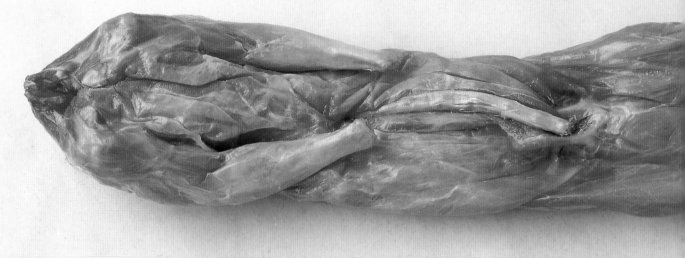

OPOSSUM
Trichosurus spp.
The lean, tightly grained meat of the wild brush-tail possum from Tasmania has a faint eucalyptus flavour. Take care to remove the four musk sacs or the meat will be inedible. Roast, barbecue, stew.

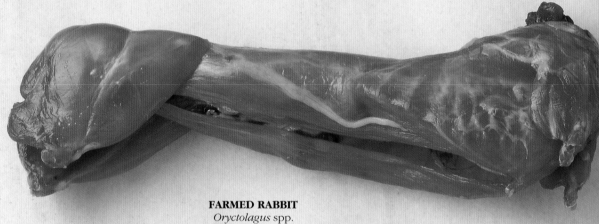

FARMED RABBIT
Oryctolagus spp.
This furry animal has lean meat and small, thin bones. The flesh of the farmed species is very pale with a delicate texture and flavour. Soak in cold, salted water for several hours before cooking. Stew, roast, sauté.

EMU
Dromaius
novaehollandiae
Emu meat was the first game meat to be farmed in Australia and the flavour is similar to, but less gamy than, venison. It is high in iron and low in cholesterol. Available as fillet or steaks. Roast, barbecue, pan-fry, smoke.

OSTRICH
Struthio camelus
Although ostrich is farmed primarily for its
feathers and skin, the lean meat is also
sold. A coarser texture than emu but,
cooked correctly, it is tender and succulent.
Roast, barbecue, pan-fry.

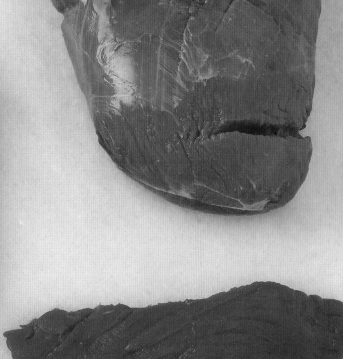

KANGAROO
Macropus spp.
The tender meat of the kangaroo is lean with a delicate flavour.
Every part of the animal may be eaten, from the head to the tail. As
with all low-fat meats, kangaroo is best when cooked rare to
medium rare. When overcooked, the meat is dry. Pan-fry, barbecue,
stir-fry, roast, casserole.

KANGAROO STEAK

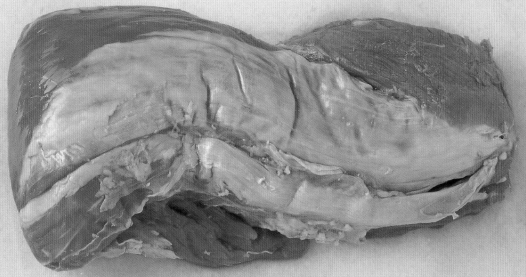

BUFFALO
Bubalus bubalus
The meat and the
individual cuts of
buffalo are similar to
beef, both in texture
and flavour.
Marinating improves
the flavour. The fillet
may be roasted or cut
into steaks and pan-
fried or barbecued.
Less tender cuts may
be casseroled.

339

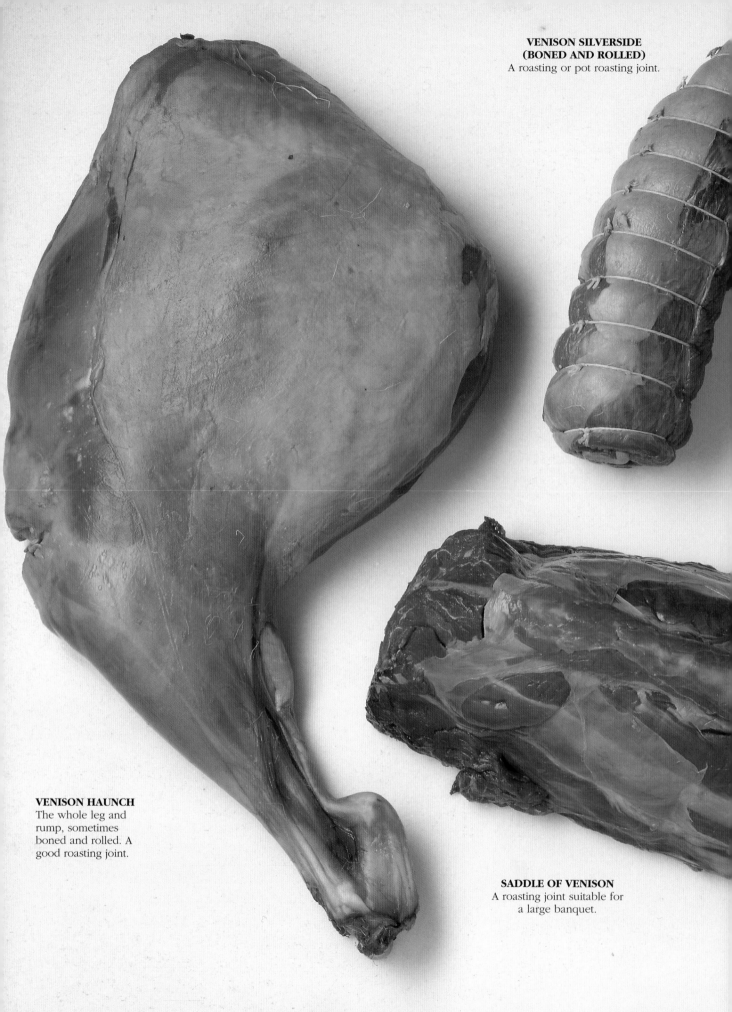

**VENISON SILVERSIDE
(BONED AND ROLLED)**
A roasting or pot roasting joint.

VENISON HAUNCH
The whole leg and
rump, sometimes
boned and rolled. A
good roasting joint.

SADDLE OF VENISON
A roasting joint suitable for
a large banquet.

340

**VENISON TOPSIDE
(BONED AND ROLLED)**
A roasting or pot roasting joint.

**VENISON
TOPSIDE STEAK**
Slices cut from the topside joint which can be
braised, or marinated and barbecued.

**VENISON HAUNCH
(BONED AND ROLLED)**
A tasty roasting joint.

341

VENISON SILVERSIDE (EX SALMON MUSCLE)
A good cut for stewing.

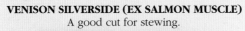

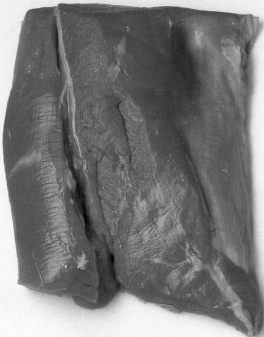

VENISON SALMON MUSCLE
The large muscle from which steaks are cut.

VENISON SILVERSIDE STEAK
A braising cut.

VENISON STRIPLOIN STEAK
Slices cut from the striploin — delicious when marinated before cooking.

DICED VENISON
Ideal for pies, terrines, pâtés, stews and soups.

VENISON SALMON STEAK
From the inside of the silverside, this is one of the most prized steaks for taste and texture. Good for grilling.

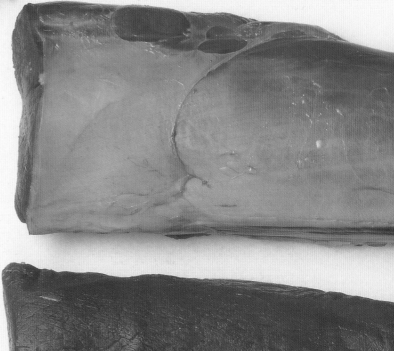

LARDER-TRIM VENISON STRIPLOIN STEAK
An extremely tender cut, sliced from the larder-trim striploin.

VENISON THICK FLANK
A prime cut for grilling or
barbecuing.

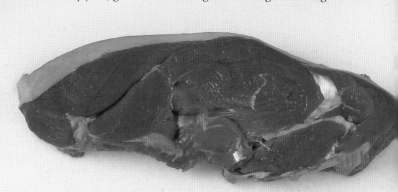

VENISON RUMP
A meaty joint, good for marinating and braising or roasting.

VENISON THICK FLANK STEAK
Also known as **toprump**, it is a prime cut which can be
rolled and roasted.

VENISON RUMP STEAK
Good for marinating and grilling or barbecuing.

VENISON SAUSAGES
Designer sausages flavoured with
herbs and spices, sometimes
including juniper.

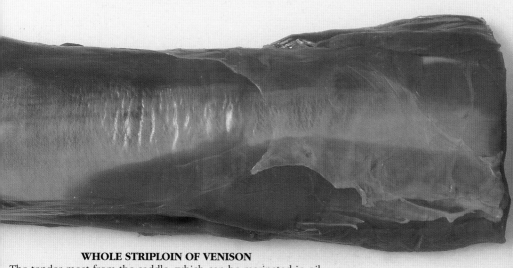

WHOLE STRIPLOIN OF VENISON
The tender meat from the saddle, which can be marinated in oil,
vinegar and juniper berries before roasting.

**LARDER TRIM
VENISON STRIPLOIN**
Prepared from the
striploin, it is cleaned of
skin, muscle and gristle,
making it an extremely
tender cut for roasting.

343

BONELESS SHOULDER OF VENISON
An excellent braising joint.

VENISON OSSO BUCCO
A modern cut similar to the original veal osso bucco, cut from across the leg with the bone remaining.

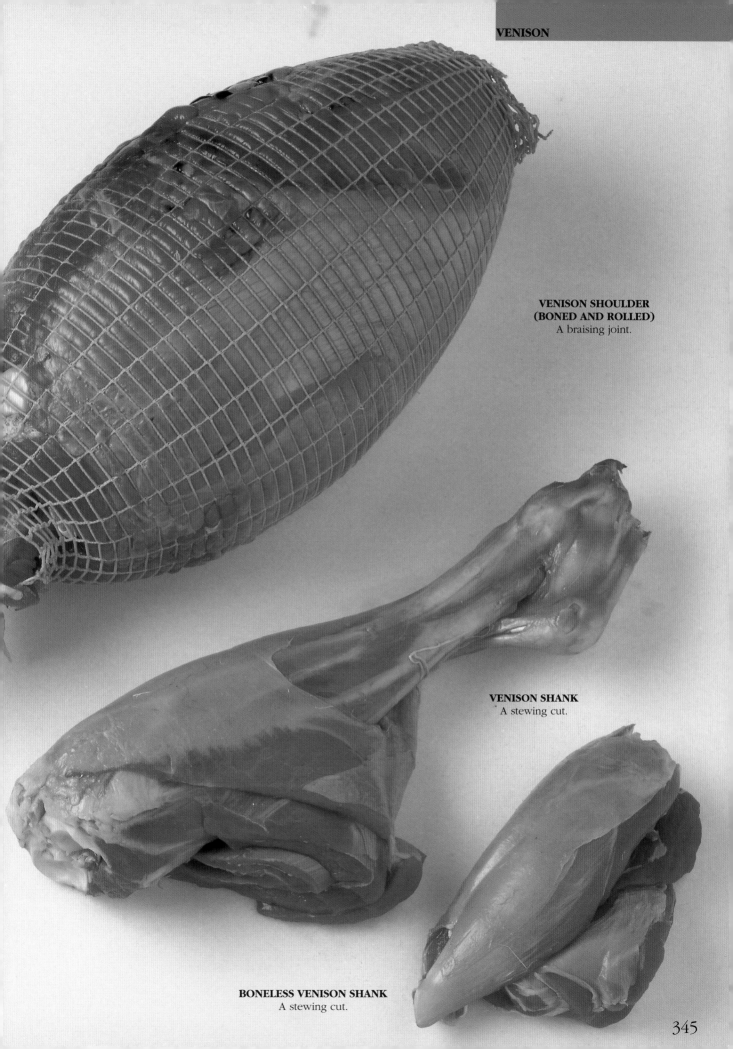

**VENISON SHOULDER
(BONED AND ROLLED)**
A braising joint.

VENISON SHANK
A stewing cut.

BONELESS VENISON SHANK
A stewing cut.

WILD BOAR AND APPLE SAUSAGES
Among the many gourmet sausages on the market, these are delicious with mash and red wine onion gravy.

WILD BOAR SADDLE
A roasting joint which benefits from
a marinade of red wine, garlic,
juniper berries and herbs.

WILD BOAR HAUNCH
The top part of the leg,
it is best roasted.

Beverages

The British are well known world-wide for their devotion to tea. In times of crisis, celebration or just for a refreshing cuppa, there is always an excuse to put the kettle on. These days, there are teas from all over the world to satisfy this thirst.

Tea drinking started in China, and records show that in the 8th century it had become so popular that tea was taxed. In England it took some time to catch on but, by the middle of the 18th century, it had become a national drink.

The most popular everyday drinking tea is usually a blend of black tea. Black tea is fermented after picking to produce a dark, strongly flavoured tea. Unfermented green tea is more delicate in flavour.

Speciality teas include those which have flower blossoms, warming spices or fruit zest in their blend. Fruit 'teas' and herbal infusions, which are not strictly teas, but brewed the same way, are also popular. Herbal teas in particular are thought to have special properties, either calming, relaxing or invigorating.

It was an Ethiopian goatherd who noticed that his charges were lively after eating particular berries. He picked some and made an infusion, then experienced the same stimulating effects when he drank it, or so legend has it. He had just invented the first cup of coffee.

Coffee comes from three types of beans. Arabica is the finest quality and is low in caffeine; robusta is strong and high in caffeine; and liberica is a medium-weight bean.

Coffee can be made from a single type of bean or it can be a blend. The taste and aroma depends on where the beans come from, the roast and the blend. High roast gives a deeply coloured, bitter, strong coffee. Medium is strong and smooth, and a light roast produces a delicate flavour.

SANTOS GREEN BEANS
Santos, the port south-east of São Paulo, is associated with the fine coffees of Brazil. These beans are extensively used in producing arabica-quality, gourmet roast coffees.

COLOMBIAN GREEN BEANS
The best-quality Colombian coffee is equal to Jamaican Blue Mountain or Costa Rican, with a good balance between flavour, richness and body, and a slight wine flavour.

NEW GUINEA GREEN BEANS
Arabica coffee grown in the New Guinea Highlands is world-renowned for its high quality and use in producing gourmet coffees.

DECAFFEINATED INSTANT COFFEE
Basically the decaffeination process is the solvent extraction of the caffeine from water-treated green beans prior to roasting. Spray-dried or freeze-dried soluble coffee can then be produced.

CARAMEL ROAST BEANS
A highly roasted coffee produced for the drinker who prefers a stronger brew. Often used in a blend and predominantly for espresso coffee.

MEDIUM-ROAST BEANS
Roasted to produce a medium-strength coffee, which is ideal for filter machines and plungers. The brew is rich and sweet with a slight acidity.

ESPRESSO GRIND
Roast coffee, ground fine in order to obtain extraction under pressure from an espresso maker.

FILTER GRIND
Medium-ground roast coffee allowing an extraction time of approximately seven minutes in a 10-cup coffee maker.

PLUNGER GRIND
Roast coffee, ground slightly coarser than medium in order to obtain quick extraction in a plunger.

ROBUSTA GREEN BEANS
A low-grade coffee primarily used in the production of instant coffee and as a blender for producing certain espresso coffees.

DECAFFEINATED GREEN BEANS
Green beans, which have either stood in water or been steamed under pressure, and then treated with solvent (methylene chloride), which penetrates the bean to extract the caffeine.

LIGHT-ROAST BEANS
Coffee roasted in the shortest amount of time required to produce light brown, dry beans. Mainly used in long-brew equipment, such as a plunger or percolator.

FRENCH MIX BEANS
Commonly known as a city roast and predominantly drunk as an espresso, it is a mix of caramel and medium-roasted beans to produce an oily brew with strength on the palate.

TURKISH GRIND
Roasted coffee, ground very fine or pulverized to produce a strong flavour. The drink is made by stirring the required amount into boiling water.

PERCOLATOR GRIND
Medium-ground roast coffee with minimum fine particles to allow for preferred brewing time to extract desired strength and flavour.

ABOUT COFFEE
Roasting coffee is simply applying the correct heat to raw coffee beans, turning them from a greenish or yellowish shade to the rich brown colour we are famililar with. As the bean is dried by the heat, it swells and the coffee flavour develops. Roasting was probably discovered by accident, and it wasn't until the middle of the 15th century that people started drinking coffee as we know it. Continental coffee-drinking habits have influenced the way we like to drink our coffee. Here are some of the popular brews:

Café au lait, made by simultaneously pouring hot coffee and boiling milk into a cup.

Caffè con leche, made by combining a 'shot' of espresso with steamed milk.

Caffè con panna, espresso with a dollop of whipped cream on top.

Caffè corretto, espresso 'corrected' with added liqueur.

Caffè crema, a 'shot' of espresso combined with cream.

Caffè freddo, chilled espresso served in a glass, usually with ice.

Caffè latte, a 'shot' of espresso combined with steamed, sometimes frothy, milk.

Caffè lungo, a long espresso made by adding boiling water to a 'shot' of espresso; also known as Americano.

Caffè macchiato, 'marked' coffee, a 'shot' of espresso in a medium cup, topped with foamy milk.

Caffè mocha, espresso combined with chocolate syrup and steamed milk, frequently topped with whipped cream and cocoa powder.

Caffè ristretto, 'concentrated' espresso, the normal amount of beans are used to make only a tiny amount of coffee.

Cappuccino, a 'shot' of espresso with enough steamed milk to half-fill the cup, topped with frothy milk.

Mochaccino, a cappuccino made with steamed chocolate milk.

Doppio, a double espresso.

Espresso, a richly concentrated coffee.

Grande, a large glass or cup of black coffee, latte or cappuccino.

Tall, a large glass of black coffee, latte or cappuccino.

Short, a medium cup of black coffee, latte or cappuccino.

INSTANT COFFEE
A coffee processed by spraying coffee extract into hot air, resulting in a dusty, light powder. Spray-drying forms a full-flowing powder of uniform-size particles, which is readily soluble in hot water.

INSTANT COFFEE GRANULES
Technically known as 'agglomerated' coffee, it is the result of melting spray-dried coffee to give it a granular appearance.

FREEZE-DRIED INSTANT COFFEE
Made by drying out deep frozen coffee extract in a vacuum at a temperature well below freezing. The final product is in an attractive granule form, reminiscent of coarsely ground, roasted coffee.

COFFEE & CHICORY ESSENCE
An alcoholic solution containing the distilled extracts of coffee and chicory. Used mainly in confectionery as a flavouring.

CHOCOLATE FOOD DRINK
A chocolate-flavoured, health-drink base, made from barley and malt extract, whey powder, sugar, glucose, cocoa, vegetable fats and egg. Mix in hot or cold milk.

COCOA
The residue of ground cocoa beans after half the cocoa butter has been extracted. Cocoa powder may be used in baking or mixed with hot milk or water and sugar for drinking chocolate. Dutched cocoa is processed to neutralize its natural acidity.

MALT FOOD DRINK
A malt-flavoured, health-drink base, made from wheatflour, malted barley, skim milk powder, malt extract and vitamins. Mix in hot or cold milk.

BEEF ESSENCE
A liquid made from beef and vegetable extracts, beef stock, yeast extract, colouring, starch, sugar, salt, spices and vitamins. May be stirred into boiling water for a drink, or used as a soup, stock or sauce base.

SOY DRINK
Made from soya beans, this non-dairy product is cholesterol- and lactose-free. May be mixed with cold water. The calcium in soy drink is not as readily absorbed as that in milk.

BRAZIL MATE
This green leaf from South America is not actually from the tea plant. It is, however, brewed as tea, can be drunk hot or cold, and contains more caffeine than coffee.

EARL GREY
A classic black tea from China or Darjeeling, scented with oil from the peel of the bergamot, a small, Cantonese orange. Sugar enhances the flavour of scented teas, but milk should be avoided.

YIN ZHEN
Classed not as a green tea, but as a white – meaning the leaves have been dried rather than steamed to promote smoothness – it is one of the most expensive teas in the world. Brew for up to 20 minutes to enjoy the delicate flavour fully.

CHAI
blend of tea from northern India where families have their own recipes and the taste varies from one to another. It is always made, however, with black tea, innamon, cardamom, ginger and cloves. It is a wonderfully warming tea.

BLOOD ORANGE
Blood orange adds sweetness and colour to this tea, which should be drunk black. Flavoured teas are usually made with black tea and one other item, for example, a fruit such as lime, peach or mango, or a spice such as cardamom or cinnamon, or even vanilla, toffee, honey, coconut or almond.

ENGLISH BREAKFAST
A stimulating and refreshing blend of tea, usually containing Assam from India and leaves from Sri Lanka (Ceylon). As the name suggests, served in the morning, often with milk.

LAPSANG SOUCHONG
A black, Chinese tea with a smoky, distinctive taste obtained by drying leaves over pine fires. Needs slow brewing and is usually enjoyed without milk or lemon.

JASMINE
A semi-fermented Chinese tea, scented with dried jasmine blossom. Served without milk.

CHAMOMILE
One of the most popular single-herb infusions today and renowned for its calming properties. Other single-ingredient infusions include peppermint, lemon grass, hibiscus and rosehips.

353

BANNOCKBURN
From Darjeeling, this is a first-flush tea, picked between March and June, which gives it a distinctly lighter flavour than the same tea harvested later in the year. It is a fine, tippy, golden, flowery, orange pekoe grade 1 leaf. An all-day drinking tea.

SINGBULLI
This is a second-flush tea from Darjeeling, harvested between July and September with a characteristically stronger, muscatel flavour than first-flush teas. The leaf is tippy, golden, flowery, orange pekoe grade 1. An all-day drinking tea.

DHELAKAT TEA
From the Assam district, the world's largest tea-producing region. A good, morning tea with a malty, dark liquor derived from tippy, golden, flowery, broken, orange pekoe leaves.

NILGIRI PARKSIDE
Nilgiri is a district in south-western India producing a soft, round, all-day, drinking tea from flowery, orange pekoe leaves.

PAI MU TAN
A white tea from China with an extremely delicate, smooth, flowery taste, appropriate for evening drinking.

GUNPOWDER TEMPLE OF HEAVEN
A green, gunpowder tea from China. This is rolled into little balls to help preserve the flavour. Often used to prepare mint tea, but also provides a highly refreshing yellow-green liquor on its own. A calming, afternoon tea.

LUNG CHING (DRAGON'S WELL)
A stimulating green tea grown on the pollution-free slopes, 200km from Shanghai. The jade-coloured liquor has a light flavour and delicate aroma. There are three grades of this tea; the younger the leaf, the better the quality.

SZECHWAN
A milder, black tea from China with a slightly earthy flavour derived from orange pekoe leaves. It is never taken with milk or sugar and is considered perfect for afternoon and evening drinking.

YUNNAN TEA
A strong, rich, black tea from China, sometimes nicknamed the 'Mocha of Teas'. It is an orange pekoe and ideal for breakfast drinking, being the only Chinese black tea to tolerate a drop of milk.

354

OOLONG SHUI HSIEN
A Formosan tea from Taiwan, combining the flavours of black and green tea leaves. It is a refreshing, cooling liquor, ideal for sipping on hot days.

PETTIAGALLA
From Sri Lanka (Ceylon), a country known for producing black, rich, astringent tea. However, pettiagalla is an orange pekoe with a surprisingly gentle, soft, round flavour.

SENCHA
The most commonly drunk green tea in Japan. Many types of sencha exist and are recognized by their pale green liquor and fresh, flowery taste.

ORANGE FLOWER OOLONG
A Formosan tea from Taiwan, this highly aromatic amber liquor is enhanced with the delicate flavour of orange flowers.

BANGLADESH
A golden, flowery, orange pekoe producing a strong liquor with a malty, earthy, slightly spicy flavour. A daytime tea which can be drunk with or without milk.

JAVA MALABAR
An orange pekoe with a strong, almost syrupy flavour. Best for breakfast drinking.

KENYA MARINYN
A golden, flowery, orange pekoe producing a malty, full, fruity flavour similar to Assam. Best drunk in the morning with milk.

NEW GUINEA GARAINA
Not as dark as black teas from other countries. It has an earthy, fresh flavour.

AUSTRALIAN DAINTREE
Similar to New Guinea Garaina, this is another lighter black tea with a fresh flavour.

From around the world

Today's cuisine would not be the same without the input of European countries or that of our migrant population. Mediterranean food, Italian in particular, has taken a very firm foothold and is part of our daily diet. Long gone are the days when a child taking a salami sandwich to school would be ridiculed by his class mates. Spanish, Greek, Moroccan and Middle-East cuisines are all increasingly popular, with wonderful oils often being the common denominator.

The increased interest in Asian cooking has brought a proliferation of cuisines to our notice, including Thai, Vietnamese, Laotian, Cambodian, Burmese, as well as the more widely known Malaysian, Chinese and Indian. Today, there are mind-boggling grower's markets and speciality shops, where you can spend many happy hours expanding your knowledge and menu repertoire,

Even in supermarkets it is common to find many varieties of chilli, unlimited Asian, Caribbean and Mexican sauces, and curry pastes, as well as unusual fruits and vegetables.

Over the past decade the cooking of Australia has become world revered. It has transformed itself from offering meat and two veg, to now offering a world-class cuisine.

Privileged by their easy access to excellent natural ingredients including all manner of seafood, fine fruit and vegetables and top quality meat, Australia's chefs have brought a spectacular change in the style of food on offer 'down under'. In addition, there is a growing interest in going back to roots and making the most of the wild produce of the Australian Bush.

Bush tucker consists of such flavourings as lemon myrtle, native mint, wattle seed and riberries, as well as the irresistible macadamia nut. Many of these ingredients are already available worldwide. Those that are not, we can look forward to seeing in the near future.

DRIED SHRIMP
These sun-dried, tiny prawns are often ground before use. They add depth of flavour, especially to fried rice, soups, condiments and stuffings. As they are usually very salty, soaking is recommended before grinding.

DRIED SPLIT ANCHOVY
Also known as **ikan bilis** or **ikan teri**. Used in the same manner as dried shrimp, to give added flavour, but also deep-fried and served as a crunchy accompaniment.

DRIED FISH SLICE
Dried fish is fried or steamed, sometimes on its own, but more often combined with other ingredients as a powerful flavouring in Asian cooking.

DASHI
A soup stock used in Japanese cooking and the base for miso soup. It is made from dried bonito flakes (*katsuo-dashi),* dried sardines (*niboshi-dashi*) or dried kelp (*konbu-dashi*). Also available in liquid or a powdered, instant form.

DRIED SHRIMP PASTE
Also known as **blachan** or **trasi**. Made from fermented prawn, this is a popular flavouring in many South-East Asian countries. Choose from a spoonable paste or a block. To use shrimp paste in uncooked dishes, wrap in a small square of foil and roast over a gas flame, or grill for a few minutes.

KRUPUK UDANG
Popular in Indonesia, Malaysia and Vietnam, these dried wafers are usually made from tapioca flour, prawns, salt and sugar. When fried in hot oil, the wafers expand and puff up into crackers. Use as a garnish, an accompaniment or a snack.

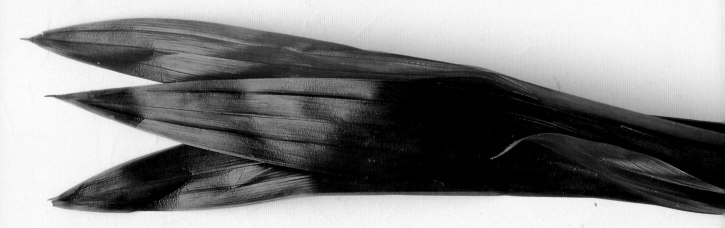

CHILLI PASTE WITH SOYA BEAN OIL
This powerful paste is used as a dipping sauce, as a base to cook meat, fish or vegetables, or stirred into hot rice and soups. Usually made with dried chillies, flavoured with sugar, fish sauce, garlic, dried shrimp and tamarind paste.

CHILLI OIL
Red chillies lend their brilliant colour to this orange oil. Use only small amounts to add heat to dishes while cooking or allow guests to help themselves.

SAMBAL
A sauce based on fresh chillies and ingredients such as dried shrimp paste, onion, garlic and tamarind. Used primarily to add extra heat to a dish at the table. There are ready-made sambals: sambal oelek and sambal badjak are two.

SALTED BLACK BEANS
Fermented, spiced and salted soya beans, available dry or canned. The dry variety needs to be rinsed before chopping to remove the salt; canned beans need to be drained from their liquid and chopped before using.

LOTUS ROOT
Used raw in salads, in stir-fries and in soups, or even candied, this buff-coloured, fibrous and starchy vegetable has a ring of decorative holes. The whole, fresh root may be refrigerated for up to three weeks. Available canned or frozen.

WATER CHESTNUT
A Chinese vegetable grown in muddy water. Its crispness is its attraction as an ingredient in stir-fries. Available canned. Once opened, keep refrigerated for up to two weeks, changing the water daily.

PANDANUS LEAF
Also known as **screw-pine leaf**. Used to wrap around food to make intricate parcels before cooking; the food is also frequently served in these parcels. A strip of leaf may be added to rice while it cooks or included in a curry, imparting a savoury/sweet flavour.

FRIED SHALLOT FLAKES
The shallot is the Orient's onion of choice. Fried shallots are used as a flavouring or sprinkled over food as a garnish. They make a wicked little snack.

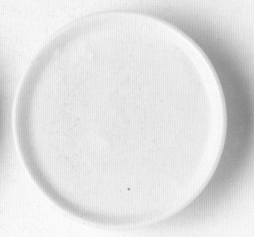

COCONUT MILK
This is not the clear liquid found inside a coconut, but the liquid extracted from grated coconut flesh. Choose from coconut cream (thick), which is the first extraction, or milk (thin), which is the second extraction.

BLACK FUNGUS
Also known as **wood fungus** or **cloud ear**. This is a tree fungus. The little black dried, curled-up chips need to be soaked to reconstitute. Check for grit and rinse well. They add a crunchy texture to Chinese dishes. Mostly sold dried.

CANDLE NUT
Known as **buah keras** in Malaysia, and as **kemiri** in Indonesia. This nut is ground to add texture and to thicken curry pastes. Macadamia nuts are a substitute.

KETJAP MANIS
This is Indonesian sweet soy sauce. If not available, use soy sauce with a small amount of brown sugar added.

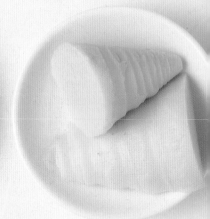

BAMBOO SHOOT
Only the fresh, young shoots are eaten. Remove the papery leaves to reveal the fibrous, cream coloured shoot. Rinse canned shoots before using to rid them of any metallic flavour.

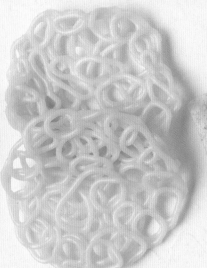

FISH CRACKER
Also known as **krupuk**, it is made with tapioca flour and flavoured with fish. When fried in hot oil, the cracker expands and puffs up. Serve as an accompaniment with meals or as a snack.

CASSAVA CRACKER
Another variety of *krupuk*, made with tapioca flour and flavoured with cassava, which gives it a sweet/tart taste. When fried in hot oil, the cracker expands and puffs up. Serve as an accompaniment with meals or as a snack.

PAPPADAM
A wafer made with lentil flour and a variety of flavourings, such as chilli, garlic and caraway. Fry in shallow, hot oil until it expands into a large, crisp cracker. Drain on paper towels before serving.

360

DRIED SHIITAKE MUSHROOM
Choose those with a thick cap and soak them in warm water for 20 minutes to reconstitute. Strain and squeeze gently to remove excess liquid. Trim and discard stalks. Reserve the soaking water to use in soups and stocks.

SOYA BEAN PASTE
This strongly flavoured, salty sauce is made from whole or mashed, fermented soya beans and may be either yellow or brown. Use as a food flavouring.

DRIED RED DATE
This sun-dried fruit is not really a date, but a **jujube**, native to the Mediterranean and China. Used in both sweet and savoury dishes as a flavouring.

HOISIN SAUCE
With a mild, garlic flavour, this slightly sweet, thick, Chinese, soya bean sauce is used in cooking and as a dip. Once opened, store in the fridge.

LUP CHONG SAUSAGE
Usually made from pork, this sausage is cured but not cooked. Keep refrigerated for up to a month, or freeze for up to two months.

AGAR-AGAR
A gelatin, made from several kinds of seaweed. Available as a fine, white powder, in strands, sticks or flakes. When soaked to soften, the agar-agar sticks may be used in salads.

361

NORI
Wafer-thin slices of seaweed, used to make *sushi* and to flavour and garnish Japanese dishes.

KRUPUK EMPING
A cracker made from the flattened kernel of the melinjo nut, with a delicious, faint bitter flavour. When fried in hot oil, it expands and puffs up. Serve as an accompaniment or snack.

FISH SAUCE
Known as **nam pla** in Thailand, **nuoc nam** in Vietnam and **patis** in the Philippines, fish sauce is used similarly to soy sauce; its salty, distinctive flavour derives from salted shrimp or fish.

PALM SUGAR
Also known as **jaggery**, the colour may range from white to dark brown. It has a delicate, distinctive flavour and is widely used in many Asian countries. Buy in wrapped chunks or in jars.

DRIED SEA VEGETABLE
Also known as **wakame**, this seaweed has been hot-water treated and salted. Add to soups or noodles just before serving, or soak in hot water for two minutes, or in cold water for five, and add to salads.

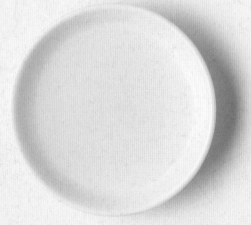

MIRIN
A Japanese, sweetened, rice wine used in cooking.

PICKLED TURNIP
Preserved in salt, this is used as a vegetable and as a flavouring ingredient, especially in soups, or stir-fries with meats, poultry or fish. If excessively salty, soak in water before using.

KRUPUK IKAN
This variety of Indonesian wafer is made from fish mixed with tapioca flour, salt and sugar. Simple, quick and easy to prepare by frying in shallow, hot oil until they expand, krupuks are a nice accompaniment to many meals, and a change from pappadams.

KONBU
Dried kelp used to make *dashi*, a soup
stock featured in Japanese cooking.
Available in long, whole sheets or smaller
pieces. Wipe with a damp cloth before
using; rinsing removes the flavour.

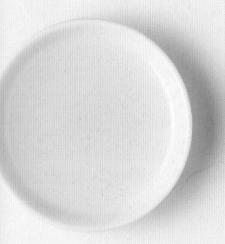

SAKE
Japanese rice wine, used both for
cooking and drinking.

BLACK BEAN PASTE
Made from fermented black soya beans
and widely used in Malaysian and Asian
cuisines. The consistency may vary from
thick and chunky to thin and smooth.
Once opened, black bean sauce should
be stored in the fridge.

SESAME PASTE
A light brown, rich, creamy paste, made
from toasted sesame seeds. It is different
from Lebanese *tahini*, which is made
from raw sesame seeds. Used in sauces
and both hot and cold dishes. Smooth
peanut butter is a substitute.

OYSTER SAUCE
A salty, sweet, thick, brown sauce
made from oysters. Widely used to
flavour all manner of Chinese
dishes, from noodles to vegetables.
Once opened, keep refrigerated.

SALTED SOYA BEANS
Preserved by cooking and fermenting with salt
and spices, they have a distinctively salty taste.
Mostly used in conjunction with garlic, ginger and
chillies in stir-fries, or in steamed and braised
dishes for a rich flavour. Chop or mash very
lightly to bring out their aroma.

SUSHI VINEGAR
Ready-to-use vinegar for *sushi*. A mixture
of rice vinegar, sugar and salt. Use to
dress rice no more than two to three
hours before required.

FLOWERING CHIVES
Allium tuberosum
Flowering chives are among several varieties of Chinese chives. They have a hollow stem, fat little buds and flat leaves. They are stronger in flavour than the chives used in Western cooking. Use as a vegetable in stir-fries, in soups and salads.

KHEE KWAI
Chrysanthemum coronarium
Known by this name in Thailand, these tender young leaves are eaten raw, while older leaves are blanched, refreshed in iced water and served as a salad. They wilt quickly so buy shortly before cooking.

HOLY BASIL
Ocimum sanctum
Known in Thailand as **bai kaprow**, this basil has thin, reddish-green leaves and a very distinct flavour. If not available, use sweet basil together with a little fresh mint.

GREEN MANGO
Mangifera indica
Both green mango and green pawpaw, when still hard and slightly sour, are used in Asian cuisines, as tenderizers and in savoury salads, pickles and chutneys.

FRESH TURMERIC
Curcuma longa
Although used dried and ground in the Western world, fresh turmeric is frequently used in many Asian cuisines for colouring, and to a lesser extent for its musty flavour. This orange-yellow rhizome resembles ginger and needs to be peeled and grated, or finely chopped, before use.

JICAMA
Pachyrhizus erosus
Also known as **yam bean** or **sweet turnip**, this vegetable closely resembles the yam. Crunchy and slightly sweet, it often replaces fresh water chestnuts in recipes. Boil, stir-fry or deep-fry. Store in the fridge up to one week.

GREEN PAWPAW
Carica papaya
The tenderizing enzyme, papain, is extracted from the unripe pawpaw and this slightly sour fruit is used in the Thai savoury salad, *som tam*.

WATER SPINACH
Ipomoea aquatica
Known as **kangkung** in Malaysia and Indonesia. Wash thoroughly as it grows in swamp areas. Frequently stir-fried with garlic and a variety of sauces or served as a side dish. Also added to soups.

KAFFIR LIME LEAF
Citrus hystrix
The fragrant leaf of the kaffir lime tree and the rind of its dark green fruit are essential ingredients in Thai soups, salads and curries. Frozen or dried leaves may be used, if fresh are not available. Fruit can be frozen in a sealed bag.

CHINESE CELERY
Apium graveolens
Similar in appearance to continental parsley, this is a stronger flavoured version of the more-familiar celery. The colour may vary from white to dark green. Use in soups, stir-fries and stews.

BIRIYANI PASTE
Mildly spiced paste used for
a composite curry of rice with meat,
fish or vegetables.

TIKKA PASTE
A red, richly flavoured paste usually
mixed with yoghurt to marinate chunks of
chicken, lamb or fish before cooking
in a tandoor.

MADRAS CURRY PASTE
A hot, spicy paste with
much chilli in evidence. Best used with
lamb or beef.

VINDALOO PASTE
One of the hottest curry pastes, made
from indigenous Indian spices and
vinegar, to give meat and poultry dishes a
sour flavour.

BALTI CURRY PASTE
A spicy paste made from ginger,
coriander, garlic, chilli, tumeric, tamarind
and creamed coconut. Use with chicken,
lamb or vegetables.

BAFAAD CURRY PASTE
A dark and aromatic paste originating in
Goa. Made from a blend of about 20
spices, it gives a rich, spicy flavour to
meat curries, and is especially
recommended for beef.

GOAN VINDALOO PASTE
A traditional, medium-hot paste flavoured
with cumin, coriander, tamarind,
cinnamon, cloves and cardamom. Mainly
used for lamb.

GOAN ONION BAGHAAR
Consisting of onion, garlic, ginger, herbs
and vinegar. It takes away the chore of
chopping onions for such dishes as
Oriental and Asian stir-fries.

**INDIAN BLACK ONION SEED
(KALONJI)**
The seeds of the nigella plant,
often used in Indian breads and in
Middle Eastern dishes.

BRINJAL PICKLE
Chopped aubergine, lightly spiced and cooked slowly to make an accompaniment for curry dishes. It is also sometimes served with pappadams as an appetiser.

CHILLI PICKLE
Made from chilli peppers, ginger, mustard, fenugreek, salt and mixed spices. It is a hot accompaniment for curries.

TAMARIND PODS
The fruit of the tamarind tree is a common ingredient in Indian cookery. The pods are soaked and sieved. The pulp is used to acidulate and flavour curries. Also available in ready-to-use paste.

THAI GREEN CURRY PASTE
Made from a mix of fresh chopped chillies, coriander, ginger, lemongrass and garlic, giving chicken, fish or vegetable dishes a fresh, spicy flavour.

THAI RED CURRY PASTE
A mix of hot red chillies, lemongrass, lime juice, coriander and shrimp paste, giving a serious blast of heat to such dishes as *tom yum* soup.

THAI GREEN CHILLI SAUCE
Made from the young chilli peppers which are medium hot, it is used to add heat and flavour to dishes, or as a dipping sauce.

THAI YELLOW CURRY PASTE
A hot paste made from galangal, chilli, turmeric, onion and garlic.A hot paste made from galangal, chilli, turmeric, onion and garlic.

PANANG CURRY PASTE
A seriously hot paste made from dried red chilli, garlic, lemon grass, shallots, galangal, Kaffir lime, shrimp paste and spices. It can be used for both chicken and fish dishes.

MATSAMAN CURRY PASTE
An extremely hot paste made from dried red chilli, garlic, shallots, spices, lemon grass and galangal. It can be used for both chicken and meat dishes.

NEW MEXICO CHILLI
Closely related to the **Anaheim**, the flavour of this versatile chilli is a great addition to chilli sauces. Mild to medium.

CASCABEL CHILLI
Cascabel means 'rattle' in Spanish; the seeds rattle when the chilli is shaken. A rich, earthy flavour when toasted; use in soups, to make salsas or in cooked tomato and tomatillo sauces. Medium hot.

HABANERO CHILLI
The intense and fruity flavour of this chilli, meaning 'from Havana', goes well with fish and seafood; also good to flavour vinegars, oils, pickles and salsas. Fiercely hot.

CHIPOTLE CHILLI
Use in soups, sauces and salsas, or grind as a seasoning. Typical use is pickled (*en escabeche*), whole or in pieces to season broth. Sometimes stuffed. Available canned in *adobo* sauce. Medium hot.

DRIED CHILLIES

These should be stored in a cool, dry place in an airtight container or frozen, securely wrapped. Buy chillies that are not completely dried to a crisp; the natural oils may have dried out as well.

To toast dried chillies: stem and seed the chillies, and dry-roast in a single layer in a dry cast-iron frying pan, or on a baking sheet in a 250°C (480°F) oven for 2–3 minutes. Do not allow the chillies to blacken or they will taste bitter.

To rehydrate dried chillies: place chillies in a bowl and add just enough water to cover them. Stand for 20 minutes or until chillies soften.

PULLA CHILLI
Related to the guajillo (below), thin-fleshed, light flavour, dry, dusty, intense heat. Seasoning for salsas and casseroles. Hot.

ARBOL CHILLI
With a nutty flavour, the smaller the hotter. Use toasted and ground with other ingredients for a hot salsa, add to fried beans or toast, and grind to a powder to sprinkle on peanuts, fruit, cucumbers and jicama. Hot.

PASILLA CHILLI
Use toasted or soaked and blend with other ingredients for cooked sauces or salsas, especially with seafood and in *moles*. It may also be rehydrated, stuffed and fried. Medium hot.

GUAJILLO CHILLI
One of the most widely used dried chillies. Use toasted and ground for salsas, chilli sauces, soups and casseroles, or ground with other ingredients as a seasoning paste. Mild to medium.

YELLOW CORNFLOUR
A flour made from yellow corn
and used to make tortillas.

MASA HARINA
A flour used to make tortillas and tamales. Corn
kernels are heated in lime juice, which makes the
skin come off easily. The kernels are dried and
ground. Masa harina can be white, yellow or other
colours, depending on the type of corn used.

BLUE CORNFLOUR
A flour made from blue corn
and used to make tortillas.

NOPALITOS
The young, fleshy pads of the
prickly pear cactus with the spines
removed; mostly used in salads, but also
in stews, with scrambled eggs
or in salsas.

MEXICAN-STYLE CHOCOLATE
Grainy, spicy tablet of cocoa, sugar,
cinnamon and, in most cases, ground
almonds. Used in chilli-rich, savoury dishes
called *moles*, particularly in the most festive
dish of Mexico, *mole poblano*.

ACHIOTE PASTE
Also known as **annato**.
The ground seeds of a tree
grown in Central and South America
mixed with vinegar, salt,
granulated garlic and spices.

MEXICAN-STYLE HOMINY
Dried, large corn kernels treated
with lime until they are plump and soft,
and have shed their skins. An earthy
flavour. Served as a side dish and
used to make into a chunky
soup called *pozole*.

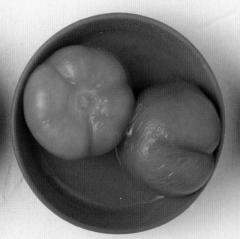

TOMATILLO
Also known as **Mexican green
tomatoes**, these tomatoes, although
green and firm, are fully ripe and
contribute a tart flavour. Used in salads,
salsas, soups and stews.

EPAZOTE
A pungent, almost medicinal-
flavoured, very typical Mexican
herb. Use in black bean dishes, stews,
soups, and with fish
and shellfish.

369

HAGGIS
The classic Scottish dish, customarily served on Burns Night (January 25),
when the dish is 'piped' in. Made from the liver, heart and lungs of sheep, mixed with
suet, oats, and mutton or beef, and stuffed sausage-like into a paunch.
Traditionally served with bashed 'neeps' and 'tatties' (turnips and potatoes). Simmer in
water until heated through, about 30 minutes.

WITCHETTY GRUB
Very rich in protein and (largely mono-unsaturated) fats, these plump
grubs feed on the witchetty bush in central Australia. Can be eaten raw, but barbecuing
or grilling makes them more palatable. A mealy texture and bland flavour,
combined with a high price, seems to indicate their future will
be restricted to the tourist trade.

SNAIL
This gastropod mollusc — one muscle, one shell — has a slightly rubbery texture.
Frequently sold canned or frozen, but occasionally available fresh. Common garden
snails can be eaten but should be starved for two days, then fed lettuce and herbs for a
fortnight. Usually cooked with masses of garlic, butter and parsley.

MASTIC
Also known as **mastiha gum**, a yellow-coloured resin from the *Pistacia lentiscus* bush. Similar in flavour to anise, mastic is used in Greek puddings and baking, in ice cream, chewing gum and liqueurs. Crush to a fine powder with a little sugar just before using.

GREATER GALANGAL
Alpinia galanga
A member of the ginger family, a rhizome with flavour reminiscent of camphor, galangal features widely in Thai cuisine, especially in curry pastes, as well as Malaysian and Indonesian cuisines. Galangal is sold in local Oriental food stores, fresh, sliced and in brine. Powdered galangal is available as Laos powder.

MAHLEPI
The inner core of sour cherry pips, this lemon-like flavouring for desserts and baked goods is popular in the Middle East. Available whole or ground.

VIETNAMESE MINT
Persicaria odorata
Not a true mint, and also known as **Cambodian mint** and **laksa leaf**, this aromatic leaf is an essential element in Singaporean laksa. In Thai cooking it's frequently found together with 'true' mint and fresh coriander, and the Vietnamese cuisine uses the leaf in salads and spring rolls.

DRIED LEMON
This dried citrus fruit is used in Middle Eastern stews. One or more are added to impart a lemony flavour. After cooking, remove and discard.

BUSH TOMATO

This small, red-brown berry has a tamarillo-caramel flavour and texture similar to a raisin. Use chopped in focaccia, antipasto, chutneys and sauces. Available dry or ready prepared in oil.

BUSH TOMATO SAUCE

This thick, orange-red sauce, with its savoury flavour, is a good substitute for tomato sauce. Use as a seafood marinade, stir-fry sauce, soup base and as a pizza or pasta sauce. Fresh oregano or basil are good herb additions.

NATIVE PEPPERMINT

A peppermint flavour with a woody eucalyptus note makes this an ideal seasoning for white meats as well as desserts. Use very small amounts. Available ground.

BUSH TOMATO CHUTNEY

Ground bush tomato in a tomato and apple base. Good with red meats, pies or vegetables. Embellish with freshly diced tomato and basil for 'bushetta' (made with mountain pepper bread).

AKUDJURA

This is the ground form of bush tomato. With its sweet/savoury taste of tamarillo and caramel, use as a flavour-enhancer, sprinkled on soups, vegetables, salads and pastries. Serve with cheddar cheese. Available as a free-flowing powder.

NATIVE MINT

A dark green, powdered herb with a strong, savoury flavour, closer to peppermint than spearmint. It is a great addition to sauces, pesto, butter, breads and vinegars. Available ground.

KAKADU PLUM

The vitamin C content of this fruit is higher than that of any other. Olive-sized, with a subtle apricot flavour, it has a stone which clings to the flesh of the fruit. Use raw strips of the fruit or pickle the whole fruit in sweet vinegar. Available frozen.

KAKADU PLUM, spreadable

Green, jam-like consistency with sweet, subtle, apricot flavour. Dilute with apple juice or white wine vinegar for sauces or glazes. Add chilli, roasted garlic, macadamia nuts, native peppermint or other herbs, depending on use.

GUMLEAF OIL

Use this pale yellow oil, with its eucalyptus flavour, in desserts with caramel or honey, or in savoury sauces with coriander, garlic or honey. When diluted, it may be brushed on to smoked salmon or barbecued meats. Use sparingly.

NATIVE PEPPERMINT OIL
A transparent, pale yellow oil. With a peppermint flavour and woody eucalyptus note, it enhances cream, milk, oil, vinegar or stock. Use sparingly for sauces, dressings or desserts.

ILLAWARRA PLUM SAUCE
Use this thick, dark purple sauce with its subtle, pine flavour as a topping for meat and vegetables or a dipping sauce for *crudités*. Use as a marinade or pizza sauce. Add chilli for an Asian-style sauce.

NATIVE PEPPERMINT, ground
Potent taste. Use in an infusion, add to cake mixes, as a flavouring in ice cream, and in a wine marinade, particularly with lamb. Sprinkle as a seasoning for seafood.

ILLAWARRA PLUM
This large, grape-sized fruit is not as sweet as a common plum. Its resinous, pure quality is enhanced with cooking. Use with chilli and garlic, as well as in sweet dishes. Try in sauces, preserves, and compotes. Available frozen.

ANISEED MYRTLE LEAF
With its subtle, aniseed flavour and sweet aftertaste, this versatile leaf is used as a garnish, to infuse vinegars and oils, or as you would kaffir lime leaves.

ANISEED MYRTLE, ground
Use to flavour biscuits, cakes, oil, white meats, stuffing, stocks, ice cream, cream cheese or breads. Ideal on fetta cheese.

RAINFOREST HERB FETTUCCINE
A semolina pasta with savoury herb flavour. Use with, but not mixed with, plain fettuccine; serve side by side or layered. Best not smothered with heavy sauces, but make a feature of the pasta flavour itself.

373

QUANDONG
With a mildly tart, apricot-and-peach flavour, this fruit is available whole, or halved with the seed removed. Use whole as a garnish or add a filling to the halves and serve as *hors d'œuvres*. Cook the halves gently in sauces for meats or desserts. Available frozen.

QUANDONG SEED
When dry-roasted, the kernel of this marble-sized seed has a strong hazelnut/roast almond flavour. Use small amounts to flavour sauces, cream, pastries or add to a crumble mix. Never use raw kernels. Available frozen.

NATIVE THYME
A light green, powdered herb reminiscen of a mixture of tarragon, thyme and rosemary. Use sparingly in soups, stuffings, pâté, herb bread, quiches, omelettes and vegetable seasoning. Available ground.

LEMON ASPEN JUICE
An economical way of adding the tart, citrus flavour of lemon aspen to dessert flavouring, toppings or a meat glaze. Use sparingly. Available frozen. Store chilled. Do not use with other citrus juices.

LEMON ASPEN SYRUP
Pale yellow syrup with a sweet, citrus flavour in grapefruit and lime tones. May be used as a dessert flavouring or topping, or as a meat glaze. When fresh coriander is added, it makes a good Thai dipping sauce. Do not combine with other citrus juices.

LEMON ASPEN FRUIT
A fruit with a tart, citrus flavour frequentl used as a garnish. Soak in sugar syrup o sweet vinegar. Do not mix with other citru Use sparingly. Available frozen.

RIBERRY
With its distinctive cinnamon-and-clove flavour, the riberry, or **lillypilly**, is used in sauces, muffins, cakes and preserves. The pink colour disappears with cooking, but returns on standing. Available frozen.

WARRIGAL GREENS
The fresh leaves are similar to spinach but must be blanched or wilted before eating. Available fresh or blanched and frozen. The frozen product may be used in pesto, quiches and stuffings.

BUNYA BUNYA NUT
Similar to the chestnut with a subtle pine
[ov]ertone. The boiled nut may be sliced and
[used] as a garnish or flavouring. The puréed nuts
[may] be fried and made into pastry or dumplings.
[Th]e shells may be used for smoking meats.
Available whole or halved, both frozen.

NATIVE PEPPERCORN
Dried form of the native pepperberry,
this Tasmanian peppercorn is said to
have the flavour of a rainforest. May be
used at the table as for black pepper, as a
seasoning and in cream sauces.

MOUNTAIN PEPPER, ground
Hot and spicy, with lots of zing, this dried,
savoury leaf is best used as a sprinkle as you
would black pepper.

NATIVE PEPPERBERRY
[Th]is black-seeded, deep purple berry gives a
[di]stinctive flavour to sauces, butter, breads,
[p]asta and game meat. It makes a striking
[g]arnish and, when used in cream sauces, it
[l]eds' an appealing burgundy colour. Effective
[s]erved with corn kernels. Available frozen.

MOUNTAIN PEPPER BBQ SAUCE
For barbecued meats, stir-fried dishes,
sausages and as a marinade, this thick,
brown sauce, with pepper and spice
flavour, possesses woody character. Use
as a finishing sauce on hot dishes to
emphasize their natural zing.

MOUNTAIN PEPPER LEAF
With flavours reminiscent of pepper and
chillies, the whole leaf can be used instead of
bay leaves in breads, butter, sauces and
desserts. When cooked, the leaf imparts a
woody character. If the zing dissipates during
cooking, add more leaves just before serving.

PAPERBARK
Use this non-edible wrap when barbecuing
white meats and fish or to line platters.
Moisten lightly to make it pliable. Wrap
food in a neat parcel and tie with vine or
twine. Increase cooking times by 10–20
per cent. Cook on high heat to blacken
bark and fully smoke contents.

375

LEMON MYRTLE LEAF
A deep green leaf with the flavours of lemon grass, lemon and lime oil. Use fresh, whole leaves in place of kaffir lime leaves, as a garnish, in bottled vinegars, in oils and on baked fish.

WILD ROSELLA SYRUP
Bright red syrup with a tart raspberry-and-rhubarb taste. Use as a dessert flavouring, topping or as a meat glaze. Add freshly chopped chilli to make a sweet dipping sauce. To make a savoury sauce, add wh[...] wine vinegar, chilli or garlic.

LEMON MYRTLE, ground
Dry, ground lemon myrtle may be added to breads, pancakes, scones, muffins, cakes and cheesecakes. Use as a flavouring on rice, fish and chicken.

WILD ROSELLA
Bright red and flower-shaped, this fruit ha[...] a tart raspberry-and-rhubarb taste. Use in sauces, pies, pastries, ice cream, sorbets, syrups and as a garnish. To reduce tartnes[...] soak in sugar syrup. Available frozen.

LEMON MYRTLE FETTUCCINE
A semolina pasta with distinctive lemon grass, lemon and lime oil flavours. Do not mix with plain fettuccine, but serve side by side or layered. No need to smother with heavy sauces, but make a feature of the flavour in the pasta itself.

LEMON MYRTLE OIL
A pale yellow oil with lemon grass, lemon and lime oil flavours. Use to flavour cream, milk, oil, vinegar or stock for sauces, dressings, soup and desserts. Use sparingly, just before serving.

ROSELLA FRUIT
Crimson red, jam-like consistency with a tart raspberry-and-rhubarb taste. Use as a cranberry sauce substitute. Dilute with apple juice to make a coulis, or with white wine vinegar and freshly chopped chilli to make a sweet, rosella, chilli sauce.

CHEESEFRUIT JUICE
A versatile juice with a fruity, blue-vein-cheese flavour. Available frozen, once defrosted, it keeps up to six weeks under refrigeration. Use small amounts in cream and cheese sauces, polenta, pasta, dips, marinades and dressings.

MUNTHARI
Pea-sized fruit has the flavour of a Granny Smith apple with a subtle, spicy finish. Use whole or chopped in muffins, fruit pies and puddings, or sauté with onions or mushrooms. This fruit stays whole, even after prolonged cooking. Use as a garnish. Available frozen.

MUNTHARI & LEMON MYRTLE CHUTNEY
Apple-spice-citrus flavour with whole munthari providing texture. As accompaniment or sauce base for chicken, fish, pork or savoury nibbles. Use as a stuffing for chicken fillets.

MACADAMIA NUT
This world-renowned 'king of nuts' may be used as a garnish, to thicken sauces or roasted and blended as for peanut butter. Roasting brings out the flavour. Although high in fat content, this nut contains no cholesterol.

WATTLESEED
This roasted, ground seed has a coffee-chocolate-hazelnut flavour. It is used as a flavouring for sweet or savoury sauces, or in batter, desserts and baked foods. Available as free-flowing, coffee-like grounds.

WILD LIME, small
The smaller, outback lime has a slightly bitter and very tart lime flavour. May be used whole as a garnish for main meals or desserts. Cook briefly so the fruit does not disintegrate. Available frozen.

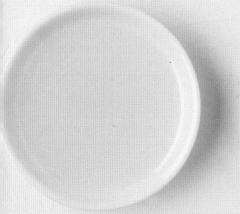

MACADAMIA NUT OIL
This transparent, yellow oil flavours salad dressings and pasta. Use as for sesame seed oil, rather as a flavouring than a cooking oil.

GUNDABLUEY MUD
A paste made from ground wattleseed. Used as a flavouring agent for dairy-based recipes such as custards, milk shakes, ice cream, yoghurt and *crème brûlée*.

WILD LIME, large
With its slightly bitter and very tart lime flavour, the larger rainforest lime is very good in marmalades, meat jams, sauces, bitter-sweet desserts and as a glacé fruit. Needs prolonged cooking. Available frozen.

377

Index

Acknowledgments

We would like to thank the following people for their assistance in the preparation of this book:

NORTHERN HEMISPHERE
Phil Howard, The Square, Bruton Street, Mayfair, London.
Billfields Food Co Ltd, The Liberty Centre, Mount Pleasant, Wembley, Middlesex.
Richard Perton, City Herbs, New Spitalfields Market, 23 Sherrin Road, Leyton, London.
Cutty Catering Specialists Limited, 57 Sandgate Street, London.
Wild Harvest Mushrooms, 31 London Stone Estate, Broughton, London.
Harrods Food Halls.
Harvey Nichols Food Halls.
Selfridges Food Halls.
M.G. & Sons (Wholesale Greengrocer) Ltd, New Covent Garden Market, London.
Neal's Yard Dairy, 17 Short's Gardens, London.
La Fromagerie, 30 Highbury Park, Highbury, London.
The Game Larder, 24 The Parade, Claygate, Surrey.
K.C. Fisheries, Oakwood Hill, Loughton, Essex.
Ken Muir, Weeley Heath, Nr Clacton-on-Sea, Essex.
Products From Spain, 89 Charlotte Street, London W1.

SOUTHERN HEMISPHERE
Liam Tomlin and Matt Kemp, Banc, 53 Martin Place, Sydney, NSW.
Molly McKenzie Food Products, 6 Kaleski Street, Moorebank, NSW.
Moses Spice Centre, 108 Brighton Boulevard, Bondi Beach, NSW.
Simon Johnson, Purveyor of Quality Foods, 181 Harris Street, Pyrmont, NSW.
Australia On A Plate, 60a Warners Avenue, Bondi, NSW.
The Cheese Shop, 797 Military Road, Mosman, NSW.
Sydney Market Authority, Parramatta Road, Flemington, NSW.
Antico's Northbridge Fruit World, 83 Sailor's Bay Road, Northbridge, NSW.
Matt Brown's Greens, 123 Regent Street Chippendale, NSW.
The Mushroom Board, Parramatta Road, Flemington, NSW.
The Chilli Press Club, 48a Queenscliff Road, Queenscliff, NSW.
B & J Lizard, Flemington Markets, Flemington, NSW.
Sunrice Rice Australia, 447 Kent Street, Sydney, NSW.
Cantarella Bros Pty Ltd, 118 Wetherill Street, Silverwater, NSW.
Arquilla Bulk Trading, 159 Allen Street, Leichhardt, NSW.
Pastabilities, 45 Albion Street, Surry Hills, NSW.
Peter's Fish, Sydney Fish Markets, Blackwater Bay, Pyrmont, NSW.
McClellands Coffee and Tea, 2 Mandible Street, Alexandria, NSW.
The Tea Centre, 135 King Street, Sydney, NSW.
The Bush Tucker Supply, 482 Victoria Road, Gladesville, NSW.
Gundabluey Bushfoods, 26 Tenterden Road, Botany, NSW.

DEDICATION
In loving memory of Peter Mirams (1929–1998).